# Forensic Cybersecurity: Protecting and Investigating Digital Data

**Mylan Rochefort**

In the ever-evolving digital age, where technology permeates every aspect of our lives, cyber threats loom larger than ever. From ransomware attacks that cripple hospitals to data breaches that expose millions of personal records, the battlefield of cyberspace grows more complex and perilous each day. At the heart of defending this virtual frontier lies forensic cybersecurity—a discipline that combines the technical rigor of digital forensics with the proactive defense strategies of cybersecurity.

Forensic cybersecurity is more than just an investigative tool—it is the cornerstone of accountability and resilience in the digital realm. It empowers organizations, law enforcement agencies, and governments to uncover the truth behind digital incidents, bring perpetrators to justice, and build robust systems to thwart future attacks. By protecting and investigating digital data, forensic cybersecurity ensures that even in a world increasingly driven by technology, integrity and trust can prevail.

This book, "**Forensic Cybersecurity: Protecting and Investigating Digital Data**," serves as your guide to this dynamic field. Whether you are a seasoned cybersecurity professional, an aspiring investigator, or simply someone curious about the mechanics of digital protection and investigation, this book is designed to illuminate the intricate processes, tools, and strategies that define forensic cybersecurity.

We begin by laying a foundation—exploring the legal and ethical frameworks that underpin digital investigations and the anatomy of cyberattacks. As the chapters unfold, we delve into the practical aspects of forensic cybersecurity, examining the tools, techniques, and methodologies that professionals use to detect, analyze, and mitigate cyber threats. Along the way, we navigate specialized domains such as malware forensics, mobile device investigations, and the unique challenges posed by cloud environments.

Through real-world case studies and expert insights, this book bridges the gap between theory and practice, offering readers a comprehensive view of forensic cybersecurity's critical role in today's interconnected world. Moreover, as we stand on the cusp of technological revolutions like artificial intelligence and quantum computing, the final chapters explore the future of this discipline and the emerging threats that lie ahead.

Cybersecurity is no longer optional—it is a necessity for individuals, organizations, and nations alike. By mastering the principles of forensic cybersecurity, you will gain not only the skills to respond to cyber threats but also the foresight to prevent them.

So, let us embark on this journey together, unraveling the mysteries of digital forensics, understanding the tactics of cybercriminals, and equipping ourselves to protect the digital landscapes of tomorrow.

**Welcome to the world of forensic cybersecurity.**

## About the Author: Mylan Rochefort

*Mylan Rochefort* is a seasoned expert in the fields of cybersecurity and digital forensics, with over a decade of hands-on experience investigating cybercrimes and fortifying digital systems against sophisticated threats. Renowned for his analytical precision and ability to translate complex technical concepts into actionable strategies, Mylan has become a trusted advisor to organizations, governments, and academic institutions worldwide.

Mylan's career began in the trenches of cybersecurity incident response, where he quickly developed a reputation for uncovering digital evidence in high-stakes cases. His expertise spans diverse domains, from malware analysis and network forensics to cloud security and artificial intelligence in cyber defense. Over the years, he has led teams in mitigating major cyberattacks, assisting law enforcement with cybercrime investigations, and advising Fortune 500 companies on building resilient cybersecurity infrastructures.

In addition to his practical experience, Mylan is a passionate educator and advocate for digital literacy. He has conducted workshops, delivered keynote speeches at international conferences, and contributed to leading industry publications. Through his work, he strives to demystify cybersecurity and empower others to navigate the ever-changing digital landscape with confidence.

**"Forensic Cybersecurity: Protecting and Investigating Digital Data"** is Mylan's debut book, born from his desire to share the knowledge and insights he has gained throughout his career. Written with clarity and depth, this book serves as both a technical resource and an accessible guide, offering readers a comprehensive understanding of the critical intersection between cybersecurity and forensics.

When not unraveling digital mysteries, Mylan enjoys delving into emerging technologies, mentoring the next generation of cyber defenders, and exploring his passion for storytelling through his writing.

Through this book, Mylan invites you to join him in uncovering the fascinating and vital world of forensic cybersecurity, equipping yourself with the tools and knowledge needed to safeguard the digital future.

# 1. Introduction to Forensic Cybersecurity

Forensic cybersecurity lies at the critical intersection of cybersecurity defense and digital forensics, combining the proactive measures needed to prevent cyber threats with the investigative techniques used to analyze and resolve incidents. This chapter introduces the fundamental principles of forensic cybersecurity, exploring its role in protecting digital assets and uncovering the truth behind cybercrimes. From its historical evolution to its modern applications in tackling real-world challenges, this chapter sets the stage for understanding how forensic cybersecurity serves as a cornerstone of digital trust and resilience in today's interconnected world.

## 1.1 Defining Forensic Cybersecurity and Its Scope.

Forensic Cybersecurity is an evolving field that integrates the disciplines of digital forensics and cybersecurity to protect, investigate, and analyze digital data. In a world where cyberattacks have become more frequent, sophisticated, and damaging, the importance of forensic cybersecurity cannot be overstated. It serves as the bridge between cybersecurity defense strategies and the investigative processes needed to trace, understand, and resolve digital crimes or security incidents. This section provides an in-depth explanation of forensic cybersecurity, its definition, scope, and the critical role it plays in both protecting digital assets and ensuring accountability in the digital age.

### What is Forensic Cybersecurity?

At its core, forensic cybersecurity is the application of cybersecurity principles and practices in the context of forensic investigations. It involves the collection, preservation, analysis, and presentation of digital evidence related to cybercrimes, data breaches, or other cybersecurity incidents. Forensic cybersecurity professionals work at the intersection of security operations and law enforcement, ensuring that evidence gathered during an investigation is legally sound and can be used to prosecute offenders or prevent future attacks.

Forensic cybersecurity is essentially a hybrid discipline that merges two important fields:

- **Digital Forensics**: The science of recovering, analyzing, and preserving evidence from digital devices, systems, and networks.
- **Cybersecurity**: The practice of protecting systems, networks, and data from digital attacks, unauthorized access, and exploitation.

Together, these fields empower organizations and investigators to detect cyber threats, analyze the scope and impact of attacks, and respond effectively to safeguard data, systems, and infrastructure.

## The Role of Forensic Cybersecurity in Investigations

Forensic cybersecurity professionals are often the first responders in the aftermath of a cyberattack, tasked with collecting evidence, identifying the nature of the threat, and determining how an attack unfolded. This process can include identifying compromised systems, tracing the origins of the attack, and recovering lost or deleted data. In some cases, forensic experts may also be called upon to provide expert testimony in legal proceedings, offering insights into the methodologies used by hackers, the extent of the damage, and how the breach was carried out.

The process of forensic investigation typically involves several stages:

- **Identification**: Detecting and identifying suspicious activities, intrusions, or breaches within a network or system.
- **Preservation**: Safeguarding the integrity of the digital evidence by following proper protocols to prevent contamination or tampering. This often involves creating digital images or backups of affected systems and data.
- **Analysis**: Analyzing the collected data to understand how the attack was carried out, the vulnerabilities exploited, and the attackers' motives.
- **Presentation**: Documenting and presenting the findings in a way that is understandable to non-technical stakeholders and, if necessary, in a court of law.

Throughout this process, forensic cybersecurity experts must adhere to legal and ethical standards, ensuring that the evidence remains admissible in court and respects privacy regulations.

## Scope of Forensic Cybersecurity

The scope of forensic cybersecurity is broad and encompasses a wide range of responsibilities and techniques. As cyberattacks become more diverse, the field of forensic cybersecurity has expanded to address a growing list of challenges. Below are some key areas within the scope of forensic cybersecurity:

**Incident Response**: Incident response is a critical component of forensic cybersecurity, as it involves the detection and mitigation of cyberattacks in real time. Forensic cybersecurity experts help organizations identify security breaches, contain threats, and limit the damage caused by cybercriminals. A key part of incident response is the investigation of the attack's origin, its methods, and its impact, which requires the expertise of forensic professionals to analyze digital evidence.

**Data Breach Investigation**: One of the most common roles of forensic cybersecurity is investigating data breaches. A data breach occurs when sensitive data, such as customer information or intellectual property, is accessed or stolen by unauthorized parties. Forensic experts analyze the breach to determine how it occurred, which data was affected, and who was responsible. Their findings are critical in understanding the scope of the breach, notifying affected parties, and implementing measures to prevent similar incidents in the future.

**Malware Analysis**: Forensic cybersecurity plays a significant role in the analysis of malware, such as viruses, worms, ransomware, and spyware. By analyzing the malware's code and behavior, forensic experts can identify how the malicious software entered a system, what vulnerabilities it exploited, and how it impacted the organization. This information is essential for neutralizing the malware, recovering lost data, and preventing future attacks.

**Digital Evidence Preservation**: Ensuring the integrity of digital evidence is one of the cornerstones of forensic cybersecurity. Evidence must be collected and preserved in a manner that maintains its authenticity and ensures that it can be used in legal proceedings if necessary. This may involve creating digital forensic images, securing hardware devices, and documenting chain-of-custody procedures to demonstrate that the evidence has not been tampered with or altered.

**Cloud and Mobile Device Forensics**: With the growing use of cloud storage and mobile devices, forensic cybersecurity must address the challenges posed by these platforms. Cloud forensics focuses on investigating data stored across cloud services, which often involves multiple jurisdictions and providers. Mobile device forensics deals with recovering evidence from smartphones and tablets, which can include encrypted communications, app data, GPS information, and more. Both areas require specialized tools and techniques to access and analyze digital evidence.

**Forensic Readiness and Proactive Defense**: Beyond reactive incident response, forensic cybersecurity also involves preparing systems for potential investigations. Forensic readiness means ensuring that digital evidence can be easily collected and analyzed in the event of a cyberattack. This involves setting up logging systems, monitoring networks, and establishing protocols for evidence collection and preservation.

Proactive cybersecurity measures, such as implementing intrusion detection systems (IDS) and endpoint monitoring, help prevent attacks and create a digital trail that can be used in forensic investigations.

**Compliance and Legal Considerations**: Forensic cybersecurity is deeply intertwined with legal and regulatory frameworks. In order to ensure that evidence is admissible in court, forensic experts must understand laws surrounding data protection, privacy, and the handling of digital evidence. This includes adhering to regulations such as the General Data Protection Regulation (GDPR) in Europe or the Health Insurance Portability and Accountability Act (HIPAA) in the U.S., which dictate how organizations must protect and report breaches involving personal data.

**Collaboration with Law Enforcement and Legal Teams**: Cybersecurity and forensics professionals frequently collaborate with law enforcement agencies, government organizations, and legal teams to track down cybercriminals, gather evidence for criminal cases, and ensure that proper procedures are followed. The intersection of law enforcement and cybersecurity requires a strong understanding of both technical and legal processes, as digital evidence often plays a central role in criminal investigations and prosecutions.

### The Importance of Forensic Cybersecurity

As cybercrime continues to evolve, forensic cybersecurity provides critical capabilities for identifying, understanding, and mitigating digital threats. Whether it's a corporation investigating a data breach, a government agency tracking a cyberespionage campaign, or a law enforcement team working on a cybercrime case, forensic cybersecurity enables professionals to piece together the puzzle of an attack, providing insight into how the attack occurred and who was behind it.

In addition, forensic cybersecurity helps build a culture of accountability and resilience within organizations. By implementing forensic-ready strategies and technologies, companies can more effectively respond to incidents, limit damage, and recover quickly. Moreover, as digital crime and cyberattacks become increasingly sophisticated, the role of forensic cybersecurity will only continue to grow, making it an essential component of any comprehensive cybersecurity strategy.

In conclusion, forensic cybersecurity is a multifaceted field that requires a blend of technical expertise, investigative skills, and legal knowledge. Its scope encompasses a broad range of activities, from incident response and malware analysis to legal compliance and proactive defense. With the growing complexity of cyber threats, forensic cybersecurity plays an integral role in safeguarding digital assets, ensuring accountability, and enabling organizations to respond effectively to cyber incidents.

# 1.2 Historical Evolution of Cyber Forensics.

The history of cyber forensics traces the development of digital evidence handling and investigation techniques, which have evolved alongside the rise of the internet and digital technologies. From its modest beginnings in the late 20th century, cyber forensics has transformed into a critical field in both cybersecurity and law enforcement. The ability to uncover digital evidence and investigate cybercrimes has become indispensable in solving complex crimes ranging from financial fraud to cyberterrorism. This section outlines the key milestones in the historical evolution of cyber forensics, examining how it has advanced in response to emerging technologies and increasing cyber threats.

**Early Beginnings (1980s – Early 1990s)**

The origins of cyber forensics can be traced to the 1980s, when computers began to play a larger role in everyday business and personal life. Early forms of digital forensics were primarily focused on the recovery of data from computer systems, particularly in cases of fraud or theft.

In the early stages, digital forensics was largely an extension of traditional criminal investigation techniques, but applied to computers and digital devices. Law enforcement agencies initially lacked the specialized knowledge and tools necessary to handle digital evidence, and investigations into computer-related crimes were few and far between. The evidence gathered from computers was primarily restricted to financial fraud and the occasional case of cyber theft.

During this period, there was a lack of formal methodologies for dealing with digital evidence, which often led to mishandling or contamination. The absence of standardized practices meant that digital evidence was susceptible to alteration, making it difficult to use in legal proceedings. The tools for analyzing digital data were also rudimentary, often requiring manual recovery techniques to retrieve files or reconstruct data from damaged or deleted files.

**The Birth of Digital Forensics (Mid-1990s – Early 2000s)**

As the internet began to expand in the mid-1990s and more businesses and individuals started to rely on digital technologies, the landscape of cybercrime also changed. This shift highlighted the need for specialized professionals who could handle the growing complexity of cybercrimes and investigate crimes that involved digital data.

During this period, digital forensics as a discipline began to formally emerge, with law enforcement agencies around the world establishing dedicated teams to investigate computer crimes. The first digital forensics tools, such as disk imaging software and data recovery programs, were developed to help recover and analyze digital evidence. These tools became essential for extracting information from hard drives, servers, and later, mobile devices.

In the United States, one of the earliest formal instances of cyber forensics was the establishment of the National Computer Crime Squad (NCCS) in the early 1990s by the FBI. The squad's mission was to handle computer-related crimes, including hacking and data theft. This marked a significant shift from traditional forensic methods to an approach that integrated technology and law enforcement, setting the stage for the broader development of cyber forensics.

By the late 1990s and early 2000s, the discipline expanded rapidly as cybercrimes such as identity theft, hacking, and online fraud became more prevalent. As the scale of cybercrime grew, law enforcement agencies faced a new set of challenges in terms of legal procedures, investigative techniques, and tools required to manage vast amounts of digital evidence.

## The Professionalization of Cyber Forensics (2000s)

The early 2000s saw the professionalization of cyber forensics as both the private sector and law enforcement began to recognize its importance. The Computer Security and Incident Response Teams (CSIRTs) emerged, bringing together private security professionals and public law enforcement to tackle cybercrime. These teams focused on not just preventing cybercrime but also on conducting forensic investigations to analyze and understand cyberattacks after they occurred.

During this period, the International Association of Computer Science and Information Technology (IACSIT) and other professional organizations began to formalize training and certification programs for digital forensic professionals. Certifications such as the Certified Computer Examiner (CCE) and Certified Forensic Computer Examiner (CFCE) were introduced, providing professionals with the specialized knowledge and skills required to handle digital evidence and investigate cybercrimes.

Meanwhile, significant developments in forensic tools began to emerge, including specialized software for file recovery, password cracking, and malware analysis. Software such as EnCase, FTK (Forensic Toolkit), and X1 Search became staples in the forensic investigator's toolkit, providing powerful, automated solutions to the labor-intensive process of digital evidence analysis.

The legal community also began to recognize the importance of digital evidence during this period. In 2000, the Federal Rules of Evidence were amended in the United States to explicitly include digital evidence as admissible in court, providing a framework for presenting and preserving digital evidence in legal proceedings.

As cyber threats became more sophisticated, forensic experts began developing more advanced techniques for handling increasingly complex cases, such as network forensics, live data analysis, and the collection of evidence from the cloud. These new challenges underscored the need for ongoing innovation in the field of cyber forensics.

**The Rise of Cybercrime and Forensic Adaptation (2010s – Present)**

The 2010s and beyond marked a period of rapid growth in cyber forensics as cybercrime became an even larger global issue. The rise of ransomware, Advanced Persistent Threats (APTs), and hacktivism created new challenges for digital forensic experts. In response, cyber forensics evolved to include advanced analysis techniques for a wider range of digital platforms, such as mobile devices, cloud computing, and social media.

During this period, mobile device forensics became one of the fastest-growing branches of digital forensics. With the widespread use of smartphones and tablets, investigators were now tasked with extracting data from a variety of mobile operating systems, including Android and iOS, which posed new challenges in terms of encryption and device security. Specialized tools such as Cellebrite and Oxygen Forensics allowed investigators to bypass security features and recover crucial evidence, such as text messages, photos, and location data, from mobile devices.

The rise of cloud computing also led to the creation of cloud forensics, as businesses and individuals moved data from local systems to the cloud. Investigating crimes involving cloud-based data storage required forensic experts to understand both traditional forensic techniques and the unique challenges posed by cloud architecture, such as multi-tenant environments and data jurisdiction issues. Tools for cloud forensics began to emerge, enabling forensic professionals to investigate crimes involving cloud-based storage and services.

Simultaneously, network forensics became more crucial as cyberattacks increasingly targeted critical infrastructure and enterprise networks. Investigators began using packet capture and traffic analysis tools to trace the origin of attacks and understand how cybercriminals moved through networks.

With cybercrime growing more complex and attacks targeting both individuals and organizations across borders, cyber forensics has expanded its scope to include international collaboration, with agencies like Europol and the FBI's Cyber Division working together on cross-border investigations. This collaboration has proven crucial in addressing large-scale global threats, such as ransomware gangs and cyberespionage campaigns.

**The Future of Cyber Forensics**

The evolution of cyber forensics is ongoing, and the future promises further advancements as emerging technologies like artificial intelligence (AI), blockchain, and quantum computing challenge traditional forensic methods. AI is expected to play a significant role in automating aspects of digital evidence analysis, helping investigators process vast amounts of data more efficiently. Blockchain, which promises enhanced security and transparency, may also provide new ways to authenticate evidence and trace transactions in financial crimes.

The continuing sophistication of cyberattacks will demand even more specialized knowledge and tools from forensic cybersecurity experts, ensuring that the field remains dynamic and critical to the fight against cybercrime.

In conclusion, the historical evolution of cyber forensics highlights its transformation from a nascent field into a complex, multifaceted discipline that continues to adapt to the challenges posed by modern digital technologies. From its early days in computer crime investigations to its current role in handling a wide array of cybercrime incidents, the evolution of cyber forensics underscores its critical importance in maintaining digital security and justice in an increasingly interconnected world.

# 1.3 Key Players in the Forensic Ecosystem: Organizations, Tools, and Experts.

The forensic cybersecurity ecosystem is made up of various organizations, specialized tools, and skilled experts, all of whom work together to investigate, analyze, and mitigate digital crimes. These key players come from a range of sectors, including law enforcement, private security firms, technology companies, and academic institutions. Each of these entities plays a crucial role in shaping the field of cyber forensics, driving innovation, and ensuring that digital evidence is handled properly. This section will provide an overview of the key players involved in the forensic cybersecurity ecosystem, categorizing them into organizations, tools, and experts.

### 1.3.1 Organizations in the Forensic Cybersecurity Ecosystem

Several organizations are central to the development, regulation, and implementation of forensic cybersecurity practices. These entities provide frameworks, standards, certifications, and support for professionals working in the field.

### 1. Government and Law Enforcement Agencies

**Federal Bureau of Investigation (FBI)** – In the United States, the FBI has a specialized Cyber Division that handles cybercrime, including investigating digital forensics cases. The FBI's Computer Crime Squad and National Cyber Investigative Joint Task Force (NCIJTF) work with other law enforcement agencies to investigate cybercrimes at both national and international levels. They also provide technical expertise and resources for handling complex forensic cases.

**Europol (European Union Agency for Law Enforcement Cooperation)** – Europol's European Cybercrime Centre (EC3) supports member states in handling cybercrime investigations, including digital forensics. Europol facilitates the sharing of information between law enforcement agencies across Europe, coordinates international investigations, and offers forensic support in complex cases.

**Secret Service** – In addition to their role in protecting high-profile individuals, the U.S. Secret Service is also involved in cybercrime investigations. They handle cases related to financial crimes, including fraud and identity theft, and work on the investigation of digital evidence.

**National Institute of Standards and Technology (NIST)** – NIST provides critical guidelines and standards for handling digital evidence and forensic investigations. They have published key documents such as the NIST Special Publication 800-101, which addresses mobile device forensics, and NIST Cybersecurity Framework, which assists organizations in managing cybersecurity risks.

### 2. Private Sector and Consulting Firms

**FireEye** – FireEye is a leading cybersecurity company that specializes in threat intelligence and digital forensics. Their team of experts conducts investigations for organizations that have suffered data breaches or cyberattacks, often helping to analyze malware, detect vulnerabilities, and recover digital evidence.

**CrowdStrike** – Known for its advanced threat detection and response services, CrowdStrike has become a key player in cyber forensics, providing support for investigating data breaches, malware analysis, and incident response. They focus on endpoint security and advanced persistent threat (APT) investigations.

**Kroll** – Kroll is a global leader in investigations and cybersecurity, specializing in digital forensics, incident response, and data recovery. Kroll's experts work with corporations and law enforcement to manage data breaches, internal fraud, and other cybercrimes.

**IBM Security** – IBM's cybersecurity division offers digital forensics services, helping clients to investigate and resolve incidents related to data breaches, hacking, and intellectual property theft. IBM's X-Force Incident Response and Intelligence Services (IRIS) provides cybersecurity professionals with the tools and expertise needed for forensic investigations.

**Hewlett Packard Enterprise (HPE)** – HPE offers forensic services through its Security Risk and Compliance practice, which provides incident response, forensics, and remediation support for organizations experiencing cyberattacks. HPE's services include digital evidence analysis and expertise in handling compliance regulations.

## 3. Academic Institutions and Research Organizations

**Carnegie Mellon University's CERT Coordination Center (CERT/CC)** – CERT/CC is a key academic player that has pioneered research in cybersecurity and digital forensics. Their team conducts research into vulnerabilities, incident response, and forensic methods to improve the overall security ecosystem. CERT/CC also offers incident response services and collaborates with government and private sectors to address cyber threats.

**The SANS Institute** – The SANS Institute is one of the world's leading cybersecurity training organizations. They offer specialized courses in digital forensics, incident response, and malware analysis, helping to train the next generation of cyber forensic experts. SANS also provides certifications like the GIAC Certified Forensic Analyst (GCFA) to establish expertise in the field.

**International Association of Computer Science and Information Technology (IACSIT)** – IACSIT is an academic association that supports the growth and research of computer science and information technology, including digital forensics. They organize conferences and provide platforms for sharing knowledge and developing best practices in the field of cybersecurity and forensics.

### 1.3.2 Tools in the Forensic Cybersecurity Ecosystem

A wide range of tools have been developed to support the work of forensic cybersecurity experts, enabling them to gather, analyze, and preserve digital evidence effectively. These tools vary in their capabilities, with some designed for specific tasks, such as malware analysis, mobile forensics, or network forensics.

### 1. Forensic Analysis Software

**EnCase** – One of the most widely used digital forensic tools, EnCase is employed by both law enforcement agencies and private sector experts. It allows investigators to acquire, analyze, and present digital evidence, including recovering deleted files, analyzing system logs, and examining file systems.

**FTK (Forensic Toolkit)** – FTK is another powerful tool for acquiring and analyzing digital evidence. FTK supports a wide range of forensic tasks, such as file recovery, password cracking, and email analysis, and is often used by both private security firms and law enforcement agencies for data breach investigations.

**X1 Social Discovery** – This tool is specifically designed for analyzing social media platforms, cloud storage, and web-based communications. X1 Social Discovery is used to collect evidence from social networks, email accounts, and websites, which is particularly useful in investigations involving cyberbullying, fraud, or defamation.

**Autopsy** – An open-source digital forensics tool, Autopsy provides investigators with a graphical interface to analyze hard drives, mobile devices, and cloud data. It includes features for timeline analysis, keyword searching, and reporting, making it an excellent tool for investigating cybercrimes.

**Cellebrite UFED** – Cellebrite is a leading provider of mobile forensics solutions, allowing investigators to extract data from smartphones, tablets, and other mobile devices. Cellebrite UFED is particularly valuable in cases involving encrypted communications, GPS data, and deleted messages, providing essential evidence in criminal investigations.

## 2. Malware and Network Forensics Tools

**Wireshark** – Wireshark is a popular open-source tool for analyzing network traffic. It allows investigators to capture and examine network packets in real-time, helping to identify suspicious activities, such as data exfiltration, malware communication, or intrusion attempts.

**Volatility** – Volatility is an advanced memory forensics tool that allows investigators to analyze volatile memory (RAM) to uncover evidence of cyberattacks, malware infections, and system compromise. Volatility is often used to conduct live memory analysis and recover evidence from compromised machines.

**Cuckoo Sandbox** – Cuckoo Sandbox is an open-source automated malware analysis tool that can be used to safely run and analyze suspicious files in a contained environment. It generates detailed reports on the behavior of the malware, including file modifications, network activity, and registry changes.

### 1.3.3 Experts in the Forensic Cybersecurity Ecosystem

In addition to the organizations and tools involved in forensic cybersecurity, experts with specialized skills and knowledge are crucial to the investigative process. These professionals play roles such as forensic analysts, incident responders, malware analysts, and legal experts, ensuring that digital evidence is properly collected, analyzed, and presented in accordance with legal standards.

**Digital Forensic Analysts** – These experts specialize in collecting, analyzing, and preserving digital evidence. They have expertise in working with various file systems, operating systems, and devices, and are skilled in recovering deleted files, examining logs, and identifying evidence of cybercrimes.

**Incident Response Teams** – Incident responders are key players in identifying and managing cyber incidents. They work with digital forensics experts to determine the cause and extent of a cyberattack, limit its impact, and recover evidence for further analysis.

**Malware Analysts** – Malware analysts focus on reverse-engineering malicious software to understand its behavior, functionality, and potential impact. Their expertise is vital in analyzing how malware spreads, how it impacts systems, and how it can be neutralized.

**Cybersecurity Consultants and Trainers** – Cybersecurity consultants provide strategic advice on how organizations can better prepare for, respond to, and recover from cyber incidents. Trainers help upskill professionals in cybersecurity and digital forensics, ensuring that organizations have the necessary expertise to handle complex threats.

The forensic cybersecurity ecosystem is a dynamic and multi-faceted landscape that involves collaboration between various organizations, tools, and experts. From government agencies and private sector firms to cutting-edge forensic tools and skilled professionals, each player has a crucial role in ensuring that digital evidence is collected, preserved, and analyzed correctly. Together, these key players enable the detection and resolution of cybercrimes, helping to protect sensitive information, maintain cybersecurity, and bring perpetrators to justice.

# 1.4 Real-World Applications of Forensic Cybersecurity.

Forensic cybersecurity plays a pivotal role in addressing and resolving digital crimes, safeguarding sensitive information, and ensuring that cybercriminals are held accountable for their actions. As the number and complexity of cyberattacks grow, the field of cyber forensics has become essential in protecting both individuals and organizations from malicious activities. In this section, we will explore the real-world applications of forensic cybersecurity across various industries, highlighting how digital forensics is used to investigate and prevent cybercrimes, protect intellectual property, and respond to incidents.

### 1.4.1 Criminal Investigations and Law Enforcement

One of the primary applications of forensic cybersecurity is in the criminal justice system, where it helps to investigate and solve crimes involving digital data. Law enforcement agencies rely heavily on digital forensics to uncover evidence of cybercrimes such as hacking, fraud, identity theft, child exploitation, and cyberterrorism.

**Investigating Cybercrime** – Forensic cybersecurity experts assist law enforcement by retrieving and analyzing digital evidence from various devices, such as computers, smartphones, and cloud storage, to identify perpetrators and understand the nature of cybercrimes. In many cases, cybercriminals use sophisticated techniques to cover their tracks, including encryption and anonymization tools. Digital forensics allows investigators to bypass these defenses and recover critical evidence, such as emails, transaction logs, browser histories, and deleted files, which can link suspects to illegal activities.

**Tracking and Prosecuting Cybercriminals** – Forensic cyber professionals also play a key role in identifying and tracking cybercriminals across borders. Cybercrime investigations often involve complex networks of perpetrators and illicit activities spanning different countries. By analyzing digital evidence, investigators can trace criminal activities, uncover organized cybercrime rings, and build a case for prosecution. The information recovered can help law enforcement authorities identify criminal networks involved in activities like online fraud, data breaches, ransomware attacks, and even terrorist activities.

**Digital Evidence in Court** – Forensic cybersecurity professionals are often called upon to present digital evidence in court as part of a legal investigation. They must follow strict procedures for collecting and preserving evidence to ensure that it is admissible in court. This may involve documenting the chain of custody, using validated forensic tools, and ensuring that evidence is not tampered with. The successful presentation of digital evidence can lead to the conviction of cybercriminals and serve as a deterrent for future cybercrimes.

### 1.4.2 Incident Response and Data Breach Investigations

Incident response teams rely heavily on forensic cybersecurity to manage and mitigate the impact of cyberattacks and data breaches. When a security breach occurs, forensic experts are called in to investigate the attack, identify the methods used by the attackers, and recover compromised data.

**Data Breach Response** – In the case of a data breach, digital forensics allows organizations to understand the scope of the attack, determine how the attackers gained access to sensitive information, and evaluate the damage caused by the breach. Investigating network logs, system vulnerabilities, and compromised accounts can help determine the cause of the breach and prevent future incidents. Forensic analysis also helps identify stolen data, such as personally identifiable information (PII), financial data, or intellectual property, enabling companies to mitigate the potential damage from identity theft, fraud, or reputational harm.

**Ransomware Investigations** – Ransomware attacks, where attackers lock access to critical systems or data and demand payment for its release, have become a significant global threat. Forensic cybersecurity professionals play an important role in investigating these attacks by analyzing how the malware infiltrated systems, mapping out the attack's progression, and identifying the files or systems that were encrypted. The analysis can also reveal whether the attackers exfiltrated any sensitive data before locking it and whether the ransomware is part of a broader criminal network. By gathering this evidence, forensic experts help organizations assess the damage and support incident recovery efforts.

**Forensics in Cloud Environments** – As businesses increasingly move their operations to the cloud, digital forensics has become essential in investigating incidents that affect cloud-based systems. Cloud forensics involves collecting and analyzing data stored in cloud environments to understand how an attack occurred, how data was compromised, and which systems were affected. This can include investigating virtual machines, storage accounts, access logs, and third-party services used in the cloud infrastructure. Cloud forensics also requires understanding multi-tenancy and shared responsibility models, which are essential when identifying whether cloud providers or customers are responsible for the breach.

### 1.4.3 Intellectual Property Theft and Corporate Espionage

Forensic cybersecurity is crucial in investigations involving the theft of intellectual property (IP) and corporate espionage. Companies that rely on proprietary information, such as trade secrets, patents, and research data, need to ensure that their intellectual property is protected from cybercriminals and competitors.

**IP Theft Investigations** – Digital forensics plays a key role in uncovering evidence of intellectual property theft. This may involve tracing the movement of sensitive documents, analyzing email communications, or reviewing network traffic to identify unauthorized access to trade secrets or proprietary information. Cyber forensic experts can track the digital footprints of suspects, uncovering whether confidential data was exfiltrated, sold, or used without permission. The analysis may reveal whether insiders, hackers, or competitors were involved in the theft.

**Corporate Espionage** – In corporate espionage cases, forensic cybersecurity experts work to gather evidence that can prove if a competitor or a disgruntled employee stole sensitive business data or sabotaged operations. This often involves analyzing emails, file transfers, and access logs to determine whether unauthorized individuals accessed confidential business plans, product designs, customer databases, or marketing strategies. Cyber forensics helps identify malicious insiders, cyber thieves, or even foreign entities involved in stealing or compromising valuable business assets.

**Digital Evidence for Litigation** – In cases of IP theft or corporate espionage, digital forensics is vital for building a case for legal action. Experts may retrieve digital evidence to support claims of intellectual property theft or unauthorized use of proprietary information. In some cases, companies may file lawsuits against cybercriminals or competitors for violating trade secrets or copyright laws, and forensic findings can provide the concrete evidence needed for litigation.

### 1.4.4 Online Fraud, Financial Crimes, and Compliance

Cyber forensics plays a critical role in detecting and preventing financial crimes, including fraud, money laundering, and identity theft. Digital evidence can be used to trace fraudulent transactions, uncover financial irregularities, and detect patterns of illegal activity.

**Online Fraud Investigations** – Forensic experts investigate various types of online fraud, such as phishing, identity theft, and credit card fraud. Forensic tools allow investigators to track fraudulent transactions, uncover email spoofing, and retrieve deleted communications that might point to the perpetrators of fraud. They may also look into digital payment systems and transaction logs to determine how stolen funds were transferred or laundered. Forensic experts are instrumental in gathering evidence for both criminal investigations and regulatory compliance.

**Money Laundering Investigations** – Digital forensics is widely used in detecting money laundering schemes, where cybercriminals move illicit funds through multiple transactions to conceal the origins of the money. Forensic analysts review transaction records, digital wallets, and blockchain data to identify patterns of money laundering. By following the digital trail, forensic professionals help law enforcement agencies trace funds, identify laundering methods, and ultimately expose criminal networks involved in illegal financial activities.

**Regulatory Compliance** – Companies in highly regulated sectors, such as banking, insurance, and healthcare, use forensic cybersecurity to ensure compliance with data protection laws, such as the General Data Protection Regulation (GDPR) or the Health Insurance Portability and Accountability Act (HIPAA). Cyber forensic experts help organizations respond to data breach incidents, perform audits, and ensure that they are adhering to required standards for the protection of sensitive data.

### 1.4.5 Cybersecurity Research and Development

In addition to its application in real-world investigations, forensic cybersecurity also contributes to research and development within the broader field of cybersecurity. Forensic experts collaborate with researchers, universities, and private companies to develop new tools, techniques, and best practices for handling digital evidence. Their work helps to advance the capabilities of forensic tools, improve incident response procedures, and ensure that digital forensic investigations keep pace with evolving cyber threats.

The real-world applications of forensic cybersecurity are vast and diverse, covering a wide range of industries and types of cybercrime. Whether it's assisting law enforcement in criminal investigations, supporting organizations in data breach responses, uncovering intellectual property theft, detecting financial crimes, or advancing research in cybersecurity, digital forensics plays a crucial role in protecting society from the growing threat of cyberattacks. As technology continues to evolve, the role of forensic cybersecurity experts will only become more integral in combating digital threats and ensuring that justice is served in the cyber world.

# 2. The Legal and Ethical Framework

Forensic cybersecurity operates within a complex web of laws, regulations, and ethical responsibilities that govern the collection, preservation, and use of digital evidence. This chapter delves into the critical legal principles that guide cyber investigations, including global standards for evidence admissibility and the importance of maintaining a chain of custody. It also explores the ethical challenges professionals face, such as balancing privacy concerns with investigative needs and navigating cross-border jurisdictional conflicts. By understanding these frameworks, readers will gain the insight needed to ensure their forensic practices are both lawful and ethically sound.

## 2.1 Overview of Cyber Laws and Digital Evidence Regulations.

The rapid expansion of the digital world has brought significant challenges to the legal landscape, particularly in the area of cybersecurity and digital forensics. As cybercrimes evolve in complexity, governments around the world have developed legal frameworks and regulations to address issues related to digital evidence and ensure that cybercrime investigations are conducted in a manner that is fair, efficient, and legally sound. This section will provide an overview of cyber laws and digital evidence regulations, discussing the importance of these legal standards in ensuring the proper handling of digital evidence, the protection of privacy, and the prosecution of cybercrimes.

### 2.1.1 Cyber Laws: A Global Perspective

Cyber laws are laws that govern activities in the digital realm, including the use of the internet, data transmission, and the protection of digital assets. These laws seek to regulate online behavior, punish cybercriminal activities, and provide a legal framework for dealing with digital crimes. The main objective is to create a legal environment that fosters innovation while safeguarding individuals, organizations, and nations against online threats.

**The Computer Fraud and Abuse Act (CFAA)** – One of the most well-known pieces of cyber legislation in the United States, the Computer Fraud and Abuse Act (CFAA) was enacted in 1986 and amended multiple times to address the evolving landscape of cybercrime. The CFAA makes it illegal to access a computer without authorization, steal data, introduce malware, or disrupt services. The law also criminalizes identity theft, hacking, and other forms of cybercrime. Under the CFAA, individuals who commit these offenses can face criminal charges and civil liabilities.

**General Data Protection Regulation (GDPR)** – The GDPR, enacted by the European Union (EU) in 2018, has set a global standard for data protection and privacy laws. The GDPR applies to organizations that process the personal data of EU citizens, regardless of where the organization is based. It lays out clear regulations regarding the collection, storage, and transfer of personal data, as well as the rights of individuals regarding their data. The law emphasizes accountability and transparency, and violations can result in severe fines. Forensic investigators must adhere to these rules when handling digital evidence, especially when dealing with personal or sensitive information.

**The Cybersecurity Information Sharing Act (CISA)** – In the U.S., the Cybersecurity Information Sharing Act (CISA), passed in 2015, promotes the sharing of cybersecurity threat information between private companies and government agencies. CISA aims to improve national cybersecurity defenses by facilitating real-time data sharing. It also provides legal protections for companies sharing cybersecurity-related information, allowing for better coordination in responding to cyber threats and attacks. Forensic experts must be aware of these legal protections when sharing digital evidence with third parties or authorities.

**The Council of Europe's Convention on Cybercrime (Budapest Convention)** – The Budapest Convention, which came into force in 2004, is the first international treaty aimed at addressing internet and computer crime. It facilitates international cooperation in cybercrime investigations, standardizes the handling of digital evidence, and promotes the harmonization of cyber laws among its member countries. The treaty covers crimes related to illegal content, cyberattacks, and data breaches and emphasizes the need for cooperation between countries in tackling cross-border cybercrimes.

**China's Cybersecurity Law** – China's Cybersecurity Law, implemented in 2017, is one of the most comprehensive sets of regulations for cybersecurity in Asia. It includes provisions for the protection of critical information infrastructure, data protection, and the regulation of online content. The law mandates that companies operating in China store certain types of data within the country and requires them to cooperate with government authorities during cybersecurity investigations. The law highlights the importance of controlling digital evidence and enforcing strict compliance in the event of a cyberattack.

### 2.1.2 Legal Frameworks for Digital Evidence

Digital evidence, which can include emails, files, system logs, network traffic, and more, plays a crucial role in the investigation and prosecution of cybercrimes. However, collecting and presenting digital evidence in court requires adherence to specific legal frameworks and protocols to ensure that the evidence is valid, admissible, and reliable.

**Chain of Custody** – The concept of chain of custody is central to the legal handling of digital evidence. It refers to the documentation of every person who has had access to the evidence, from the time it is collected until it is presented in court. Ensuring an unbroken chain of custody is essential to prove that the evidence has not been tampered with or altered in any way. Failure to establish a valid chain of custody can lead to the evidence being excluded from court, undermining the investigation and prosecution of cybercrimes.

**The Federal Rules of Evidence (FRE)** – In the United States, the Federal Rules of Evidence (FRE) govern the admissibility of evidence in federal courts. Digital evidence is subject to the same rules as physical evidence, but it must be handled with additional care due to its intangible nature. For example, forensic experts must demonstrate that the digital evidence is authentic, relevant, and collected in a way that preserves its integrity. The FRE Rule 902 specifically addresses the admissibility of digital evidence and allows for the use of electronic records and data as evidence in court.

**The Electronic Communications Privacy Act (ECPA)** – The Electronic Communications Privacy Act (ECPA), enacted in 1986 in the U.S., is designed to protect the privacy of communications in electronic formats. It sets forth rules governing the interception of electronic communications, such as emails, phone calls, and text messages. Forensic investigators must navigate the provisions of the ECPA to ensure that evidence gathered from communication devices or platforms complies with privacy standards and legal requirements.

**International Cooperation and Mutual Legal Assistance Treaties (MLATs)** – Cybercrimes often span multiple jurisdictions, requiring international collaboration to investigate and prosecute offenders. Mutual Legal Assistance Treaties (MLATs) are agreements between countries that provide a framework for the exchange of evidence and legal assistance in criminal matters, including cybercrimes. MLATs play an essential role in cross-border investigations by facilitating the sharing of digital evidence, even when the crime involves servers, data, or suspects located in different countries.

**Digital Evidence Standards and Guidelines** – Several national and international organizations have developed standards and guidelines for handling digital evidence to ensure consistency and reliability in forensic investigations. In the U.S., the National

Institute of Standards and Technology (NIST) provides a comprehensive set of guidelines for forensic experts. NIST's Special Publication 800-101 addresses mobile device forensics, while NIST 800-86 provides guidelines on the forensic examination of digital evidence. Similarly, the International Organization on Computer Evidence (IOCE) provides the IOCE Guidelines to ensure the integrity of digital evidence during the collection, preservation, and analysis phases of an investigation.

### 2.1.3 Privacy Considerations and Ethical Issues

While cyber laws and digital evidence regulations are essential for enforcing the law and prosecuting cybercrimes, they must be balanced with privacy protections. Investigators must carefully navigate the fine line between gathering evidence to support legal proceedings and respecting individuals' privacy rights.

**Privacy Laws and Data Protection** – Laws such as the GDPR in Europe and the California Consumer Privacy Act (CCPA) in the United States set strict rules on how personal data can be collected, stored, and shared. These laws require that digital evidence is handled in ways that do not violate the privacy of individuals, particularly when it involves personal or sensitive data. For example, personal data collected during a cyber investigation must be anonymized, encrypted, and protected to prevent unauthorized access.

**Search and Seizure of Digital Evidence** – In many cases, law enforcement must obtain a search warrant before seizing digital devices or accessing digital data. The Fourth Amendment in the U.S. protects citizens from unreasonable searches and seizures, and any search of electronic devices must comply with this constitutional right. Digital forensics experts must ensure that searches are conducted in compliance with legal requirements, and that evidence is only seized if there is probable cause to believe that it is related to criminal activity.

**Ethical Guidelines for Digital Forensics** – Ethical guidelines in forensic cybersecurity emphasize the need for impartiality, confidentiality, and respect for privacy. Forensic investigators must ensure that their actions do not violate the rights of individuals or compromise the integrity of the investigation. The International Society of Forensic Computer Examiners (ISFCE) and the Digital Forensics Association (DFA) provide codes of conduct to guide forensic professionals in adhering to ethical standards during investigations.

The legal landscape surrounding cyber laws and digital evidence regulations is complex, as it must balance the need for effective crime investigation and prosecution with the protection of privacy and civil liberties. As technology advances and cybercrime becomes more sophisticated, these legal frameworks will continue to evolve to address new challenges. Forensic cybersecurity professionals must stay up-to-date on relevant laws, privacy regulations, and ethical guidelines to ensure that they handle digital evidence in a lawful, ethical, and professional manner. By doing so, they contribute to the integrity of the legal process and help safeguard the rights of individuals and organizations in the digital world.

## 2.2 Chain of Custody: Principles and Best Practices.

In forensic cybersecurity, chain of custody refers to the process of documenting and safeguarding the integrity of evidence throughout its collection, handling, storage, and eventual presentation in court. Maintaining an unbroken and verifiable chain of custody is essential to ensure that digital evidence remains uncontaminated and admissible in legal proceedings. Without proper documentation, the credibility of digital evidence can be compromised, which can undermine the entire investigation. This section will explore the principles of chain of custody, the importance of adhering to these principles, and the best practices to follow in order to maintain the integrity of digital evidence.

### 2.2.1 Principles of Chain of Custody

The principles of chain of custody are rooted in the need for transparency, accountability, and reliability in the handling of evidence. These principles ensure that every step in the process—from the collection of evidence to its presentation in court—is documented and conducted in a manner that preserves the integrity of the evidence.

**Documentation and Recording** – The chain of custody begins with meticulous documentation. Every person who handles the evidence, from the moment it is collected until it is presented in court, must be recorded. This includes recording the date, time, and specific actions taken during each handoff or transfer of the evidence. Each individual involved in the process must sign a custody form or log that confirms their possession and handling of the evidence. This record is crucial in demonstrating that the evidence has not been tampered with or altered.

**Security and Control** – The integrity of evidence is maintained through strict control and security measures. Once digital evidence is collected, it must be securely stored in a controlled environment that minimizes the risk of unauthorized access or tampering. In the context of digital forensics, this may involve using password-protected storage, encryption, or physical security measures such as locked storage devices or secure rooms. It is critical that only authorized personnel have access to the evidence at each stage of the investigation.

**Traceability** – Forensic investigators must ensure that the evidence can be traced back to its source at any point in the investigation process. This includes ensuring that every transfer of evidence is documented and that any change in the location or status of the evidence is recorded. If the evidence is moved, it must be tracked to show who moved it, when, and for what reason. Traceability also involves maintaining records of any analysis or testing done on the evidence, which allows investigators and legal professionals to track how the evidence has been used or processed.

**Preservation of Integrity** – The fundamental principle of chain of custody is to preserve the integrity of the evidence, ensuring that it has not been altered, contaminated, or destroyed. This principle requires forensic professionals to follow standardized procedures for collecting and handling digital evidence. For example, when collecting digital data from a computer, investigators may create a forensic image (a bit-by-bit copy of the original data) to preserve the original data in its unaltered state. This allows them to work with a duplicate of the data while ensuring the original remains intact for legal proceedings.

**Admissibility in Court** – The ultimate goal of maintaining a proper chain of custody is to ensure that digital evidence is admissible in court. In legal proceedings, the prosecution or defense must be able to show that the evidence presented is the same as the evidence collected at the scene of the crime and has not been tampered with or altered in any way. A robust chain of custody is essential to prove this, as any gaps or inconsistencies can lead to the exclusion of the evidence from the case.

### 2.2.2 Best Practices for Maintaining Chain of Custody

In order to ensure that the integrity of digital evidence is preserved throughout the investigative process, forensic cybersecurity professionals must follow a set of best practices for chain of custody. These best practices are designed to minimize risks, maintain transparency, and ensure compliance with legal standards.

**Secure Collection of Evidence** – The first step in maintaining the chain of custody is the secure collection of digital evidence. When collecting evidence, investigators should avoid making any changes to the original data, especially if it is located on a live system. For instance, investigators should use write-blockers to ensure that no data is inadvertently written to the device during the collection process. Additionally, a detailed record should be made of the device's condition, the location of the evidence, and any relevant circumstances surrounding the collection.

**Forensic Imaging** – In digital forensics, creating a forensic image of the original device or storage medium is one of the most effective ways to preserve evidence. A forensic image is an exact bit-by-bit copy of the data on the device, which can be used for analysis without altering the original data. This practice is crucial because it ensures that investigators can analyze the data while maintaining the integrity of the original evidence. Forensic images must also be verified using hash values (such as MD5 or SHA-1), which serve as digital fingerprints to confirm that the image is identical to the original data.

**Clear Labeling and Identification** – Each piece of evidence must be clearly identified and labeled to prevent confusion or mishandling. This includes assigning unique identifiers, such as evidence numbers or barcodes, and clearly marking each item with information such as the date, time, case number, and a brief description of the evidence. This ensures that all digital evidence can be traced back to the specific case and that there is no ambiguity regarding its provenance.

**Proper Storage and Handling** – Once digital evidence has been collected and imaged, it must be stored in a secure environment to prevent unauthorized access or tampering. This may involve physical storage, such as locked cabinets or safes for hard drives and flash drives, or digital storage, such as encrypted databases or servers for cloud-based data. Access to the evidence should be restricted to authorized personnel only, and any transfer or handling should be documented and logged.

**Documenting Every Transfer** – Every time evidence changes hands, it must be logged in a chain of custody form or logbook. This includes recording the name of the person receiving the evidence, the time and date of the transfer, the reason for the transfer, and the condition of the evidence at the time. If evidence is transported between different locations, the transfer must be documented with the same level of detail. This ensures transparency and provides a clear audit trail for investigators, legal teams, and the courts.

**Use of Secure Digital Evidence Management Systems** – To streamline the management of evidence and ensure consistency in handling, forensic investigators should make use of digital evidence management systems (DEMS). These systems provide a secure platform for logging, tracking, and managing evidence, and often integrate features such as automatic timestamping, access controls, and audit trails. By using a DEMS, investigators can minimize human error, reduce the risk of lost or tampered evidence, and ensure that evidence is properly documented and preserved.

**Periodic Audits and Reviews** – To ensure that the chain of custody is maintained and that no unauthorized access has occurred, forensic investigators should conduct periodic audits and reviews of the evidence. This may involve reviewing the logs to ensure all transfers were properly documented and that no evidence has been accessed without proper authorization. Audits can help identify any potential issues early in the process, allowing corrective actions to be taken before evidence is compromised.

**Training and Awareness** – Maintaining a proper chain of custody requires the involvement of all parties handling the evidence, from the initial collection to its final presentation in court. As such, training and awareness are crucial for forensic professionals, law enforcement personnel, and legal teams. Regular training on chain of custody procedures, legal requirements, and the potential consequences of mishandling evidence is essential to ensure that everyone involved is aware of their responsibilities and the importance of maintaining the integrity of digital evidence.

### 2.2.3 Challenges and Solutions in Maintaining Chain of Custody

Maintaining a flawless chain of custody can be challenging, particularly when dealing with digital evidence. Digital data is easily copied, altered, or transferred, which presents unique risks that do not exist with physical evidence. Some common challenges include:

**Remote or Cloud-Based Evidence**: Evidence stored in the cloud or accessed remotely can be more difficult to secure and track. Investigators may not have direct access to physical devices or servers, which complicates the process of documenting and controlling the evidence. One solution is to work closely with service providers to ensure proper procedures for evidence retrieval and handling, and to implement secure, encrypted channels for data transfer.

**Multiple Hands on Evidence**: In large investigations, multiple individuals may handle the same piece of evidence. In such cases, it becomes critical to ensure that all interactions are meticulously documented and that there are no lapses in the custody process. Using digital evidence management tools can help minimize human error and create a centralized log for all activities related to the evidence.

The chain of custody is a foundational element of forensic cybersecurity, ensuring that digital evidence remains untainted, reliable, and admissible in legal proceedings. By following established principles and best practices—such as secure evidence collection, forensic imaging, clear documentation, and restricted access—investigators can protect the integrity of the evidence and contribute to the successful prosecution of cybercriminals. Maintaining a strong chain of custody is not only essential for legal compliance but also critical for building trust in the investigative process and ensuring that justice is served in the digital realm.

## 2.3 Ethical Challenges in Cyber Forensics.

As the field of cyber forensics continues to grow in complexity, professionals in this area are increasingly faced with a range of ethical challenges. Cyber forensics involves the collection, analysis, and presentation of digital evidence to investigate and prosecute cybercrimes. However, the digital realm presents unique issues when it comes to ethical decision-making. These issues are amplified by the need to balance effective law enforcement with the protection of individual rights and privacy. This section will explore some of the most pressing ethical challenges in cyber forensics, including privacy concerns, bias, and the responsibilities of forensic professionals, and will offer guidance on how to navigate these dilemmas.

### 2.3.1 Privacy and the Right to Confidentiality

One of the most significant ethical concerns in cyber forensics is the potential violation of privacy rights. Investigating cybercrimes often requires accessing sensitive data on personal computers, mobile devices, or cloud storage. This data may contain private information such as personal communications, financial records, health information, and more. As forensic professionals sift through digital evidence, they are tasked with respecting the privacy of individuals while still fulfilling their duty to uncover relevant evidence.

**Informed Consent**: In some cases, cyber forensics professionals may be authorized to collect digital evidence through a warrant or subpoena, but the question arises: should individuals be informed that their data is being examined? Ethical dilemmas often occur when forensic professionals have to decide whether to disclose to individuals the extent of the data being examined. In some jurisdictions, there are exceptions to informed consent when it comes to law enforcement investigations, but it remains a critical ethical consideration. Ethical investigators must always ensure that they respect the limits of their mandate and avoid overreaching beyond what is legally authorized.

**Minimizing Intrusiveness**: The principle of minimizing intrusiveness guides the forensic investigation of digital data. Forensic professionals must focus only on the specific information relevant to the investigation and avoid unnecessary exploration of personal or irrelevant data. If investigators unnecessarily access private files or sensitive information not related to the case, they risk violating an individual's rights. This calls for clear boundaries, with investigators ensuring that their actions are targeted and proportionate to the investigation at hand.

**Confidentiality and Data Protection**: The handling of sensitive information during the forensic process also presents a significant ethical responsibility. Cyber forensics experts must ensure that the data they handle is secure and confidential. Cyber forensics professionals often work with data from victims of crimes, and mishandling or unauthorized disclosure of this data could have detrimental consequences for individuals involved. They must also adhere to relevant data protection regulations such as the General Data Protection Regulation (GDPR) in the European Union, which mandates strict privacy safeguards and confidentiality protocols.

### 2.3.2 Balancing Law Enforcement with Individual Rights

Another key ethical challenge lies in balancing the need for effective law enforcement with respect for individuals' constitutional rights. While digital forensics is essential for identifying and prosecuting cybercriminals, it is crucial that investigations do not infringe on civil liberties, such as the right to privacy, freedom of expression, or protection from unreasonable search and seizure.

**Overreach and Scope of Investigation**: Ethical concerns can arise if law enforcement agencies or forensic professionals exceed the scope of their investigation. For example, investigators may be authorized to examine one device or account in relation to a specific crime but may end up analyzing unrelated files, communications, or accounts without proper authorization. In such cases, forensic professionals must exercise restraint and ensure they do not engage in fishing expeditions, where evidence unrelated to the crime is sought or exploited. Respecting the boundaries of warrants and search orders is essential to prevent unethical conduct.

**Protection of Innocent Parties**: While a cyber forensics investigation may be focused on a suspected criminal, it is common for innocent individuals to have their data accessed as part of the investigation. Ethical investigators must take care to protect the privacy and data of these individuals. This is particularly important when metadata or cloud-based data is involved, as such data may not always be clearly linked to the suspect. Forensic professionals must carefully differentiate between the suspect's data and the data belonging to innocent parties to avoid unnecessary violations of their rights.

**Balancing Public Safety with Personal Rights**: In cases where digital evidence can be used to prevent imminent harm or loss of life (e.g., during a cyberterrorism investigation), forensic professionals may face difficult ethical decisions. The investigation may require accessing sensitive information quickly, but this should always be weighed against potential privacy violations. In such cases, a balance must be struck between achieving the goals of law enforcement while safeguarding individuals' rights.

### 2.3.3 Data Integrity and Evidence Manipulation

Ensuring the integrity of digital evidence is paramount in cyber forensics. The ethical responsibility to preserve the accuracy and authenticity of evidence is central to the role of a forensic professional. Manipulating or altering evidence, either intentionally or accidentally, undermines the investigation and can lead to miscarriages of justice.

**Accidental Alterations**: In digital forensics, even the simplest actions—such as opening a file, accessing a computer, or copying data—can inadvertently alter or destroy evidence. For example, opening a file can modify its metadata or delete logs of previous activity. Ethical challenges arise when forensic professionals make decisions about how to interact with data during the investigation. To avoid any unintentional alteration, forensic professionals use write-blockers or create forensic images of the data to work with copies rather than the original evidence.

**Intentional Manipulation of Evidence**: While rare, there are cases where evidence is intentionally altered or fabricated to secure a conviction or to mislead investigators. This type of misconduct can occur at any stage of the investigation, from evidence collection to data analysis. Ethical investigators must remain impartial and committed to uncovering the truth, even when the outcome is not favorable to their investigation. Intentional manipulation of evidence violates the ethical code of forensic experts and can lead to severe legal consequences.

**Transparency and Documentation**: Ethical cyber forensics professionals must ensure that their methods and processes are transparent and well-documented. Maintaining accurate records of the procedures followed during the collection and analysis of evidence ensures that their actions can be verified and scrutinized. Documentation provides an audit trail that can help prevent misunderstandings or accusations of malpractice. Furthermore, forensic experts should be willing to testify in court and explain their methods and findings in clear, understandable terms.

### 2.3.4 Bias and Objectivity in Cyber Forensics

Another ethical issue in cyber forensics is the potential for bias in the investigation and analysis of digital evidence. Cyber forensics professionals must remain objective and impartial, as any signs of bias can compromise the investigation and damage the credibility of the evidence.

**Confirmation Bias**: Confirmation bias occurs when an investigator seeks evidence that supports a preconceived hypothesis or theory, rather than examining the evidence objectively. This bias can lead to selective analysis, where only certain data is considered while potentially exonerating information is overlooked. To mitigate confirmation bias, forensic professionals should follow a systematic and thorough analysis process, documenting all relevant findings, even if they do not support the hypothesis.

**Cultural and Personal Bias**: Investigators, like anyone else, may carry their own biases based on their background, beliefs, or experiences. These biases can inadvertently influence the interpretation of evidence. For instance, a forensic expert may interpret a piece of evidence in a way that reflects their personal views, rather than an objective analysis of the facts. To counteract this, forensic professionals should engage in continuous education and reflection to recognize and mitigate the effects of their biases.

**Independence and Objectivity**: Forensic professionals must be independent and act impartially. They must avoid situations where their judgment could be compromised by external influences, whether from law enforcement agencies, corporate entities, or other stakeholders. To maintain objectivity, forensic experts should adhere to established forensic methodologies, industry standards, and ethical guidelines, avoiding any actions or decisions that could unduly influence the outcome of the investigation.

### 2.3.5 The Role of Professional Ethics and Codes of Conduct

To navigate these ethical challenges, cyber forensics professionals must adhere to established ethical frameworks and codes of conduct. Various organizations, such as the International Society of Forensic Computer Examiners (ISFCE) and the Digital Forensics Certification Board (DFCB), provide professional codes of ethics to guide investigators in making ethical decisions. These guidelines emphasize principles such as impartiality, confidentiality, transparency, and the preservation of data integrity. Adhering to such standards not only enhances the professionalism of forensic experts but also ensures that investigations are conducted with the highest ethical standards.

Ethical challenges in cyber forensics are complex and multifaceted, involving considerations of privacy, fairness, data integrity, and impartiality. Forensic professionals must navigate these challenges with care, adhering to legal standards while also respecting individual rights. By following best practices, maintaining transparency, and upholding professional ethical standards, forensic experts can conduct investigations that are both effective and ethical. The ability to address these ethical dilemmas is vital to ensuring that the field of cyber forensics remains credible, trusted, and capable of serving justice in the digital age.

# 2.4 Evidence Admissibility in Global Jurisdictions.

In cyber forensics, evidence admissibility refers to the standards and rules governing whether digital evidence can be accepted by a court of law. Since cybercrimes can span multiple regions and jurisdictions, determining the admissibility of evidence in various global contexts becomes a complex and critical issue. Different countries and regions have different legal frameworks for handling digital evidence, each with its own rules, procedures, and standards for what constitutes admissible evidence. Understanding how evidence is treated in different jurisdictions is essential for forensic investigators who operate in a global environment. This section will explore the key factors that influence evidence admissibility in cyber forensics across different countries, international agreements, and the challenges of handling digital evidence in a globalized digital world.

### 2.4.1 Legal Frameworks and Standards for Admissibility

The admissibility of digital evidence varies significantly across global jurisdictions, influenced by national laws, international agreements, and specific legal standards. Key principles governing evidence admissibility include reliability, authenticity, and chain of custody. However, each jurisdiction may apply these principles in different ways, which can create challenges for investigators working in cross-border cases.

**United States: The Federal Rules of Evidence and the Daubert Standard**

In the United States, digital evidence must comply with the Federal Rules of Evidence (FRE), which outline the legal criteria for the admission of evidence in federal court. Forensic evidence, including digital data, must be reliable, relevant, and authentic. A key standard used in federal courts to determine the admissibility of forensic evidence is the Daubert Standard, which provides guidelines for expert testimony. The standard requires that scientific methods and techniques, including those used in digital forensics, be tested, peer-reviewed, and widely accepted in the relevant field. This ensures that the methods used to collect and analyze digital evidence are both scientifically sound and legally admissible.

**European Union: The General Data Protection Regulation (GDPR) and the E-Privacy Directive**

The European Union (EU) has specific privacy protections that complicate the admissibility of digital evidence. The General Data Protection Regulation (GDPR), which governs the processing of personal data, mandates strict standards for how data is collected, stored, and used. The E-Privacy Directive provides additional protections regarding electronic communications. Forensic investigators working within the EU must ensure that they comply with these regulations to avoid violating individuals' privacy rights, particularly when dealing with data that crosses borders or is stored in the cloud. As a result, the admissibility of evidence collected without consent or in violation of these rules may be questioned in EU courts. Additionally, the European Convention on Human Rights (ECHR) ensures the protection of individuals' privacy, requiring investigators to demonstrate that their activities respect privacy rights.

**United Kingdom: The Police and Criminal Evidence Act (PACE) 1984 and the Regulation of Investigatory Powers Act (RIPA)**

In the United Kingdom, the Police and Criminal Evidence Act (PACE) 1984 provides the legal framework for the admissibility of evidence, including digital evidence, in criminal cases. Under PACE, evidence must be obtained legally and must be preserved without contamination, particularly in relation to digital devices and data. Additionally, the Regulation of Investigatory Powers Act (RIPA) regulates the use of surveillance and interception of communications, further impacting the collection and admissibility of digital evidence. Forensic professionals must ensure they have the proper legal authorization before accessing or sharing digital evidence to avoid challenges to its admissibility.

**Australia: The Australian Evidence Act 1995 and the Telecommunications (Interception and Access) Act 1979**

In Australia, the Australian Evidence Act 1995 governs the admissibility of evidence, including digital forensics. Like other jurisdictions, evidence must be reliable, authentic, and collected following the appropriate legal procedures. Forensic experts must ensure they adhere to the Telecommunications (Interception and Access) Act 1979, which regulates the interception of communications and the collection of electronic data. In addition, Australia has stringent rules regarding the admissibility of data obtained from overseas, making cross-border data access and the handling of digital evidence from foreign jurisdictions a potential challenge.

**2.4.2 International Treaties and Agreements on Evidence Admissibility**

In a globalized digital world, cybercrimes often span multiple countries, making it necessary to deal with international treaties and mutual legal assistance agreements (MLAAs). These agreements provide mechanisms for international cooperation in investigating and prosecuting cybercrimes, including the collection and sharing of digital evidence.

## The Budapest Convention on Cybercrime

The Council of Europe's Budapest Convention on Cybercrime (also known as the Cybercrime Treaty) is the first international treaty aimed at addressing internet and computer crime. It sets out guidelines for the cross-border exchange of digital evidence and cooperation between signatory countries in investigating cybercrime. The convention encourages parties to harmonize their domestic laws regarding the investigation and prosecution of cybercrimes, which helps establish a shared legal framework for handling digital evidence. However, countries must still adapt their local legal systems to the convention's principles, leading to varying degrees of compliance and enforcement.

## The European Union's Mutual Legal Assistance Treaties (MLATs)

The European Union and other countries have established Mutual Legal Assistance Treaties (MLATs) to facilitate the sharing of evidence between jurisdictions. MLATs provide a formal process for one country to request evidence from another, ensuring that the evidence is collected and handled in accordance with the laws of the requesting country. However, these treaties can be slow and cumbersome, especially when dealing with digital data, which can be easily transmitted across borders without physical constraints. As a result, the handling of digital evidence often requires careful attention to ensure that it complies with the legal frameworks in both the requesting and providing countries.

## The CLOUD Act (Clarifying Lawful Overseas Use of Data Act)

In the United States, the CLOUD Act allows U.S. law enforcement agencies to access data stored overseas, provided that the data is stored by companies subject to U.S. jurisdiction. The CLOUD Act allows for direct requests for data without going through the traditional process of mutual legal assistance, but this has raised concerns regarding international data sovereignty and privacy. While the CLOUD Act has made it easier for U.S. authorities to obtain digital evidence from companies operating in the U.S., it has also sparked international debates about the ability of foreign governments to access data that is held by companies within U.S. jurisdiction. Some countries, such as the EU, have expressed concerns over the implications of this law for privacy and data protection.

### 2.4.3 Challenges in Admissibility of Cross-Border Digital Evidence

Handling cross-border digital evidence presents a number of challenges for forensic investigators. Evidence obtained in one jurisdiction may not automatically be admissible in another, and there are potential conflicts between local privacy laws and international evidence-sharing agreements. Key challenges include:

**Jurisdictional Issues**: In cybercrime cases, it is often unclear which country has jurisdiction over the evidence, especially when the evidence is stored in the cloud or on servers located in a different country. Jurisdictional disputes can delay investigations and complicate the admissibility of evidence. Courts may need to determine which jurisdiction's laws apply to the evidence, and different countries may have conflicting rules regarding what constitutes admissible evidence.

**Privacy Laws and Sovereignty**: Privacy regulations in one country may not align with those in another. For instance, the European Union's GDPR requires strict adherence to privacy protections, which may not be compatible with the less stringent privacy standards in other countries. This creates difficulties when attempting to share digital evidence across borders, as one country's legal requirements may conflict with another's. Forensic professionals must navigate these challenges by ensuring compliance with all relevant laws and considering potential conflicts between national and international standards.

**Data Integrity and Preservation**: When digital evidence crosses borders, it must be preserved in a way that ensures its integrity and authenticity. Investigators may face challenges in ensuring that digital evidence remains unaltered during transit, particularly when dealing with data transfers between countries with differing legal frameworks. Preserving the chain of custody is vital to ensure that evidence remains admissible in court, but this can be more difficult in cross-border cases where different jurisdictions may not have compatible procedures.

Admissibility of digital evidence in global jurisdictions is a complex and evolving issue, shaped by national laws, international treaties, and the growing importance of digital data in cybercrime investigations. Forensic professionals must understand the different legal frameworks governing evidence collection, handling, and admissibility in various jurisdictions to ensure the evidence is valid in the eyes of the law. While international cooperation through treaties and agreements helps facilitate the exchange of digital evidence, challenges remain, particularly when it comes to navigating conflicting privacy regulations, jurisdictional issues, and ensuring the preservation of evidence across borders. Addressing these challenges requires careful attention, expertise, and adherence to both local and international legal standards to maintain the credibility and admissibility of digital evidence in a globalized world.

# 3. Anatomy of a Cyberattack

Every cyberattack follows a structured path, from reconnaissance to execution, leaving traces that forensic experts must decipher. This chapter unpacks the lifecycle of a cyberattack, providing a detailed look at common attack vectors like phishing, ransomware, and Advanced Persistent Threats (APTs). It explores the techniques used by hackers to infiltrate systems, escalate privileges, and exfiltrate sensitive data. By dissecting the attacker's mindset and methods, readers will gain a deeper understanding of how cyber threats unfold and how forensic investigations can uncover the truth behind the breach.

## 3.1 Common Attack Vectors and Methods.

In the world of cybersecurity, understanding the various attack vectors and methods used by cybercriminals is critical to developing effective strategies for prevention, detection, and response. Attack vectors are the pathways through which attackers gain unauthorized access to systems, networks, or devices. These vectors are often exploited to initiate attacks that can lead to data breaches, financial loss, system downtime, or other malicious consequences. By recognizing the most common attack methods, cybersecurity professionals can better prepare defenses and identify vulnerabilities before they are exploited.

This section will explore the primary attack vectors and the methods commonly used by attackers to exploit these vulnerabilities, providing insight into how cybercriminals operate and the risks they pose to both individuals and organizations.

### 3.1.1 Phishing and Social Engineering Attacks

One of the most prevalent and effective methods of attack is phishing, a form of social engineering that manipulates individuals into revealing sensitive information, such as login credentials, personal identification data, or financial details. Phishing relies on exploiting human trust rather than technological vulnerabilities, making it particularly dangerous and difficult to defend against.

**Email Phishing**: The most common form of phishing is email phishing, where attackers send emails that appear to come from legitimate sources such as banks, government agencies, or popular services. These emails often contain malicious links or attachments that, when clicked, lead to the installation of malware or the theft of credentials. Phishing emails may also direct recipients to fake websites that closely resemble legitimate login pages, tricking users into entering their personal information.

**Spear Phishing**: Unlike broad, generic phishing campaigns, spear phishing is highly targeted and often involves thorough research on the victim. Attackers may gather information from social media profiles, corporate websites, or other publicly available sources to craft a convincing email that appears to come from someone the victim knows, such as a colleague, boss, or trusted vendor. This method makes it even harder for the victim to detect the attack, as it is personalized to their interests or professional environment.

**Whaling**: A specific form of spear phishing that targets high-level executives or individuals in positions of power (often referred to as "big fish" or "whales"). Whaling attacks are often more sophisticated and convincing, leveraging social engineering to exploit the victim's authority or responsibilities. For example, attackers might impersonate a CEO requesting urgent financial transfers or sensitive information from a subordinate, knowing that the urgency of the request will prompt immediate action.

**Vishing and SMiShing**: Vishing (voice phishing) and SMiShing (SMS phishing) are variations of phishing that use phone calls or text messages to trick individuals into revealing confidential information. In vishing attacks, attackers may impersonate banks or government agencies over the phone and ask for personal details or security codes. SMiShing works similarly, where attackers send text messages containing links to fake websites or instructions to call a fake customer service number.

### 3.1.2 Malware Attacks

Malware, short for malicious software, is any software intentionally designed to cause harm to a computer system, network, or device. Cybercriminals use malware to infiltrate systems, steal data, disrupt operations, or cause other damage. Various types of malware can be delivered through different attack vectors, such as email attachments, malicious websites, or infected software downloads.

**Viruses**: A virus is a type of malware that attaches itself to a legitimate program or file and spreads when the infected program or file is executed. Once executed, the virus can alter, delete, or corrupt data, and it can spread further to other files or systems. Some viruses are designed to trigger only under specific conditions, making them difficult to detect until they are activated.

**Trojans**: A Trojan horse (or simply, Trojan) is a type of malware that disguises itself as a legitimate or useful program but performs malicious actions once installed. Trojans often rely on social engineering to trick users into downloading and installing them, with the malware functioning silently in the background. Unlike viruses or worms, Trojans do not replicate themselves but can still cause significant damage, such as stealing data or providing remote access to attackers.

**Ransomware**: Ransomware is a form of malware that locks or encrypts a victim's files or entire system, making them inaccessible until a ransom is paid to the attacker. Ransomware attacks typically involve a demand for cryptocurrency (e.g., Bitcoin) in exchange for the decryption key or unlocking the files. Modern ransomware can spread rapidly across networks, causing widespread disruption and financial losses. Notable examples of ransomware include WannaCry and Ryuk.

**Spyware and Adware**: Spyware is malicious software that secretly monitors a user's actions, such as logging keystrokes, tracking browsing habits, or stealing personal information. Adware is a type of malware that displays intrusive advertisements, often in the form of pop-up windows or unwanted redirects. While adware is often seen as a nuisance, spyware poses a more serious threat as it can compromise sensitive data, including login credentials or financial information.

### 3.1.3 Distributed Denial of Service (DDoS) Attacks

A Distributed Denial of Service (DDoS) attack is an attempt to make an online service or website unavailable by overwhelming it with massive amounts of traffic. DDoS attacks are typically carried out by networks of compromised computers, known as botnets, which are controlled by the attacker to send a flood of traffic to the target. The goal of a DDoS attack is not to breach or steal data but to cause service disruption or downtime.

**Volumetric Attacks**: These attacks aim to consume the target's bandwidth by flooding the network with large amounts of data, often through methods such as ICMP floods or UDP floods. Volumetric attacks are effective at crippling a website's ability to serve legitimate traffic, as the sheer volume of traffic exceeds the target's capacity to handle requests.

**Application Layer Attacks**: Application layer attacks focus on specific aspects of a web application, such as sending requests to overload web servers or database connections. Unlike volumetric attacks, which are based on traffic volume, application layer attacks are designed to exhaust the resources of a specific application or service, making it slow or unavailable.

**Amplification Attacks**: In amplification DDoS attacks, attackers use vulnerable systems or services to amplify the traffic sent to a target. For example, an attacker might send small requests to a vulnerable server, which in turn sends large responses to the victim. By exploiting these amplifying systems, attackers can launch large-scale DDoS attacks with minimal effort.

### 3.1.4 Exploiting Software Vulnerabilities

Many cyberattacks are based on the exploitation of software vulnerabilities that allow attackers to gain unauthorized access or control over systems and applications. These vulnerabilities are typically flaws or weaknesses in software code that can be exploited to bypass security controls, execute malicious code, or steal sensitive data.

**Zero-Day Exploits**: A zero-day exploit refers to a vulnerability in software that is unknown to the software vendor or security community. Because the flaw is undiscovered, there is no patch or fix available, making it an attractive target for attackers. Zero-day exploits are highly valuable to cybercriminals and are often used in advanced persistent threats (APTs) to gain undetected access to systems.

**SQL Injection**: SQL injection occurs when an attacker is able to inject malicious SQL code into a vulnerable database query, allowing them to manipulate the database and access, modify, or delete sensitive data. SQL injection attacks often target web applications that fail to properly sanitize user inputs, allowing attackers to execute arbitrary queries on the backend database.

**Cross-Site Scripting (XSS)**: XSS is a vulnerability in which an attacker injects malicious scripts into a web page that are executed by other users' browsers. This can allow attackers to steal session cookies, redirect users to malicious websites, or perform actions on behalf of a user without their consent. XSS is particularly dangerous because it can target users directly, allowing attackers to steal sensitive information or compromise accounts.

**Privilege Escalation**: Privilege escalation attacks occur when an attacker exploits a vulnerability to gain elevated access rights or administrative privileges within a system. These attacks often begin with the attacker compromising a low-level user account and then exploiting flaws to escalate their privileges, eventually gaining full control of the system or network.

Cybercriminals utilize a wide range of attack vectors and methods to compromise systems and steal data. The attacks outlined in this section—phishing, malware, DDoS, and the exploitation of software vulnerabilities—represent just a few of the most common and dangerous techniques. As technology evolves, so too do the methods used by attackers. By understanding these attack vectors and methods, cybersecurity professionals can better prepare for, detect, and mitigate the risks posed by cybercriminals, ensuring stronger protection for their organizations and individuals. As the threat landscape continues to grow, staying vigilant and proactive remains essential for defending against evolving cyber threats.

## 3.2 The Cyber Kill Chain: Phases of an Attack.

The Cyber Kill Chain is a model developed by Lockheed Martin that outlines the stages of a cyberattack from initial reconnaissance to the final exfiltration of data or damage to the target system. It provides a structured approach to understanding the sequence of steps that attackers typically follow when launching a cyberattack. By breaking down the attack process into distinct phases, security professionals can identify vulnerabilities at each stage and implement strategies to prevent, detect, and respond to attacks more effectively. This model has become an essential framework in cybersecurity for threat intelligence, incident response, and forensics.

The Cyber Kill Chain consists of seven stages, each representing a different phase in the lifecycle of an attack. Understanding each of these phases is crucial for improving defensive measures, identifying malicious activities early, and preventing attackers from succeeding in their objectives.

### 3.2.1 Phase 1: Reconnaissance (Preparation)

The reconnaissance phase is the first step in the cyber kill chain and is often referred to as the pre-attack phase. During this stage, the attacker gathers information about the target organization, its systems, employees, and infrastructure. This phase can be either active or passive, depending on the methods used.

**Passive Reconnaissance**: In this type of reconnaissance, attackers collect publicly available information from sources such as social media platforms, websites, DNS records, and WHOIS databases. They may learn about the target's employees, technologies in use, or vulnerabilities in publicly accessible systems. This information can be invaluable in planning a more focused attack.

**Active Reconnaissance**: In contrast, active reconnaissance involves more direct interaction with the target system, such as scanning networks or probing for vulnerabilities. This stage is riskier for the attacker because it involves direct engagement with the target and increases the likelihood of detection by security systems. Tools like Nmap or Shodan can be used to map out the target network and identify open ports, services, and weaknesses.

Reconnaissance is critical because it allows attackers to understand the target environment and plan their attack with precision, choosing the best vector and method to exploit vulnerabilities.

### 3.2.2 Phase 2: Weaponization

The weaponization phase occurs once the attacker has gathered sufficient information about the target. In this stage, the attacker prepares the malicious payload and pairs it with an exploit that will allow them to deliver the attack. Essentially, the attacker takes a vulnerability discovered during reconnaissance and develops a weaponized attack that can take advantage of it.

**Malware Creation**: The attacker may create malware such as viruses, Trojans, ransomware, or exploits to be delivered to the target. This can include social engineering tactics, such as designing phishing emails that contain malicious attachments or links that, when clicked, execute the payload.

**Exploit Development**: The attacker often customizes the exploit based on the vulnerabilities identified in the target system. This could involve developing a zero-day exploit (a vulnerability previously unknown to the vendor) or modifying an existing exploit to suit the target's configuration.

During weaponization, the goal is to craft a tailored attack that has the highest chance of success based on the vulnerabilities of the target. It is during this phase that attackers refine their tactics to maximize impact.

### 3.2.3 Phase 3: Delivery

The delivery phase is the stage where the attacker attempts to deliver the weaponized payload to the target system or network. This is typically the first stage in which the target becomes aware that something may be amiss, although the delivery itself is not always immediately visible to the target.

**Phishing Emails**: A common method for delivering malware is through phishing emails, where the attacker sends an email with a malicious attachment or link. When the victim opens the attachment or clicks the link, the malicious code is executed.

**Drive-by Downloads**: In some cases, attackers use websites or advertisements to infect a user's device. This technique, called a drive-by download, happens when a victim visits a compromised website that automatically downloads malware onto their computer without their knowledge.

**Exploiting Network Vulnerabilities**: Attackers may also deliver exploits directly to the target through vulnerable web servers, or by using Remote Desktop Protocol (RDP) brute-force attacks to gain access to the network.

Once the payload is delivered, the attacker's next goal is to execute it, ideally without detection by the target's security defenses.

### 3.2.4 Phase 4: Exploitation

In the exploitation phase, the attacker's weaponized payload is activated to exploit the specific vulnerabilities of the target system. The goal of this phase is to gain unauthorized access to the system or network.

**Execution of Malware**: If the attacker used a phishing email with a malicious link or attachment, the malware would now execute once the victim interacts with it. Similarly, if the attacker used a vulnerability to deploy a backdoor or shell, that's when they would gain access to the system.

**Privilege Escalation**: Once inside the target system, the attacker will attempt to escalate their privileges. This can involve exploiting additional vulnerabilities in the system to gain higher-level access, such as administrator or root privileges, which give the attacker full control of the system.

**Payload Execution**: If the goal is data theft, the attacker might now have the ability to access confidential files. If the goal is a DDoS attack, this might be the stage where the attacker executes the code to flood the target server with traffic.

The exploitation phase is where the attacker gains control over the target system, making it the most critical part of the kill chain. Success in this phase gives the attacker the ability to carry out further actions, such as moving laterally within the network.

### 3.2.5 Phase 5: Installation

Once the attacker has gained access to the target system, the installation phase involves ensuring that the attacker has a persistent foothold within the network. The attacker will aim to install tools or software that allow them to maintain access to the system, even if the initial exploit is discovered and mitigated.

**Backdoors**: Attackers often install backdoors—malicious software that provides an entry point into the system at a later time. This allows them to bypass security measures and return to the system when needed without having to re-exploit the initial vulnerability.

**Rootkits**: A rootkit is a type of malware designed to hide the presence of malicious activity on a system. Rootkits can disguise files, processes, or network connections used by the attacker, making detection much more difficult for security professionals.

The installation phase is critical for maintaining control over the target system, ensuring the attacker can continue to exploit the system even after the initial attack vector is closed.

### 3.2.6 Phase 6: Command and Control (C2)

In the command and control (C2) phase, the attacker establishes a communication channel with the compromised system to issue commands, exfiltrate data, or perform further malicious activities. This phase is crucial for attackers who want to maintain control over the target environment and potentially deploy additional malware.

**C2 Servers**: Attackers often set up remote C2 servers that allow them to issue instructions to the compromised systems. These servers may use encrypted channels to avoid detection by security systems.

**Botnets**: Attackers often leverage compromised systems to form botnets—networks of infected machines that can be controlled remotely to launch coordinated attacks, such as DDoS or spam campaigns.

Command and control enables the attacker to keep their presence undetected while issuing commands or spreading their attack further.

### 3.2.7 Phase 7: Actions on Objectives

The final phase of the cyber kill chain, actions on objectives, is when the attacker achieves their end goal. This could be data exfiltration, destruction of data, financial theft, or system disruption, depending on the nature of the attack.

**Data Exfiltration**: Attackers often steal sensitive data during this phase, including financial records, intellectual property, or personal identifying information (PII).

**Destruction of Data**: In some cases, attackers may choose to destroy or corrupt data, either as part of a ransomware attack (where data is encrypted until a ransom is paid) or as an act of sabotage.

**Lateral Movement**: Attackers may also move laterally within the network, compromising additional systems and further extending their control.

This phase represents the attacker achieving their objectives, which could have severe consequences for the target organization, ranging from financial loss to reputational damage and legal liabilities.

The Cyber Kill Chain offers a structured framework for understanding how cyberattacks unfold, from reconnaissance to achieving the attacker's objectives. By identifying and addressing each phase of the kill chain, organizations can develop better detection and prevention strategies at each step, potentially stopping attackers before they can exploit vulnerabilities. Implementing strong security measures, such as intrusion detection systems, endpoint protection, and network monitoring, can help organizations disrupt the kill chain and prevent cybercriminals from achieving their malicious goals. Understanding the phases of a cyberattack and applying countermeasures at each stage is crucial for building a resilient defense against modern cyber threats.

## 3.3 Understanding Advanced Persistent Threats (APTs).

An Advanced Persistent Threat (APT) represents a sophisticated and sustained cyberattack where an adversary gains unauthorized access to a network and remains undetected for a prolonged period. APTs are highly targeted, often involving a combination of multiple attack vectors and advanced techniques to infiltrate, maintain access, and achieve specific goals such as espionage, intellectual property theft, or data exfiltration. Unlike typical cyberattacks that are often opportunistic and short-lived, APTs are methodical, persistent, and aim for long-term infiltration, making them one of the most dangerous types of cyber threats.

This section explores the concept of APTs, their characteristics, the stages involved in an APT attack, and how organizations can defend against these highly complex and evasive threats.

### 3.3.1 Defining Advanced Persistent Threats

At its core, an APT is an organized, often state-sponsored or highly motivated group that carries out targeted cyberattacks to achieve strategic, political, or financial goals. The "advanced" in APT refers to the use of sophisticated tools, techniques, and methodologies that make these attacks difficult to detect and mitigate. The term "persistent" underscores the fact that APTs involve continuous and prolonged efforts to remain inside the victim's network over time, with attackers working to avoid detection and gradually achieve their objectives.

An APT attack typically involves the following characteristics:

**Targeted**: APTs are not random; they focus on specific organizations, industries, or even individuals. Attackers often conduct extensive reconnaissance to gather intelligence on their target before launching an attack. This focus makes APTs particularly dangerous because the attackers are highly skilled and have a clear understanding of the target's vulnerabilities.

**Sophisticated**: APT attackers use highly advanced tools and techniques, often custom-built, to bypass security measures and maintain stealth. This includes leveraging zero-day vulnerabilities, exploiting unpatched software, and using encryption or obfuscation methods to conceal their activities.

**Persistent**: Unlike typical cyberattacks, APTs are long-term operations. Once attackers gain access to the target network, they work to maintain that access indefinitely, often using techniques like backdoors, rootkits, and other tools that allow them to stay undetected for months or even years.

**Multi-stage**: APT attacks unfold in multiple stages over a significant amount of time, with the attackers gradually escalating their activities and objectives. Attackers often establish initial access and then move laterally across the network, escalating privileges and avoiding detection as they gather sensitive data or deploy malware.

### 3.3.2 Phases of an APT Attack

While every APT is unique, they generally follow a series of stages that mirror the classic Cyber Kill Chain. These phases describe the various actions an attacker takes to infiltrate a network, maintain access, and achieve their goals. The following are the typical stages of an APT:

### Initial Reconnaissance and Target Identification:

The first step in an APT attack involves reconnaissance, where the attacker gathers information about the target. This could include mapping the target's network, identifying employees, analyzing software used, or finding weaknesses in external defenses such as firewalls or public-facing services. This information is often gathered using both active (direct probing) and passive (open-source intelligence) methods.

### Weaponization and Exploit Development:

Once the attacker understands the target's environment, they develop a weaponized payload tailored to exploit specific vulnerabilities in the target's network. This may involve exploiting zero-day vulnerabilities (previously unknown security flaws) or using commonly available tools to create customized exploits. The goal is to silently gain access to the system without triggering security alerts.

### Delivery and Exploitation:

Attackers often deliver their malicious payload via methods like phishing emails, malicious attachments, or drive-by downloads. Once the payload is delivered, it's executed, allowing the attacker to gain initial access to the target's systems. In some cases, attackers use social engineering tactics to trick employees into running malware or providing credentials.

### Establishing Command and Control (C2):

After exploitation, the attacker establishes a command and control (C2) channel, typically using encrypted communication channels to avoid detection. This allows them to remotely control the compromised system, issue further instructions, and maintain access over time. This phase is critical for long-term persistence, as the attacker may install backdoors or other tools to remain undetected.

### Lateral Movement and Privilege Escalation:

To deepen their foothold, attackers move laterally across the network, escalating privileges as they go. By exploiting vulnerabilities or using stolen credentials, they gain access to additional systems, databases, and sensitive resources. Lateral movement helps the attacker avoid detection by remaining within a network segment that may not have robust monitoring.

**Data Exfiltration or Sabotage:**

The ultimate goal of most APTs is to exfiltrate valuable data, whether it's intellectual property, financial records, or government secrets. In some cases, attackers may sabotage systems or delete critical data, causing operational disruption. They often compress and encrypt stolen data to avoid detection by security monitoring systems. If the objective is espionage, the exfiltrated data may be transmitted back to the attacker's servers, often in small, undetectable chunks to evade detection.

**Covering Tracks and Persistence:**

Throughout the attack, APT attackers work to avoid detection by covering their tracks. This may involve deleting logs, using rootkits to hide their activities, and ensuring that any traces of their presence are erased. Attackers also focus on maintaining long-term access to the target network, ensuring that even if their initial foothold is discovered, they can reinfiltrate the network quickly.

### 3.3.3 Characteristics of APT Attackers

APT attackers are typically well-resourced and skilled, often belonging to nation-state actors, cybercriminal syndicates, or highly organized hacker groups. These attackers are different from opportunistic hackers or common cybercriminals in several key ways:

**High Levels of Expertise**: APT groups are composed of highly skilled individuals, often with backgrounds in computer science, cryptography, or networking. They employ a variety of technical and strategic methods, including reverse engineering, social engineering, and custom malware development, to gain access and maintain control over targeted networks.

**Organized and Coordinated Efforts**: APT attacks are usually carried out by well-coordinated teams of cybercriminals working over an extended period. These attacks are meticulously planned, and each team member plays a specific role, from reconnaissance to data exfiltration, making it a highly organized operation.

**Resource Availability**: Nation-state actors, for example, have access to significant resources, including advanced tools, funding, and infrastructure. These resources allow APT groups to sustain long-term operations and develop sophisticated tools to evade detection.

**Clear Objectives**: Unlike typical cybercriminals who may target systems for financial gain, APT attackers usually have strategic goals, such as espionage, intellectual property theft, political motives, or sabotage. Their actions are driven by the desire to gain intelligence, disrupt operations, or destabilize their targets.

### 3.3.4 Detection and Mitigation of APTs

Detecting and mitigating APTs requires a proactive and multi-layered approach to cybersecurity. Traditional security measures, such as firewalls and antivirus software, are often insufficient because APT attackers are skilled at evading these defenses. However, several strategies can help detect and neutralize APT threats:

**Network Monitoring and Anomaly Detection**: Continuous network monitoring is essential for detecting unusual patterns of behavior that could indicate an APT. Intrusion detection systems (IDS) and Security Information and Event Management (SIEM) solutions can help identify suspicious activities, such as unexpected data transfers, unusual user behavior, or failed login attempts.

**Endpoint Detection and Response (EDR):** EDR tools monitor endpoint devices for signs of compromise, including malware, unauthorized access, and unusual system behavior. These tools provide a deeper level of visibility into endpoints and can help detect hidden backdoors and lateral movement.

**Threat Intelligence Sharing**: Organizations can benefit from collaborating with other entities by sharing information about new threats and vulnerabilities. By participating in information sharing programs or threat intelligence platforms, organizations can stay ahead of emerging APT tactics and techniques.

**Incident Response and Containment**: Once an APT is detected, a rapid response is essential. This includes isolating compromised systems, conducting a thorough investigation, and ensuring that all traces of the attack are removed from the network. Forensically sound procedures should be followed to understand how the attack occurred and identify any data exfiltrated.

**Zero Trust Architecture**: Adopting a Zero Trust security model, where every user and device is treated as a potential threat and must be authenticated and authorized continuously, can help limit the damage of an APT attack. This model reduces the attack surface and limits lateral movement once an attacker gains initial access.

Advanced Persistent Threats (APTs) are among the most sophisticated and dangerous types of cyberattacks, characterized by long-term persistence, highly targeted objectives, and advanced attack techniques. Unlike typical attacks, APTs are methodical and strategic, making them difficult to detect and defend against. Understanding the phases of an APT attack, recognizing the unique characteristics of these threats, and implementing a multi-layered defense strategy are crucial for organizations aiming to protect themselves from these persistent and advanced cyber adversaries.

# 3.4 Behavioral Analysis of Hackers and Threat Actors.

Understanding the behavior of hackers and threat actors is a critical aspect of cybersecurity and forensic investigations. By analyzing the motivations, tactics, and patterns of cybercriminals, organizations can better anticipate potential attacks, improve their defensive strategies, and identify vulnerabilities before they are exploited. In this section, we explore the psychological and strategic behaviors of hackers and threat actors, categorize different types of attackers, and discuss how their actions can be predicted and mitigated.

### 3.4.1 Categorizing Hackers and Threat Actors

Hackers and threat actors vary in their methods, motivations, and targets. Understanding the types of threat actors is crucial in identifying potential attackers and determining the most effective ways to defend against them. Cybercriminals typically fall into one of the following categories:

**Hacktivists:**

- **Motivation**: Hacktivists are individuals or groups that use cyberattacks as a form of protest or to promote political or social agendas. Their actions are often driven by ideology rather than financial gain.
- **Behavior**: Hacktivist attacks typically include website defacement, DDoS (Distributed Denial-of-Service) attacks, and data breaches aimed at embarrassing or discrediting the target. The focus of these attacks is on creating public awareness or disruption, rather than financial gain.

- **Example**: Groups like Anonymous are often associated with hacktivism, engaging in cyberattacks on organizations that they believe are unethical or politically opposed to their values.

## Cybercriminals:

- **Motivation**: Cybercriminals are motivated primarily by financial gain. They engage in activities such as ransomware attacks, phishing, identity theft, and credit card fraud.
- **Behavior**: Cybercriminals often target individuals, small businesses, or large enterprises with the intention of stealing sensitive financial information, holding systems hostage, or disrupting operations for monetary reward.
- **Example**: A notorious example of cybercriminal behavior is the operation of ransomware gangs, such as REvil or Conti, which infect systems, encrypt files, and demand payment in exchange for the decryption key.

## State-Sponsored Actors:

- **Motivation**: State-sponsored hackers are typically driven by national or geopolitical objectives. Their goal is often to spy on governments, steal sensitive intelligence, or disrupt critical infrastructure.
- **Behavior**: These actors are highly sophisticated, often using advanced malware, zero-day exploits, and persistent infiltration tactics to gather intelligence or sabotage an adversary's systems. They can remain undetected for long periods while executing their operations.
- **Example**: One of the most well-known examples of state-sponsored hacking is the Stuxnet attack, allegedly carried out by U.S. and Israeli hackers, which targeted Iran's nuclear enrichment facilities.

## Insiders:

- **Motivation**: Insiders are individuals within an organization who abuse their access to systems for personal, financial, or malicious reasons. Their motivations may range from financial gain to revenge or espionage.
- **Behavior**: Insider threats are particularly dangerous because they exploit legitimate access privileges. Insider attacks may involve data theft, fraud, or sabotage. These actors are often difficult to detect, as they can blend in with normal operations.

- Example: The Edward Snowden case, where a former National Security Agency (NSA) contractor leaked classified information, is a well-known instance of insider threat.

**Script Kiddies:**

- **Motivation**: Script kiddies are typically inexperienced hackers who use pre-written tools or scripts to exploit vulnerabilities, often without a full understanding of how the attack works. Their motivation is often the desire for recognition, fun, or proving their skills.
- **Behavior**: These attackers tend to focus on easy targets and are usually not as sophisticated as other threat actors. They engage in activities like defacing websites, spamming, or launching basic denial-of-service attacks.
- **Example**: Many small-scale attacks attributed to SQL injection or DDoS attacks are carried out by script kiddies using open-source tools available on the dark web.

**Cyber Espionage Actors:**

- **Motivation**: Cyber espionage actors are primarily motivated by gaining access to sensitive information, such as intellectual property, corporate secrets, or classified government data. These attacks are typically carried out by state-sponsored groups or corporate competitors.
- **Behavior**: Cyber espionage actors engage in long-term infiltration campaigns, carefully avoiding detection while they gather intelligence. Their attacks are highly targeted and involve multiple techniques such as social engineering, spear-phishing, and advanced malware.
- **Example**: The APT28 group, also known as Fancy Bear, has been linked to cyber espionage campaigns targeting government organizations, think tanks, and political entities in the U.S. and Europe.

### 3.4.2 Motivations Behind Hacking

The behavior of hackers is often shaped by underlying motivations, which can vary widely depending on the attacker's objectives. Some of the most common motivations include:

**Financial Gain:**

Many cyberattacks are financially motivated. Cybercriminals target individuals and organizations to steal money, credit card information, or intellectual property. They may use techniques such as ransomware, banking Trojans, or credit card fraud to extract financial value from their victims.

**Political or Ideological Objectives:**

Hacktivists and some state-sponsored actors are motivated by a desire to influence political events, promote social causes, or destabilize governments or industries they perceive as unethical. These attackers often use cyberattacks as a tool for protest or to disrupt the operations of entities they view as adversaries.

**Espionage:**

Corporate espionage and government-sponsored espionage are common in both the private and public sectors. Attackers target organizations to steal trade secrets, proprietary technologies, or sensitive government intelligence. Espionage attackers are typically well-funded, organized, and skilled in maintaining long-term access to targeted systems.

**Revenge or Personal Vendettas:**

Insiders, disgruntled employees, or individuals with a personal vendetta may engage in malicious activities to retaliate against an organization or individual. These attacks can range from data theft to the destruction of critical systems or intellectual property.

**Demonstration of Skill or Recognition:**

Script kiddies and some hacktivists are driven by the desire to demonstrate their hacking skills, gain recognition, or challenge others in the hacking community. These attackers typically engage in smaller-scale attacks or high-profile cyber disruptions to make a name for themselves.

### 3.4.3 Identifying Hacker Behavior Patterns

Behavioral analysis of hackers involves identifying indicators of compromise (IoCs) and understanding the tactics, techniques, and procedures (TTPs) used during attacks. By observing patterns in cyberattacks, defenders can predict the likely next move of a hacker, anticipate their tactics, and improve response strategies.

**Reconnaissance Behavior:**

Hackers often begin by gathering information about the target. This could include scanning for vulnerabilities, gathering intelligence through social engineering, or using tools to map the network. Recognizing this pattern early on through network logs or suspicious scanning activity can allow defenders to detect potential attacks.

**Infiltration and Exploitation:**

Once reconnaissance is completed, attackers proceed to infiltrate the network, often using phishing or exploiting software vulnerabilities. Attackers may attempt multiple methods of access, including spear-phishing emails, exploiting unpatched software, or using brute-force attacks to crack passwords. Identifying unsuccessful login attempts or anomalies in network traffic can indicate attempts to gain access.

**Lateral Movement:**

After initial access is gained, attackers often move laterally within the network, looking for higher privileges or access to sensitive data. Behavioral indicators include unusual file transfers, unusual user activities, or connections to systems outside the normal working environment.

**Data Exfiltration or Destruction:**

The final behavior to observe is the exfiltration of data or destruction of critical systems. Exfiltration behaviors may include large data transfers or encrypting files for ransom. Destructive behavior often involves deleting logs, wiping systems, or deploying ransomware to disable operations.

**3.4.4 Mitigating and Defending Against Threat Actor Behavior**

Understanding hacker behavior is crucial for improving detection and defense mechanisms. The following approaches can help organizations mitigate and respond to these evolving threats:

**Continuous Monitoring:**

By continuously monitoring network traffic, logs, and endpoints, organizations can detect early signs of suspicious behavior that may indicate a threat actor is present. Implementing tools like Security Information and Event Management (SIEM) and Endpoint Detection and Response (EDR) solutions can help spot anomalous patterns in real time.

**Behavioral Analytics:**

Leveraging User and Entity Behavior Analytics (UEBA) systems can help detect deviations from normal user activity. These systems use machine learning algorithms to identify suspicious activities that may indicate an attacker is moving laterally, escalating privileges, or exfiltrating data.

**Training and Awareness:**

Since social engineering is one of the most common tactics used by hackers, educating employees about phishing, spear-phishing, and other social engineering techniques can help prevent initial compromises.

**Red and Blue Team Exercises:**

Red teaming involves simulating cyberattacks to test an organization's defenses, while blue teaming focuses on defending against these simulated attacks. By engaging in regular exercises, organizations can better understand hacker tactics and improve their response strategies.

Behavioral analysis of hackers and threat actors provides invaluable insights into the nature of cyberattacks. Understanding the motivations, tactics, and behaviors of different types of attackers enables organizations to predict and defend against evolving threats. By leveraging detection systems, continuous monitoring, and cybersecurity best practices, organizations can strengthen their defenses and mitigate the risks posed by various threat actors.

# 4. Foundations of Digital Evidence

Digital evidence is the backbone of forensic cybersecurity, serving as the key to understanding, analyzing, and resolving cyber incidents. This chapter examines the fundamental principles of digital evidence, distinguishing between volatile and non-volatile data and exploring its various sources, from computers and mobile devices to network logs and IoT gadgets. Readers will learn how to locate, preserve, and authenticate digital evidence while adhering to strict legal and procedural standards. With a focus on integrity and reliability, this chapter lays the groundwork for effective and admissible forensic investigations.

## 4.1 Categories of Digital Evidence and Their Characteristics.

In forensic cybersecurity, digital evidence plays a crucial role in investigating cybercrimes, data breaches, or any unauthorized access to digital systems. Digital evidence is any data that can be used to establish facts, identify perpetrators, or prove the occurrence of a crime. Unlike traditional physical evidence, digital evidence exists in the form of electronic data and can be stored, transmitted, or accessed in multiple ways, making it both unique and complex to handle. This section outlines the main categories of digital evidence, their characteristics, and the challenges that forensic investigators face when collecting and analyzing them.

### 4.1.1 Types of Digital Evidence

Digital evidence can be broadly classified into several categories based on its nature, source, and relevance to the investigation. These categories are essential for understanding the context of evidence, determining its chain of custody, and establishing its admissibility in legal proceedings.

**Computer Data:**

**Description**: Computer data refers to information stored on traditional computing devices, such as desktops, laptops, and servers. This data can include a wide range of information, such as files, documents, databases, emails, system logs, and configuration settings.

**Characteristics:**

- Computer data is typically stored on hard drives, solid-state drives (SSDs), or external storage devices (USB drives, network-attached storage).
- It can include both active and deleted data. Even when a file is deleted, it may remain recoverable unless it has been overwritten by new data.
- Digital forensic tools can recover deleted or hidden files from storage media, revealing crucial information that could help trace the actions of a suspect.

## Challenges:

- Data fragmentation and encryption techniques can make it difficult to retrieve all relevant information.
- Some data may be intentionally hidden through steganography or other methods, requiring specialized tools to uncover.

## Network Data:

**Description**: Network data encompasses information transmitted across a network, including internet traffic, logs, and metadata associated with network communications. This category includes data captured from routers, firewalls, network appliances, and network interfaces.

## Characteristics:

- Network data provides valuable insight into an attacker's actions, including IP addresses, port numbers, timestamps, and the source and destination of communications.
- Logs generated by network devices (e.g., routers, intrusion detection systems, and firewalls) can be critical in understanding how a cyberattack was executed and identifying compromised systems.
- Network traffic can be captured via packet sniffing and network monitoring tools, which can help reveal encrypted communications, traffic patterns, or malicious payloads.

## Challenges:

- Capturing and analyzing large volumes of network data can be time-consuming and require significant storage resources.
- Encryption, VPNs, or anonymizing services (like Tor) can obfuscate the traffic, making it harder to analyze or trace.

**Mobile Device Data:**

**Description**: Mobile devices, including smartphones, tablets, and wearable technology, are common sources of digital evidence. They store information such as call logs, text messages, photos, location data, and app usage histories.

**Characteristics:**

- Mobile devices often contain a variety of sensitive data, including user credentials, browsing history, location information, and application-specific data.
- Mobile device data can be found in both volatile (e.g., RAM) and non-volatile storage (e.g., internal storage or external SD cards).
- The use of cloud synchronization and apps that backup data to remote servers makes mobile devices an essential source for investigating user behavior and communication patterns

**Challenges:**

- Mobile devices are often protected by encryption and biometric security features, which can complicate access.
- Device-specific operating systems (iOS, Android) and frequent software updates require specialized forensic tools for analysis.
- Limited physical access to a mobile device can hinder forensic analysis.

**Cloud Data:**

**Description**: Cloud data refers to information stored or processed via cloud-based services such as Google Drive, Dropbox, Amazon Web Services (AWS), or Microsoft Azure. As cloud services become more ubiquitous, the data stored in the cloud becomes an increasingly important source of evidence.

**Characteristics:**

- Cloud data can include emails, files, logs, databases, backup information, and system configurations.
- Unlike data stored on physical devices, cloud data is often hosted on remote servers, making it accessible from any internet-connected device.
- Cloud providers typically maintain data logs and access records, which can be helpful in determining when and where an incident occurred and who was responsible for accessing or manipulating the data.

**Challenges:**

- The jurisdiction of cloud services can complicate legal procedures, as data might be stored in different countries with varying laws and regulations.
- Cloud service providers may delete or overwrite data after a certain period, making it challenging to recover older information unless proper preservation procedures are followed.
- The shared responsibility model of cloud computing (where providers are responsible for the infrastructure, and customers are responsible for data) can create confusion over which entity is accountable for data security.

**Emails and Instant Messaging Data:**

**Description**: Emails, text messages, and instant messaging data from platforms like Slack, WhatsApp, or Skype can serve as important digital evidence, particularly in cases of fraud, harassment, or espionage.

**Characteristics:**

- Email and messaging data can include timestamps, attachments, metadata, and the content of the messages themselves.
- This data provides evidence of communication between individuals, which can establish intent, motive, or an alibi in criminal investigations.
- Metadata, such as the sender, recipient, time of transmission, and IP address, can often be traced back to an attacker.

**Challenges:**

- Encryption (such as end-to-end encryption used by services like WhatsApp) can prevent the forensic extraction of message content.
- Some email systems use retention policies, automatically deleting older messages or attachments, which may impact the availability of evidence.

**Digital Images and Videos:**

**Description**: Digital images and videos, which include photographs, video recordings, and audio files, can serve as crucial evidence in investigations, particularly in cases involving harassment, exploitation, or evidence of physical security breaches.

**Characteristics:**

- Digital images contain metadata, such as the time, date, GPS coordinates, and device information that can provide useful context in investigations.
- Forensic investigators can analyze image and video files for digital signatures, modifications, or hidden information (such as steganography).

**Challenges:**

- The use of image editing tools can lead to the manipulation of files, making it difficult to authenticate their origin.
- Large image or video files may require specialized tools and significant computing resources for analysis.

**Logs and System Files:**

**Description**: System logs and configuration files are vital for understanding the behavior of a compromised system. These can include operating system logs, application logs, access logs, and error logs.

**Characteristics:**

- Logs provide a detailed record of system activities, user logins, network connections, file access, and application usage.
- They are essential for detecting unusual or unauthorized activities, such as malware execution, privilege escalation, or data exfiltration.

**Challenges:**

- Logs can be easily deleted, altered, or tampered with, particularly by sophisticated attackers who aim to cover their tracks.
- Analyzing log data can be overwhelming due to the sheer volume, making it difficult to pinpoint the most relevant evidence.

### 4.1.2 Characteristics of Digital Evidence

The characteristics of digital evidence determine how it is handled, analyzed, and preserved in a forensic context. Some of the most important characteristics include:

**Volatility:**

Digital evidence can be classified as volatile (e.g., RAM, live network data) or non-volatile (e.g., hard drives, cloud storage). Volatile data is highly susceptible to being lost when a device is powered off, making it crucial for forensic investigators to capture this data as soon as possible.

**Authenticity and Integrity:**

Digital evidence must maintain its integrity from the moment it is collected to ensure it is admissible in court. Proper documentation of the chain of custody, along with verification techniques (e.g., hashing), helps ensure that the evidence is authentic and has not been tampered with.

**Searchability:**

Unlike physical evidence, digital evidence can be quickly searched and analyzed using forensic tools. However, this searchability can also make it easy for perpetrators to hide or destroy evidence (e.g., encryption, file wiping).

**Relevance:**

Not all digital evidence is relevant to a particular investigation. The key to successful forensic analysis is identifying the most pertinent evidence and properly correlating it with the timeline of the crime or incident.

Digital evidence is a broad and diverse category, encompassing various types of data from computers, mobile devices, networks, cloud services, and even communication platforms. Each type of evidence has unique characteristics that influence how it is collected, analyzed, and preserved. Forensic investigators must understand the nature of different digital evidence and employ appropriate tools and techniques to ensure that it is handled correctly, preserving its integrity and ensuring its usefulness in an investigation.

## 4.2 Locating and Preserving Evidence Across Devices.

In forensic cybersecurity, one of the most critical steps in any investigation is the process of locating and preserving evidence. Unlike physical evidence, which can be easily seen and secured, digital evidence often exists across multiple devices, networks, and storage mediums. The challenge for forensic investigators lies in identifying where critical evidence resides, how to access it, and ensuring its integrity is maintained throughout the process.

This section provides an overview of the key principles, tools, and techniques used to locate and preserve digital evidence across various devices such as computers, mobile phones, cloud storage, and network environments. Additionally, we discuss the best practices for handling and securing evidence to ensure it remains valid and usable in court.

### 4.2.1 Identifying the Potential Sources of Evidence

Before starting the process of locating evidence, forensic investigators need to first identify the potential sources of evidence. This step is based on the nature of the cybercrime or breach being investigated. Evidence can be found across a wide range of devices and systems, each with its own set of challenges in terms of access and preservation. Common sources of evidence include:

**Computers and Servers:**

- **Hard Drives**: These often contain files, system logs, and traces of user activities.
- **Network Servers**: Servers may store large volumes of sensitive data, system logs, and application logs that are crucial to an investigation.
- **System RAM**: Volatile memory may hold critical evidence of a cyberattack, especially when dealing with malware or active intrusions.

**Mobile Devices:**

- **Smartphones and Tablets**: These devices hold a wide range of information, including text messages, social media activity, photos, videos, and GPS data. They may also contain apps and backups with critical evidence.
- **Wearables**: Devices like smartwatches or fitness trackers may contain health-related data, locations, and communications that can aid investigations.

**Cloud Storage:**

- **Cloud Services**: Data stored in cloud environments, such as emails, documents, photos, and logs, can be crucial. Cloud storage can sometimes be a more challenging environment to access, especially when considering jurisdictional issues and encryption.

- **Cloud Metadata**: Logs from cloud services can also be vital to trace who accessed specific data and when.

## Network and Communication Devices:

- **Routers and Firewalls**: These devices maintain logs and records of network traffic that may help trace the origin of an attack or the movement of data within a network.
- **Intrusion Detection Systems (IDS):** Logs from IDS devices can help identify when and how an intrusion took place.
- **Email and Messaging Systems**: Emails, instant messaging, and communication platforms like Slack or WhatsApp may hold valuable communication trails.

## Peripheral Devices:

- **External Storage Devices**: USB drives, external hard drives, and other forms of removable storage often contain data that may be involved in the cybercrime.
- **Printers, Scanners, and IoT Devices**: These devices may leave behind logs or other indirect evidence that can provide clues about activities or interactions.

### 4.2.2 Techniques for Locating Evidence Across Devices

Once potential sources of evidence have been identified, forensic investigators need to use specific tools and techniques to locate evidence within those devices. The process of locating evidence varies depending on the device type and the nature of the data being sought.

## Data Acquisition Tools:

- **Disk Imaging Tools**: Tools like FTK Imager, EnCase, and dd allow investigators to make bit-by-bit copies (or forensic images) of hard drives and other storage media. These tools are essential for ensuring that the evidence is preserved in its original state.
- **Memory Dumping Tools**: For volatile data, investigators use memory acquisition tools like Volatility or FTK Imager to capture the contents of system RAM. This is particularly important in malware analysis and active cybercrime investigations.
- **Mobile Forensic Tools**: Tools such as Cellebrite or XRY can be used to extract data from mobile phones and tablets, even when the device is locked or encrypted.

## Log Analysis:

- **Network Traffic Analysis**: By capturing and analyzing network traffic using tools like Wireshark or tcpdump, investigators can trace the flow of data, identify malicious activities, and pinpoint the source of an attack. Logs from routers, switches, and firewalls can also be useful in locating evidence of network-based attacks.
- **System and Application Logs**: Logs from operating systems (Windows Event Logs, Linux syslogs) and applications can help investigators trace activities, such as file access, login attempts, and network connections. These logs can pinpoint the time and date of critical events, helping to establish a timeline of the attack.

**Cloud Forensics Tools:**

- **Cloud Data Recovery Tools**: Tools like X1 Social Discovery and CloudFuze are used for recovering and analyzing data from cloud services like Google Drive, Dropbox, or Amazon S3. Investigators can download or access data stored in the cloud, including files, metadata, and activity logs.
- **Cloud Service Provider Logs**: Many cloud providers offer logs that can provide information about when and how users accessed certain data. These logs can be valuable for tracing evidence back to a specific user or determining the scope of a breach.

**Browser History and Artifacts:**

- **Web Browsing Artifacts**: Evidence of internet activity can be found in browser history, cookies, and cached files. Investigators often use tools like Browser Forensics Toolkits (e.g., WebBrowserForensic or Internet Evidence Finder (IEF)) to extract information on visited websites, downloads, and logins to online services.
- **Social Media and Instant Messaging**: If relevant, tools like Social Media Investigation or OSINT (Open Source Intelligence) tools can be used to trace digital footprints across social networks or messaging apps, helping identify communications and interactions that may be evidence of criminal activity.

### 4.2.3 Best Practices for Evidence Preservation

The integrity and authenticity of digital evidence must be maintained throughout the collection, preservation, and analysis process. Failure to properly preserve evidence can lead to questions about its validity, potentially rendering it inadmissible in legal proceedings. The following best practices should be followed when preserving evidence:

**Document the Chain of Custody:**

- Maintaining an accurate chain of custody is one of the most critical aspects of preserving digital evidence. Every person who handles the evidence must be logged, and the condition and handling of the evidence must be documented at each stage.
- Digital evidence should be stored securely and tamper-proof measures, such as hashing, should be used to ensure its integrity.

**Create Forensic Copies (Imaging):**

- Before analyzing any digital device, forensic investigators should create an exact copy of the storage media (forensic image). This ensures that the original data remains untouched and can be used as a reference if necessary.
- Tools like EnCase, FTK Imager, or dd should be used to create images that are cryptographically hash-verified (e.g., using MD5 or SHA1 hashes) to confirm the integrity of the original data.

**Avoid Modifying Original Evidence:**

- Investigators should never work directly with the original device or data. Instead, all analyses should be performed on forensic copies, preserving the original evidence.
- When collecting evidence from devices, investigators should take steps to minimize interaction with the device. For example, devices should be powered off if they are not actively needed for data extraction, preventing any data from being altered or deleted.

**Secure Evidence Storage:**

- All evidence, including forensic images and physical devices, should be stored in a secure environment. This could include locked rooms, safes, or other tamper-proof containers.
- Digital evidence should also be encrypted if stored digitally to prevent unauthorized access.

**Handle Encrypted and Password-Protected Data Properly:**

If the evidence is encrypted, investigators should attempt to retrieve the password or decryption keys from the suspect. Tools like Oxygen Forensics or Passware can assist in breaking passwords or decrypting data, though investigators must ensure that this is done legally and ethically.

### 4.2.4 Overcoming Challenges in Locating and Preserving Evidence

While the techniques and tools discussed above can help in locating and preserving digital evidence, forensic investigators often face several challenges during this process:

**Encryption**: Many devices and cloud services use strong encryption methods, making it difficult to access and retrieve data without the proper decryption keys. Investigators may need to work with service providers or employ advanced decryption methods, which can be time-consuming and complex.

**Cloud Jurisdiction Issues**: Cloud providers often store data across multiple geographic regions, and the legal and regulatory framework surrounding this data can vary significantly between countries. Investigators may need to work with international legal authorities to obtain the necessary permissions for accessing cloud-based evidence.

**Rapid Technological Changes**: As technology evolves, new devices and storage methods emerge, creating challenges for investigators who must continually adapt to these changes. New encryption techniques, data storage formats, and cloud services may require updated tools and methods for analysis.

**Data Overload**: With the vast amount of data generated by modern devices and networks, investigators may be overwhelmed with information. Using advanced tools and techniques, such as machine learning algorithms or automated data analysis, can help streamline the process and highlight the most relevant evidence.

Locating and preserving digital evidence is a complex, multi-faceted process that requires careful planning, specialized tools, and adherence to best practices. By identifying key sources of evidence, using appropriate tools to capture data, and ensuring the integrity of the evidence through proper handling and storage, forensic investigators can build a strong case that holds up in court. However, the rapidly evolving nature of technology and the sophistication of cybercriminals pose continuous challenges, requiring investigators to stay updated with the latest methods and technologies in digital forensics.

# 4.3 Legal Standards for Evidence Collection and Preservation.

In forensic cybersecurity, adhering to legal standards for evidence collection and preservation is critical to ensuring that the digital evidence obtained can be used effectively in court. Unlike traditional physical evidence, digital evidence is unique in its volatility and susceptibility to alteration or destruction. Therefore, the process of collecting and preserving digital evidence requires careful attention to detail and compliance with various legal guidelines. Failing to meet these standards can lead to the evidence being excluded from legal proceedings, rendering the investigation ineffective.

This section provides an overview of the key legal standards that govern evidence collection and preservation in forensic cybersecurity, including the roles of laws, regulations, and protocols, as well as the importance of maintaining the chain of custody and ensuring evidence integrity.

### 4.3.1 The Chain of Custody: Legal Framework

One of the most fundamental principles in evidence handling is the chain of custody. The chain of custody refers to the documented and unbroken trail of evidence, outlining everyone who handled the evidence from the moment it was collected until it is presented in court. It ensures that the evidence has not been tampered with, altered, or substituted.

**Legal Requirements**: Courts require that evidence be handled in a way that preserves its integrity. A break in the chain of custody can lead to evidence being considered inadmissible or compromised. The chain of custody must clearly document:

- The name of the person who collected the evidence.
- The date and time of collection.
- Where and how the evidence was collected.
- How it was transferred or stored between handlers.
- Any handling or testing performed on the evidence.

**Chain of Custody Documentation**: Every individual who handles or transports the evidence must sign a chain of custody log to verify their interaction with the evidence. This documentation ensures that there is a clear, traceable record of the evidence's movement and integrity throughout the investigation.

**Legal Impact**: In court, if the chain of custody is not well-documented or is found to have gaps, it could result in the evidence being inadmissible, as the court may not be able to trust its authenticity. Proper documentation and handling of digital evidence thus play a pivotal role in ensuring that it can withstand legal scrutiny.

### 4.3.2 Adherence to National and International Legal Standards

Digital forensics must comply with a variety of national and international laws that govern how evidence can be collected, stored, and presented. While specific regulations vary by jurisdiction, certain core principles are consistent across many legal systems.

### National Laws:

- In the United States, digital evidence collection is governed by laws such as the Fourth Amendment, which protects individuals from unreasonable searches and seizures, and the Computer Fraud and Abuse Act (CFAA), which addresses computer-related crimes. Digital forensics investigators must ensure they obtain evidence in a way that respects constitutional rights, particularly the right to privacy.
- The Federal Rules of Evidence (FRE) provide guidance on how digital evidence should be handled in the U.S. court system, particularly around issues like admissibility, authentication, and integrity.
- Other countries have their own sets of digital evidence regulations, such as the Data Protection Act in the UK or the General Data Protection Regulation (GDPR) in the European Union, which regulate the collection and handling of personal data.

### International Standards:

In addition to national laws, international conventions and agreements, such as the Budapest Convention on Cybercrime, offer guidance on how digital evidence should be handled across borders. This convention facilitates international cooperation in combating cybercrime and sets out standards for handling evidence that is stored or transmitted across different countries.

Intergovernmental agencies like INTERPOL and Europol also provide frameworks for cross-border evidence collection, ensuring that investigators from different countries can share evidence and cooperate effectively while complying with each nation's legal standards.

### 4.3.3 Search Warrants and Consent

The legality of evidence collection often hinges on whether proper authorization was obtained. In the context of digital evidence, obtaining a search warrant is typically necessary to legally access private or protected data on a device or network.

**Search Warrants**: In many jurisdictions, law enforcement must present a probable cause that a crime has been committed in order to obtain a search warrant from a judge. This includes providing evidence that justifies the need to access specific digital evidence. The warrant will typically specify:

- The devices or locations to be searched.
- The types of evidence being sought.
- The timeframe during which the search is authorized.

A search warrant protects the rights of individuals against unreasonable searches and ensures that investigators can legally access evidence.

**Consent**: In some cases, the owner of the device or system being investigated may voluntarily consent to the search and seizure of evidence. However, consent must be informed and given without coercion. Investigators must also ensure that consent is documented to avoid challenges to the evidence's validity.

**Challenges with Consent**: When it comes to digital evidence, consent can be complicated by encryption, password protection, or other privacy measures that may require additional steps to access. In these cases, investigators must still ensure they follow legal procedures, such as obtaining a warrant or court order to bypass these protections.

### 4.3.4 Compliance with Privacy Laws and Data Protection Regulations

As the collection and analysis of digital evidence often involve accessing personal or sensitive data, investigators must also comply with privacy laws and data protection regulations to safeguard individuals' rights.

**General Data Protection Regulation (GDPR):**

- For investigators working in or with the European Union, the GDPR governs how personal data must be handled, stored, and processed. The regulation applies not only to companies based in the EU but also to entities outside of the EU that process data of EU citizens.

- GDPR mandates that personal data be collected for specific, legitimate purposes, stored securely, and not kept longer than necessary. It also grants individuals the right to access their data and request its deletion.
- Forensic investigators must ensure that data is only collected for legitimate investigative purposes, and any personal information that is not relevant to the case must be handled according to GDPR principles, such as anonymization.

## Data Minimization:

The principle of data minimization under the GDPR emphasizes collecting only the data necessary for the investigation. Forensic investigators should avoid over-collecting personal data when conducting forensic analysis. This principle also aligns with other privacy-focused regulations, including the California Consumer Privacy Act (CCPA) in the U.S.

## Data Security:

Privacy laws typically require investigators to take appropriate technical and organizational measures to protect data from unauthorized access, alteration, or destruction. This includes encrypting evidence, using secure storage methods, and restricting access to the data to authorized personnel only.

### 4.3.5 Digital Evidence Authentication and Admissibility

Once digital evidence is collected, it must be properly authenticated and preserved to be admissible in court. Legal standards for evidence admissibility require that digital evidence be proven to be both relevant and authentic.

## Authentication:

- Authentication refers to proving that the digital evidence presented in court is what it is claimed to be. This can be done by verifying the hash values of the digital evidence (using algorithms like SHA-1 or MD5) to ensure the data has not been altered since it was collected.
- In some cases, experts may be called upon to testify about the methods and tools used to collect and analyze the evidence, explaining how it was preserved and ensuring its integrity.

## Admissibility:

- In most legal systems, digital evidence must meet certain criteria to be admissible in court. For example, in the U.S., the Federal Rules of Evidence and Daubert Standard require that the evidence be relevant, reliable, and obtained through legally permissible means.
- Additionally, courts may assess the validity of digital evidence based on the methods used to collect and analyze it. Any deviation from established legal standards could result in the evidence being excluded.

The collection and preservation of digital evidence are integral to the success of any forensic cybersecurity investigation. Legal standards and guidelines provide a framework for investigators to follow to ensure that the evidence is legally collected, preserved, and admissible in court. Adhering to these standards not only protects the rights of individuals involved in the investigation but also helps ensure that justice is served. Investigators must be meticulous in documenting the chain of custody, obtaining proper authorization, and handling evidence in a way that maintains its integrity, all while complying with applicable privacy laws and regulations. By doing so, they help create a solid foundation for the legal proceedings that follow.

# 4.4 Avoiding Contamination and Tampering in Evidence Handling.

In forensic cybersecurity, maintaining the integrity of digital evidence is paramount. Unlike physical evidence, which can often be physically secured and protected, digital evidence is highly susceptible to contamination and tampering during the collection, handling, and analysis processes. Even a small modification to digital evidence can compromise its authenticity, making it inadmissible in court or rendering it useless for investigative purposes. Therefore, forensic investigators must follow stringent protocols to ensure that evidence remains unaltered from the moment it is collected until it is presented in a legal setting.

This section discusses the importance of avoiding contamination and tampering in evidence handling, outlining key strategies and best practices to ensure the integrity of digital evidence is maintained throughout the forensic process.

### 4.4.1 Understanding Contamination and Tampering

Before delving into preventive measures, it is essential to define what constitutes contamination and tampering of digital evidence:

Contamination refers to any unintentional alteration, modification, or addition to the evidence during the process of collection, transportation, or storage. This could include accidental overwriting of data, failure to secure the evidence properly, or improper handling of devices.

Tampering, on the other hand, is intentional manipulation or modification of evidence, usually with the aim of misleading the investigation. This can include unauthorized access, deletion, or alteration of files and data.

Both contamination and tampering can lead to serious legal consequences, including the exclusion of evidence in court, the collapse of a case, or even criminal charges against investigators or involved parties. Therefore, it is critical to have strict protocols in place to prevent such occurrences.

### 4.4.2 Best Practices for Preventing Contamination

To avoid contamination of digital evidence, forensic investigators must take numerous precautions during each stage of the evidence handling process: from initial collection to long-term storage. Below are some key best practices designed to preserve the integrity of evidence.

**Minimize Interaction with Evidence:**

- The golden rule in digital forensics is to avoid interacting with the evidence unless absolutely necessary. Any interaction with the device, system, or data could potentially alter the evidence.
- If possible, investigators should make a forensic copy or disk image of the device or data before analyzing it. This ensures that the original evidence is left untouched and preserved in its unaltered state.
- In cases where it is essential to access a device (e.g., to prevent encryption or password protection from activating), investigators should do so in a way that leaves no trace on the device's storage, using tools designed to capture data without modifying it.

**Use Write-Blockers:**

- When collecting data from hard drives, USB drives, or other storage devices, forensic investigators must use write-blockers. Write-blockers are devices or software tools that allow investigators to access the data on a drive without the risk of writing or modifying anything on it.

- Write-blockers are essential tools for preventing inadvertent changes to the data and are considered an industry standard when dealing with potentially volatile digital evidence.

## Document Everything:

Thorough documentation is crucial to ensure the transparency of the evidence handling process and to provide a verifiable record of each step taken. This includes:

- Documenting the condition of the evidence upon receipt.
- Noting the time, date, and individuals involved in the evidence collection and analysis.
- Recording the specific tools and methods used during the collection process.
- Keeping a chain of custody log, as discussed in earlier sections, to ensure that each transfer of evidence is properly recorded.
- Proper documentation reduces the risk of contamination by providing a clear record of all actions taken and serves as evidence in case any allegations of tampering arise.

## Secure Evidence Storage:

- Once evidence is collected, it should be stored in a secure, tamper-proof location to prevent unauthorized access or accidental exposure to environmental factors that could alter the data (e.g., power surges, humidity, or extreme temperatures).
- Physical storage should be restricted to authorized personnel only, and evidence should be stored in containers such as evidence bags or lockboxes that are designed to prevent tampering.

## Isolation of Evidence:

Evidence should be isolated from external systems, networks, or devices to prevent accidental contamination or tampering. For instance, devices containing potential evidence should not be connected to the internet or local networks, as doing so may inadvertently introduce malware, alter timestamps, or even trigger automatic updates that can change the evidence.

## 4.4.3 Best Practices for Preventing Tampering

While contamination is often the result of accidental actions, tampering involves deliberate manipulation or destruction of evidence. To prevent tampering, forensic investigators must implement measures that guarantee the evidence's security and authenticity.

## Hashing and Digital Signatures:

- One of the most effective ways to ensure evidence remains unaltered is through the use of cryptographic hashing. When a forensic image of a device or storage medium is created, investigators should generate a hash value (such as MD5, SHA-1, or SHA-256) of the data. This hash value serves as a unique digital fingerprint of the data.
- Every time the evidence is accessed, investigators can compare the hash value to verify whether the evidence has been altered. If the hash value changes, it indicates that the evidence has been tampered with
- Digital signatures can also be used in conjunction with hashing to authenticate the evidence's origin and integrity.

## Restricted Access and Controlled Handling:

- To prevent unauthorized access or tampering, evidence should only be accessible to individuals with a legitimate need to handle it. Access to evidence should be tightly controlled and documented in a chain of custody.
- When evidence is transferred between individuals or locations, it should be done securely, with both parties verifying the identity and integrity of the evidence at each step.

## Tamper-Evident Seals and Tags:

- Physical evidence containers should be equipped with tamper-evident seals or tags that will visibly show if someone has attempted to open or alter the container. These seals can be a simple mechanism, such as a sticky tape that leaves marks when disturbed, or more advanced digital seals that track when and by whom evidence was accessed.
- In addition to physical seals, digital evidence can be protected using encryption or digital rights management (DRM) systems to prevent unauthorized access.

## Monitoring and Surveillance:

- In cases where evidence is stored or handled over an extended period, investigators can use surveillance or monitoring systems to track who is accessing the evidence and when. This can include video surveillance in storage areas or the use of software logs that track user access to digital evidence.
- Access logs should also be generated and monitored for any suspicious activity, such as attempts to bypass security protocols or unauthorized access to evidence storage systems.

**Secure Communication:**

When evidence is communicated or transferred, it is vital that the communication channels remain secure. For example, when sending evidence between agencies or jurisdictions, investigators should use encrypted communication platforms (e.g., encrypted email, secure file transfers, or virtual private networks (VPNs)) to prevent interception or unauthorized alteration of the evidence.

### 4.4.4 Training and Awareness for Investigators

Ensuring that digital forensic investigators are properly trained in handling evidence is essential in preventing contamination and tampering. Investigators should be familiar with the legal and technical standards for evidence collection and preservation, as well as the tools and techniques available to safeguard the evidence.

**Ongoing Education**: The field of digital forensics is constantly evolving with new technologies and emerging threats. Regular training programs and certifications, such as those offered by the International Association of Computer Investigative Specialists (IACIS) or GIAC (Global Information Assurance Certification), can help ensure investigators are up to date with the latest best practices.

**Protocols and SOPs**: Investigative teams should have established Standard Operating Procedures (SOPs) for evidence handling, which all team members must follow. These protocols should address all stages of the evidence lifecycle, from collection to court presentation, with clear rules for minimizing contamination and preventing tampering.

Avoiding contamination and tampering in evidence handling is a fundamental responsibility of forensic cybersecurity investigators. By following established best practices, including minimizing interaction with evidence, using write-blockers, maintaining a strict chain of custody, and securing evidence storage, investigators can ensure that digital evidence remains intact, unaltered, and legally admissible. Furthermore, by employing cryptographic tools, controlling access, and providing proper training to investigators, the risk of deliberate tampering can be significantly reduced. Maintaining the integrity of digital evidence is crucial not only for the success of the investigation but also for the fair administration of justice.

# 5. Tools and Techniques for Cyber Forensics

The success of a forensic investigation hinges on the tools and techniques used to analyze digital evidence. This chapter explores the essential software and hardware tools that forensic experts rely on, such as disk imaging tools, data recovery software, and specialized forensic suites like EnCase and FTK. It also covers key forensic techniques, including hashing, imaging, and log analysis, to ensure the integrity and authenticity of collected data. By understanding the full range of tools and methodologies, readers will gain practical insights into how cyber forensics is conducted in real-world investigations.

## 5.1 Overview of Industry-Standard Forensic Tools.

In the rapidly evolving field of forensic cybersecurity, having the right tools to collect, analyze, and preserve digital evidence is essential to ensuring the integrity and reliability of an investigation. Forensic tools are software and hardware solutions specifically designed to assist in identifying, preserving, analyzing, and presenting digital evidence in a way that meets legal and procedural standards. These tools allow forensic investigators to extract data from a wide variety of digital devices, including computers, smartphones, servers, and network equipment, while maintaining the integrity of the evidence.

This section provides an overview of the industry-standard forensic tools used in cybersecurity investigations. It discusses the various types of tools available, highlighting their primary functionalities and the scenarios in which they are typically used.

### 5.1.1 Types of Forensic Tools

Forensic tools can be broadly categorized into several types based on their function within the investigation process. The following are the primary categories of forensic tools commonly used in cybersecurity investigations:

**Disk Imaging Tools:**

Disk imaging is the process of creating an exact copy, or image, of a storage device (such as a hard drive, SSD, or USB flash drive). This image preserves all the data on the device, including deleted files, file systems, and unallocated space, which may contain crucial evidence.

**Popular Tools:**

- **FTK Imager**: A widely used forensic tool for creating disk images of hard drives, memory cards, and other storage devices. FTK Imager allows users to create bit-by-bit copies of drives and to extract individual files or file partitions.
- **dd (Disk Duplicate):** A command-line tool that is part of many UNIX-based operating systems. It allows investigators to create raw bit-for-bit copies of drives or partitions, preserving all data, including deleted and hidden files.
- **X1 Social Discovery**: A tool designed for creating disk images from social media and other online sources, ideal for cases involving cyberbullying, defamation, or other social media-based crimes.

## Data Recovery Tools:

Data recovery tools are used to recover files that may have been deleted, damaged, or corrupted, allowing investigators to restore data that might otherwise be inaccessible.

## Popular Tools:

- **R-Studio**: A professional-grade data recovery tool that can recover lost files, partitions, or drives from damaged or deleted sources. It works with a wide range of file systems, including FAT, NTFS, exFAT, and HFS.
- **Recuva**: A simple and effective tool for recovering deleted files from storage devices. While less comprehensive than professional recovery tools, Recuva is often used in less complex cases.
- **EnCase Forensic**: Another industry-leading tool, EnCase offers advanced data recovery and file carving features, along with comprehensive support for various operating systems, including Windows, macOS, and Linux.

## File Carving and Data Analysis Tools:

File carving is the process of recovering files without file system metadata, often used when a file system is damaged or has been deleted. File carving tools can scan raw disk images to search for files based on their known signatures, structure, or data patterns.

## Popular Tools:

- **Scalpel**: An open-source file carving tool that is often used by digital forensics professionals to recover files from unallocated disk space. It works with a wide range of file types and can be customized to search for specific signatures.

- **Sleuth Kit and Autopsy**: Sleuth Kit is an open-source collection of command-line tools used for analyzing disk images and carving out files from unallocated space. Autopsy is a graphical user interface (GUI) built on top of Sleuth Kit, making it easier for investigators to manage and analyze evidence.
- **ProDiscover Forensic**: ProDiscover is a comprehensive forensic tool that combines file carving with the ability to perform detailed forensic analysis of file systems, partitions, and digital devices.

**Mobile Device Forensics Tools:**

As mobile devices become increasingly important sources of evidence, forensic tools for mobile devices are essential for investigators. These tools allow the extraction of data from smartphones, tablets, and other mobile devices, including call logs, text messages, app data, and multimedia content.

**Popular Tools:**

- **Cellebrite UFED**: One of the most well-known mobile forensics tools, Cellebrite UFED enables investigators to extract, decode, and analyze data from a wide variety of mobile devices, including both iOS and Android phones, as well as feature phones.
- **XRY**: A mobile forensics tool used to extract and analyze data from mobile devices, including smartphones, tablets, and GPS devices. XRY is known for its ability to bypass security features like passwords and encryption to retrieve data.
- **Oxygen Forensic Detective**: A powerful tool for mobile forensics that offers comprehensive data extraction, decoding, and analysis capabilities. It supports a wide range of devices and can recover deleted messages, contacts, images, and more.

**Network Forensics Tools:**

Network forensics tools are used to capture and analyze network traffic to investigate incidents, identify malicious activity, and trace cyberattacks back to their source. These tools allow investigators to monitor, capture, and analyze packets of data transmitted over a network, which can be crucial in tracing the path of an attack.

**Popular Tools:**

- **Wireshark**: One of the most widely used network protocol analyzers, Wireshark allows forensic investigators to capture and examine network traffic in real-time. It is valuable for investigating network intrusions and identifying anomalous traffic patterns indicative of cyberattacks.

- **NetworkMiner**: An open-source network forensics tool that allows investigators to analyze PCAP files and extract files, images, and credentials from network traffic. It supports several protocols and is particularly useful for incident response investigations.
- **SolarWinds Network Performance Monitor**: While primarily a network monitoring tool, SolarWinds also has forensic capabilities that allow investigators to track network traffic, detect unusual activity, and identify potential security breaches.

## Memory Analysis Tools:

Digital forensics often involves analyzing the volatile memory (RAM) of a computer or device, as this can contain valuable evidence such as running processes, system logs, network connections, and traces of malware. Memory analysis is particularly useful in cases of active cyberattacks or to track the behavior of malicious software.

## Popular Tools:

- **Volatility**: An open-source memory forensics tool that allows investigators to analyze volatile memory dumps for artifacts like running processes, network connections, and system information. Volatility supports a wide range of operating systems and is widely used for analyzing memory images.
- **FTK Imager**: In addition to disk imaging, FTK Imager can also be used to create memory dumps of running systems, which can then be analyzed for evidence of malware or attack activity.
- **Memoryze**: A tool developed by Mandiant (now part of FireEye) that enables investigators to analyze memory images and identify artifacts left by malware, including rootkits, Trojans, and other malicious software.

## Encryption and Decryption Tools:

Many cybercriminals use encryption to protect their communications and data. Forensic investigators may need to decrypt evidence to make it accessible for analysis. Specialized tools are required to handle encrypted data, especially when dealing with advanced encryption algorithms or password-protected files.

## Popular Tools:

- **Passware**: A popular tool for decrypting password-protected files, including documents, spreadsheets, and disk images. Passware supports a wide range of encryption formats and can recover passwords through dictionary or brute-force attacks.
- **ElcomSoft**: A suite of tools for breaking encryption on hard drives, mobile devices, and online accounts. ElcomSoft's tools are widely used in digital forensics for decrypting encrypted data.

### 5.1.2 Tool Selection Criteria

Selecting the appropriate forensic tool depends on several factors:

- **Case Requirements**: Different investigations may require different types of tools depending on the nature of the cyberattack or crime. For example, a case involving malware may require memory analysis tools, while a financial fraud investigation may necessitate the use of file recovery and disk imaging tools.
- **Device Compatibility**: Forensic tools must be compatible with the devices or operating systems being analyzed. For example, certain tools work better with specific mobile devices or file systems.
- **Reliability and Legal Admissibility**: Investigators should choose tools that are known for their reliability and have been tested in courts of law. Tools that meet industry standards and can demonstrate their adherence to evidence handling best practices are more likely to be admissible in court.

Industry-standard forensic tools are vital for performing thorough and reliable investigations in the field of cybersecurity. From disk imaging and data recovery to mobile device analysis and network forensics, these tools enable forensic investigators to capture, preserve, and analyze digital evidence in a manner that supports the legal and procedural standards necessary for effective legal action. As technology advances, the tools available to forensic professionals continue to evolve, ensuring they remain capable of addressing the increasingly sophisticated nature of cybercrime.

# 5.2 Imaging and Hashing Techniques for Data Integrity.

In forensic cybersecurity, preserving the integrity of digital evidence is critical to ensuring its validity in investigations and legal proceedings. The techniques of imaging and hashing are two fundamental practices that forensic investigators use to maintain and verify the authenticity of evidence. These techniques allow investigators to create reliable copies of digital data, ensuring that the original data is not altered during analysis, and provide a method for verifying that the evidence has remained unchanged throughout the investigation process.

This section delves into imaging and hashing, explaining their importance in maintaining data integrity and their roles in forensic investigations.

### 5.2.1 Data Imaging: Creating Exact Copies of Digital Evidence

Imaging is the process of creating a bit-for-bit copy of a digital device's storage medium, such as a hard drive, flash drive, or memory card. The goal is to replicate the entire storage content, including the operating system, files, file system, deleted data, and unallocated space, while maintaining the original evidence's integrity. Imaging is an essential step in digital forensics because it allows investigators to work on a copy of the data rather than the original device, ensuring that the integrity of the original evidence is prooorvod.

### 5.2.1.1 The Importance of Data Imaging

**Non-Invasive Analysis**: By creating a duplicate of the storage medium, investigators can analyze the data without making any changes to the original device. This is crucial in ensuring that the evidence remains intact and unaltered, which is especially important in legal cases where evidence authenticity is scrutinized.

**Preservation of Volatile Data**: Some digital evidence, such as system memory (RAM), can be volatile and may change or be lost when the device is powered down. Imaging allows investigators to preserve the state of a system, including active files and system processes, which may be crucial for understanding the sequence of events in an attack or investigation.

**Efficiency in Investigation**: Once a digital image is created, investigators can conduct detailed analysis, including data recovery and file carving, on the copy, without the risk of damaging the original evidence. This allows for a more thorough investigation of the data and ensures that no information is inadvertently lost or altered.

### 5.2.1.2 Imaging Tools and Techniques

To create an accurate and reliable digital image, forensic investigators must use specialized tools and follow established procedures. Common forensic imaging tools include:

**FTK Imager**: A widely used tool for creating disk images from hard drives and other storage devices. FTK Imager allows users to create images in multiple formats (e.g., E01, DD, AFF), which are then used for analysis in forensic investigations.

**dd (Disk Duplicate):** A versatile command-line tool commonly used in UNIX-based systems. It creates an exact byte-by-byte copy of storage devices and can be customized for specific needs (e.g., copying only certain partitions or files).

**X1 Social Discovery**: Designed to capture digital evidence from social media and other online sources, X1 can create digital images from websites, chat logs, and social media accounts to preserve potential evidence of cybercrimes involving online activities.

When performing imaging, it's critical to follow a strict procedure to ensure the image is accurate and complete:

- **Use Write-Blockers**: To prevent any changes to the device's data during the imaging process, investigators should use write-blockers, which ensure that data can be read but not modified.
- **Verify Image Integrity**: After creating the image, investigators must verify that the image is a true and complete copy of the original device. This is where hashing (discussed below) comes into play.

### 5.2.2 Hashing: Ensuring Data Integrity and Authenticity

Hashing is a cryptographic process that generates a unique identifier (hash value) for a file or data set. This identifier is typically a fixed-size string of characters that uniquely corresponds to the content of the file. Even a tiny change in the data will result in a completely different hash value. In forensic cybersecurity, hashing is used to verify that digital evidence, such as disk images, has not been altered during the collection, storage, or analysis process.

### 5.2.2.1 The Role of Hashing in Data Integrity

**Verification of Integrity**: Hash values are used to verify that a digital image or piece of data has not been modified. When investigators create a disk image, they compute the hash value of both the original data and the image. If the hash values match, it confirms that the image is an exact copy of the original data, ensuring its integrity.

**Evidence Authentication**: Hash values are often included in evidence documentation and chain of custody logs. Since the hash value uniquely represents the original data, it can be used in court to prove that the evidence has not been tampered with. If any modification occurs to the evidence, the hash value will change, indicating tampering.

**Preventing Tampering and Contamination**: Hashing acts as a safeguard against tampering. If someone tries to alter the evidence, even slightly, it would be immediately evident because the new hash value would not match the original. This provides a way to detect and prevent evidence contamination.

### 5.2.2.2 Common Hashing Algorithms

Several cryptographic hash functions are commonly used in forensic investigations, each generating a unique value based on the content of the data. The most commonly used hashing algorithms in digital forensics include:

**MD5 (Message Digest Algorithm 5)**: One of the earliest and most commonly used hashing algorithms, MD5 generates a 128-bit hash value. While it is fast and efficient, MD5 has vulnerabilities and is not recommended for cases requiring the highest level of security or where integrity is critical.

**SHA-1 (Secure Hash Algorithm 1)**: SHA-1 produces a 160-bit hash value and is considered more secure than MD5. However, it is also vulnerable to certain types of attacks, such as collision attacks, where two different pieces of data can produce the same hash value.

**SHA-256**: Part of the SHA-2 family of hashing algorithms, SHA-256 generates a 256-bit hash value. It is currently considered one of the most secure and widely used hashing algorithms for forensic purposes due to its resistance to collisions and other vulnerabilities.

### 5.2.2.3 Hashing Procedures in Forensics

When applying hashing techniques in digital forensics, investigators must follow a precise and methodical approach:

**Generate Hash of Original Data**: Upon receiving or acquiring the original data or storage device, investigators generate a hash value for the data. This value is recorded as part of the evidence documentation and is used for future verification.

**Generate Hash of the Forensic Image**: Once a disk image is created, investigators generate a hash value for the image. The hash of the image should match the hash of the original data, confirming that the image is a perfect replica of the original.

**Regular Hashing Throughout the Investigation**: Investigators should periodically hash both the image and any extracted data during the investigation to ensure the integrity of the evidence is maintained. This is especially important if the evidence is being transferred between systems or individuals.

**Chain of Custody Logs**: Hash values are often recorded in the chain of custody log to verify that no modifications have occurred during the handling of the evidence. If any discrepancy is found between the hash values, it indicates that the evidence has been tampered with.

### 5.2.2.4 Use of Hash Databases for Known Data

In addition to verifying data integrity, hashes can be used to identify known files and data, such as operating system files or known malware. Forensic investigators can compare the hashes of files found in a system with databases of known hashes, such as the National Software Reference Library (NSRL) or Hash Sets. This helps identify and filter out irrelevant or known files, focusing on the unique and potentially criminal data.

### 5.2.3 Challenges and Limitations of Imaging and Hashing

While imaging and hashing are powerful tools for preserving and verifying data integrity, there are some challenges and limitations:

- **Corrupted or Inaccessible Data**: In some cases, the data may be damaged or inaccessible due to hardware failure, encryption, or corruption. This can complicate the imaging process, requiring specialized tools and techniques.
- **Hashing Collisions**: Although rare, hashing algorithms can sometimes produce the same hash value for different inputs (a collision). This is a known vulnerability in older algorithms like MD5 and SHA-1, which is why newer algorithms like SHA-256 are preferred.
- **Encryption and Password Protection**: If the evidence is encrypted or password-protected, forensic investigators must have the necessary decryption keys or passwords to generate a hash of the data. Without this information, hashing alone may not be sufficient for verifying data integrity.

Imaging and hashing are critical techniques in forensic cybersecurity, ensuring that digital evidence remains intact and reliable throughout the investigation process. Imaging allows forensic investigators to work with an exact replica of digital data, while hashing ensures the authenticity of that data by providing a unique identifier that can be used to verify the evidence's integrity. Together, these techniques form the foundation of a robust forensic process, enabling investigators to preserve, protect, and analyze digital evidence with confidence that it will stand up in court. As cyber threats and forensic techniques continue to evolve, these practices will remain central to the success of any digital investigation.

## 5.3 The Role of Log Analysis in Investigations.

Log analysis is a fundamental component of digital forensics and cybersecurity investigations. Logs are records generated by computer systems, applications, and network devices that document activity within a system or across a network. These logs contain crucial information about system events, user actions, and network communications, which can be vital for uncovering evidence of cyberattacks, understanding the timeline of an incident, identifying malicious behavior, and tracing unauthorized access. Log analysis plays a pivotal role in ensuring that investigators can reconstruct events, detect breaches, and establish a clear chain of actions that lead up to and follow a security incident.

In forensic cybersecurity investigations, logs serve as the digital breadcrumbs that can provide insights into an attack, the attacker's methods, and the compromised systems. This section discusses the importance of log analysis, the tools used to collect and analyze logs, and how it fits into the overall forensic process.

### 5.3.1 Importance of Log Analysis in Cybersecurity Investigations

Logs are crucial for understanding what occurred before, during, and after an incident, and they help investigators answer several key questions:

- **What happened?** Logs capture system, network, and application events that can tell investigators what actions occurred on a system—whether a login attempt, data access, or a file modification.
- **When did it happen?** Logs typically include timestamps, allowing investigators to create a timeline of events. This is especially important for tracking an attacker's movements, understanding the duration of the attack, and identifying the point of entry.

- **Who did it?** Logs often contain user identifiers, IP addresses, and device information that can link specific actions to a particular user or attacker, assisting in attribution efforts.
- **How did it happen?** Logs can also provide detailed data on the techniques and methods employed in an attack, such as exploitation of vulnerabilities, use of remote access tools, or malware execution.

The ability to correlate logs from various sources—such as firewalls, intrusion detection systems, servers, and endpoint devices—is essential for creating a comprehensive picture of an attack. Log analysis can reveal the full scope of an incident, including any lateral movement within a network or additional compromised systems.

### 5.3.2 Types of Logs in Forensic Cybersecurity Investigations

Logs can come from a wide range of sources, each providing unique and valuable information in an investigation. Some of the key types of logs used in forensic cybersecurity are:

**System Logs:**

Generated by operating systems (Windows, Linux, macOS) and provide a record of system-level events, including logins, shutdowns, application errors, and security alerts. They can reveal unauthorized login attempts, failed password attempts, and system misconfigurations that attackers may exploit.

**Examples**: Windows Event Logs, syslog (Linux), macOS Unified Logs.

**Application Logs:**

These logs capture events related to specific software applications or services running on the system. Application logs can be especially useful for identifying application vulnerabilities or suspicious activity within specific services.

**Examples**: Web Server Logs (Apache, Nginx), Database Logs, Email Server Logs.

**Network Logs:**

Network logs provide data on traffic flowing through network devices such as routers, firewalls, and intrusion detection systems (IDS). They can help investigators track malicious network activity, identify connections between compromised systems, and trace back the origin of an attack.

**Examples**: Firewall Logs, VPN Logs, Network Intrusion Detection System (NIDS) Logs, Router and Switch Logs.

## Security Logs:

Specialized logs generated by security devices and tools that monitor and protect systems and networks. These logs are key to detecting malicious activities such as attempts to bypass security measures, exploits, or malware behavior.

**Examples**: IDS/IPS Logs (Intrusion Detection/Prevention Systems), Antivirus Logs, SIEM (Security Information and Event Management) Logs.

## Authentication and Access Logs:

These logs capture details of user logins, authentication attempts, and access to sensitive resources. They are essential for identifying unauthorized access attempts and understanding an attacker's behavior, such as using stolen credentials or exploiting weak authentication systems.

**Examples**: SSH (Secure Shell) Logs, RDP (Remote Desktop Protocol) Logs, Access Control Logs.

## Cloud Logs:

As more organizations migrate to the cloud, cloud service logs become an important source of evidence in investigations. Cloud logs track access and activity within cloud-based services, including computing, storage, and network management systems.

**Examples**: AWS CloudTrail Logs, Google Cloud Logs, Azure Activity Logs.

### 5.3.3 How Log Analysis Supports Forensic Investigations

Log analysis is often one of the first steps in a digital forensic investigation. When a cybersecurity incident is detected or suspected, logs can help investigators identify the root cause of the breach, track the attacker's movements, and gather evidence that may lead to the attacker's identification or uncover additional compromised systems. The following outlines the core functions of log analysis in forensic investigations:

**Incident Detection:**

Logs are often the first place where signs of a cyberattack can be found. Unusual activity, such as a sudden spike in failed login attempts, anomalous network traffic, or the execution of unexpected processes, can be detected through log analysis. Identifying these indicators early can help investigators respond more quickly to minimize damage.

**Timeline Reconstruction:**

Creating a timeline of events is critical in understanding the sequence of actions leading up to, during, and after a cyberattack. By analyzing logs from various sources, investigators can accurately reconstruct when the attacker entered the system, what actions they took, and when they were detected or removed.

**Attribution and Identification:**

Logs can contain valuable information that helps identify the attacker, such as IP addresses, user accounts, and other identifiers. By cross-referencing this data with other logs, investigators can build a profile of the attacker's behavior and attempt to link the attack to specific threat actors or groups.

**Tracking Attack Progression:**

Cyberattacks often evolve over time, with attackers gaining initial access and then moving laterally across the network to compromise additional systems. Logs provide the evidence necessary to track this progression and identify the extent of the compromise. This can include monitoring for unusual access to critical systems, changes to files or configurations, and evidence of privilege escalation.

**Malware Analysis:**

Logs may also reveal signs of malware activity, such as the execution of malicious files, communication with external command-and-control servers, or the installation of backdoors. Log analysis can help identify the type of malware, how it was deployed, and whether it was successful in its objectives.

**Post-Incident Analysis and Reporting:**

After an incident is contained, logs play a crucial role in conducting a thorough investigation and creating a report detailing the findings. This report may be used for internal purposes, legal proceedings, or to improve future security measures. Log analysis helps provide the evidence needed to support these reports.

### 5.3.4 Tools for Log Analysis

Various tools are available to assist investigators in analyzing large volumes of logs and identifying relevant data quickly. These tools help automate the parsing, correlation, and search of log data, enabling investigators to efficiently sift through vast amounts of information.

**SIEM (Security Information and Event Management) Systems:**

SIEM platforms, such as Splunk, ArcSight, and QRadar, aggregate and correlate logs from various sources, providing real-time alerts and insights. SIEMs are particularly useful for detecting patterns of attack and generating alerts based on predefined rules.

**Log Aggregators:**

Tools like ELK Stack (Elasticsearch, Logstash, and Kibana) and Graylog help collect, centralize, and visualize logs from different devices and systems. These tools allow investigators to search logs, generate dashboards, and analyze trends over time.

**Log Analysis Software:**

Specialized software like LogRhythm or SolarWinds Log Analyzer can assist investigators in performing deep forensic analysis of logs, detecting anomalies, and identifying signs of intrusion or attack.

**Manual Tools:**

Sometimes, a manual approach is necessary to dig through log files. Tools like grep (for Linux/Unix systems) or LogParser (for Windows) can help investigators search through logs and filter out relevant information.

### 5.3.5 Challenges in Log Analysis

While log analysis is a powerful tool, it comes with its own set of challenges:

- **Volume of Data**: Logs can generate an overwhelming amount of data, especially in large enterprise networks. Sorting through this data can be time-consuming and requires powerful tools and methodologies to identify relevant events.
- **Log Format Variability**: Logs can come in many different formats, and inconsistencies between systems can make it difficult to standardize log analysis. Investigators must often spend time transforming or normalizing data before analysis can begin.
- **Log Retention**: Logs may be overwritten or deleted if they are not properly archived or retained. This can limit the ability to investigate past incidents, especially if logs are not regularly backed up.

Log analysis is an essential component of forensic cybersecurity investigations, providing invaluable insights into the timeline, methods, and scope of cyberattacks. By analyzing logs from various sources such as operating systems, applications, firewalls, and intrusion detection systems, forensic investigators can piece together the events of an attack, identify the attacker, and understand the techniques used. Effective log analysis requires the use of specialized tools, but it also requires skill and expertise in identifying relevant data amidst large volumes of logs. As cyberattacks become increasingly sophisticated, the role of log analysis in cybersecurity investigations will continue to be critical in detecting, responding to, and preventing future incidents.

# 5.4 Open-Source Tools vs. Proprietary Solutions.

In the field of forensic cybersecurity, tools are essential for collecting, analyzing, and preserving digital evidence. These tools can either be open-source or proprietary solutions, each offering distinct advantages and limitations based on their functionality, cost, and usability. Understanding the differences between these two types of tools is crucial for cybersecurity professionals, as it impacts the effectiveness of investigations, the choice of tool based on available resources, and the overall security posture of an organization.

In this section, we will explore the differences between open-source tools and proprietary solutions in the context of forensic cybersecurity, highlighting the key characteristics, benefits, drawbacks, and real-world use cases for each.

### 5.4.1 Open-Source Tools

Open-source forensic tools are publicly available software applications whose source code is open for modification, distribution, and collaboration by anyone. These tools are developed and maintained by communities of developers, enthusiasts, or organizations. Open-source tools are often free to use, although some may offer premium features or services.

**Advantages of Open-Source Tools:**

**Cost-Effectiveness:**

One of the biggest benefits of open-source tools is that they are typically free to use. For smaller organizations, educational institutions, or government agencies with limited budgets, these tools can provide access to powerful forensic capabilities without the financial burden of expensive licenses.

**Transparency and Customizability:**

Open-source tools offer full transparency, allowing users to review and audit the source code for security flaws, vulnerabilities, and backdoors. Additionally, users can modify the software to suit their specific needs, integrating additional functionality or enhancing the tool's compatibility with custom environments. This can be especially valuable for organizations with unique investigative requirements.

**Community Support and Development:**

Open-source tools often have large, active user communities that contribute to their development. Forums, documentation, and online resources help users troubleshoot issues, share use cases, and continuously improve the tools. With many eyes on the code, the development process is generally quicker, and issues can be addressed rapidly.

**Flexibility Across Platforms:**

Many open-source tools are cross-platform, meaning they can run on various operating systems such as Windows, Linux, and macOS. This is particularly important for forensic investigations, as investigators may encounter a variety of systems and environments during their analysis.

**Disadvantages of Open-Source Tools:**

**Lack of Formal Support:**

While community support is valuable, it does not always provide the same level of reliability or promptness as professional, paid support. In some cases, users may struggle to resolve issues without official assistance, especially in high-pressure investigative situations.

**Limited Documentation:**

Despite the availability of community resources, many open-source tools may lack comprehensive, well-structured documentation. Investigators may face challenges in learning how to use the tool effectively or troubleshooting advanced functionalities.

**Inconsistent Updates and Maintenance:**

Open-source tools may not be updated as frequently as proprietary solutions, and maintenance can be irregular, particularly if a tool's development team disbands or loses interest. This can lead to compatibility issues with new technologies, platforms, or digital evidence formats.

**Potential for Security Vulnerabilities:**

While transparency allows for auditing, open-source tools may also have undiscovered vulnerabilities or security flaws that could be exploited by malicious actors. Investigators must be cautious about using open-source tools in high-risk environments where security is paramount.

**Popular Open-Source Forensic Tools:**

- **Autopsy**: A digital forensics platform that supports a wide variety of file systems and digital evidence analysis, including imaging, hash analysis, and keyword searching.
- **Volatility**: A memory forensics framework that helps investigators analyze volatile memory (RAM) to uncover evidence of malware, rootkits, and other attack artifacts.
- **FTK Imager (Open-Source Version)**: A lightweight, open-source tool used for imaging, creating disk images, and verifying the integrity of evidence with hash algorithms.
- **Sleuth Kit**: A collection of command-line tools and a library for examining disk images and file systems, providing basic forensic functionalities.

### 5.4.2 Proprietary Solutions

Proprietary solutions are commercial software applications developed by private companies. These tools are sold under license and offer a range of forensic capabilities, typically supported by customer service, technical support, and regular software updates. Proprietary tools are commonly used by law enforcement, private investigation firms, and large corporations due to their reliability, professionalism, and comprehensive features.

**Advantages of Proprietary Solutions:**

**Comprehensive Support and Training:**

Proprietary tools often come with formal support from the developer. This includes direct access to customer service, dedicated technical support teams, and detailed user guides or training programs. This is particularly beneficial for organizations with high standards for incident response and those conducting high-stakes investigations, where time is critical.

**Robust Functionality:**

Commercial tools tend to be feature-rich, offering advanced capabilities such as automated analysis, real-time monitoring, high-level reporting, and seamless integration with other enterprise tools. Proprietary solutions also tend to have a user-friendly interface, which can reduce the learning curve for investigators, making them ideal for teams that require efficiency in handling complex investigations.

**Regular Updates and Maintenance:**

Proprietary software is typically updated regularly, ensuring that it stays compatible with the latest operating systems, file formats, and investigative needs. The development teams behind these tools are usually proactive in identifying and fixing bugs, adding new features, and improving tool functionality, ensuring they are reliable for long-term use.

**Advanced Security Features:**

Commercial forensic tools often come with advanced security features such as encryption, authentication, and compliance with legal standards. These features make proprietary tools suitable for use in legally sensitive investigations, such as criminal cases, where the integrity of the evidence must be safeguarded at all times.

**Disadvantages of Proprietary Solutions:**

## High Cost:

One of the major drawbacks of proprietary solutions is their cost. Licensing fees can be substantial, particularly for large organizations or government agencies. This can limit access to these tools for smaller firms or individuals who lack the financial resources to purchase and maintain them.

## Limited Customization:

Unlike open-source tools, proprietary solutions are typically closed systems that cannot be modified by the end user. Investigators are limited to the functionality provided by the vendor and cannot easily customize the tool to meet their specific needs unless the vendor offers specific customization services at an additional cost.

## Vendor Lock-In:

With proprietary solutions, organizations may become dependent on the vendor for future updates, patches, and support. If the vendor discontinues the tool or significantly alters the software's pricing structure, organizations may be left with limited options or be forced to transition to a new solution, which can be both costly and disruptive.

## Learning Curve:

While proprietary solutions are often user-friendly, they can be complex and require training to use effectively. Large, feature-rich forensic tools may have steep learning curves that require significant time and resources to master.

## Popular Proprietary Forensic Tools:

- **EnCase Forensic**: A leading tool for disk-level investigations, supporting the acquisition, analysis, and reporting of digital evidence across various systems.
- **X1 Social Discovery**: A specialized tool for collecting, analyzing, and preserving social media evidence, commonly used in legal investigations.
- **Cellebrite UFED**: A mobile forensic tool for extracting and analyzing data from mobile devices, including smartphones, tablets, and GPS units.

### 5.4.3 Open-Source vs. Proprietary Tools: Choosing the Right Tool for the Job

When deciding whether to use open-source or proprietary forensic tools, investigators and organizations need to consider several factors:

- **Budget**: Open-source tools are ideal for organizations with limited budgets, as they provide essential functionality without the financial burden of licensing fees.
- **Complexity of the Investigation**: For high-stakes investigations requiring advanced features, professional support, and long-term reliability, proprietary solutions may be more appropriate.
- **Customization Needs**: If an organization requires tools that can be tailored to specific needs or integrated into a unique infrastructure, open-source solutions offer the flexibility to modify and extend the software.
- **Legal and Compliance Requirements**: For investigations that must meet strict legal or regulatory standards, proprietary tools with proven certifications and compliance features may be the best choice.

Both open-source tools and proprietary solutions offer significant value in forensic cybersecurity, depending on the specific needs of the investigation. Open-source tools provide flexibility, transparency, and cost-effectiveness, making them ideal for smaller operations or those with specialized requirements. On the other hand, proprietary tools offer comprehensive functionality, support, and reliability, making them suitable for large organizations or high-profile investigations. By understanding the strengths and weaknesses of each, cybersecurity professionals can make informed decisions about which tools best fit their forensic needs.

# 6. Network Forensics and Incident Response

In the world of cyber threats, network forensics and incident response are critical for identifying, mitigating, and recovering from attacks. This chapter examines how network traffic is monitored and analyzed to detect anomalies and trace malicious activity. It covers the tools and techniques used for packet inspection, log analysis, and intrusion detection systems (IDS), helping readers understand how to capture and reconstruct events leading to a breach. Additionally, the chapter walks through the steps of effective incident response, from initial detection to containment and recovery, offering strategies for minimizing damage and preparing for future threats.

## 6.1 Key Concepts in Network Traffic Analysis.

Network traffic analysis is a critical skill in forensic cybersecurity, playing a central role in detecting, investigating, and mitigating cyber threats. It involves monitoring and interpreting data transmitted across a network, such as packet-level information, protocols, and communications between devices. The goal is to uncover any suspicious activity, identify potential breaches, or understand the behavior of attackers. This process can provide vital insights into how an attack was initiated, how it spread, and what systems were compromised.

Network traffic analysis serves as the backbone of many incident response and forensic investigations. It allows cybersecurity professionals to reconstruct attack scenarios, pinpoint entry points, trace the flow of malware or data exfiltration, and even establish timelines of events. In this section, we will explore the key concepts that underlie network traffic analysis and its role in forensic investigations.

### 6.1.1 Traffic Flow and Protocols

At the heart of network traffic analysis is understanding the flow of data within a network and how it is structured. When a device communicates over a network, it sends and receives data in the form of packets, which are small chunks of information broken down for efficient transmission. Each packet contains essential information, including the source and destination IP addresses, the protocol used, and the data being transmitted.

The two fundamental elements to understand here are:

- **Protocols**: Protocols define the rules for communication between devices on a network. Some of the most common protocols relevant to network traffic analysis include:
- **TCP/IP (Transmission Control Protocol/Internet Protocol):** This is the foundational protocol suite that governs most network communications. It is responsible for breaking data into packets and ensuring that they are transmitted reliably.
- **UDP (User Datagram Protocol):** Unlike TCP, UDP is a connectionless protocol that does not guarantee delivery, order, or error checking. It is often used in real-time applications like VoIP (Voice over IP) or video streaming.
- **HTTP/HTTPS (HyperText Transfer Protocol/Secure):** These protocols are the backbone of web traffic, allowing browsers to request and receive web content. HTTPS adds an encryption layer using SSL/TLS to secure the communication.
- **DNS (Domain Name System):** This protocol translates human-readable domain names (like www.example.com) into IP addresses that computers can use to communicate with each other.
- **SMTP (Simple Mail Transfer Protocol):** This protocol is used for sending emails over a network.
- **Traffic Flow**: Traffic flow refers to the pattern or path data takes as it moves across a network, from its origin to its destination. Analyzing traffic flow helps identify abnormal patterns that could indicate malicious activity, such as data exfiltration, botnet communications, or DDoS (Distributed Denial of Service) attacks.

### 6.1.2 Packet Analysis and Deep Packet Inspection (DPI)

In network traffic analysis, investigators often focus on packet analysis to gain detailed insights into the data being transmitted. A packet is composed of several components, each of which provides critical information:

- **Header**: The header contains routing information, such as the source and destination IP addresses, ports, and the protocol used (TCP, UDP, etc.).
- **Payload**: The payload contains the actual data being transmitted, which could be anything from an email message to a file or command.
- **Checksum**: A checksum is used to verify the integrity of the packet, ensuring that it hasn't been altered during transmission.

Deep Packet Inspection (DPI) is a sophisticated method of analyzing packets in greater detail. DPI goes beyond just looking at the headers of packets and examines the payload, allowing analysts to detect:

- Malware embedded within the payload.
- Exploited vulnerabilities or unusual traffic patterns that may indicate malicious behavior.
- Data exfiltration, where sensitive information is being sent out of a network to an external destination.
- DPI tools are often used by intrusion detection systems (IDS), intrusion prevention systems (IPS), and firewalls to actively inspect and filter traffic based on specific rules or signatures.

### 6.1.3 Analyzing Network Topology and Segmentation

Network topology refers to the physical and logical arrangement of a network's devices and how they are connected. Understanding network topology is important for forensic investigators because it helps determine the paths that data travels and the potential vulnerabilities that could be exploited during an attack. Some key topologies include:

- **Star topology**: All devices are connected to a central hub or switch.
- **Mesh topology**: Devices are interconnected, and data can travel through multiple paths, improving redundancy.
- **Hybrid topology**: A combination of different topologies tailored to specific network needs.

Network segmentation is the practice of dividing a network into smaller, isolated sections (subnets), each with its own security measures. This reduces the risk of lateral movement by attackers, limiting their access to critical systems. Analyzing network segmentation can help forensic investigators identify compromised areas and prevent further damage.

In the context of forensics, network topology and segmentation are critical for understanding the flow of malicious traffic, especially when attackers use techniques like pivoting to move across network segments undetected.

### 6.1.4 Anomalies and Patterns in Network Traffic

One of the primary goals of network traffic analysis is to identify anomalies that might signal a security breach or ongoing attack. Some of the most common anomalies include:

- **Unusual Traffic Volume**: A sudden spike in traffic, especially outbound traffic, can indicate a DDoS attack or data exfiltration. Monitoring the volume of traffic over time can help detect such changes.

- **Unusual Source or Destination**: Traffic directed to unfamiliar IP addresses or countries that don't normally access the network can be a sign of a compromised system or communication with a Command-and-Control (C2) server in a botnet attack.
- **Port Scanning**: Attackers often scan open ports on a network to identify vulnerable services. This scanning generates distinctive patterns of small, repeated requests that can be detected during analysis.
- **Suspicious Protocols**: Some attack methods use uncommon or non-standard protocols to bypass detection. Identifying and investigating unknown or suspicious protocols can uncover malicious activity.
- **Lateral Movement**: Attackers often move laterally across a network to access additional systems after breaching an initial target. Anomalies in traffic patterns that suggest unusual communications between internal systems should be examined closely.
- **Data Exfiltration**: Unusually large file transfers, especially over encrypted channels like HTTPS or FTP, can indicate that an attacker is exfiltrating data from the network.

### 6.1.5 Tools for Network Traffic Analysis

A wide range of tools are available for network traffic analysis. Some of the most popular include:

**Wireshark**: An open-source, packet-sniffing tool that allows investigators to capture and analyze network traffic. Wireshark is one of the most widely used tools for network forensics because of its ability to decode and display detailed packet-level data in a user-friendly interface.

**tcpdump**: A command-line tool used for capturing and analyzing network traffic. While not as visually intuitive as Wireshark, tcpdump provides powerful filtering options and is commonly used for network troubleshooting and incident response.

**NetFlow**: A network protocol that collects IP traffic information as it passes through a router or switch. NetFlow data provides insight into traffic patterns, allowing forensic investigators to analyze flows of data across the network to detect potential anomalies.

**Suricata**: An open-source IDS/IPS that performs real-time traffic analysis, including deep packet inspection. It is designed to detect and prevent a wide range of attacks, including exploits, DDoS, and botnet traffic.

**Snort**: Another popular IDS/IPS that provides real-time traffic analysis, alerting security personnel about potential security incidents. Snort is highly configurable and can be used to detect a range of known attack signatures.

### 6.1.6 Correlation with Other Forensic Evidence

Network traffic analysis does not happen in isolation. It is part of a broader forensic ecosystem that includes host-based evidence (e.g., system logs, files) and external evidence (e.g., cloud activity, external devices). By correlating network traffic data with other types of evidence, investigators can establish a comprehensive understanding of the attack.

For example, a spike in network traffic may correlate with suspicious activity on a compromised system, such as the execution of malware or unauthorized access to sensitive files. Correlating such data helps forensic experts piece together the events surrounding an attack, ensuring that all aspects of the incident are accounted for.

Network traffic analysis is a cornerstone of forensic cybersecurity investigations. By understanding the protocols, traffic flow, and patterns of communication within a network, forensic professionals can uncover critical information about security breaches, attacks, and malicious activities. The ability to analyze network traffic effectively requires knowledge of packet analysis, deep packet inspection, traffic anomalies, and the use of various analysis tools. With this skill, investigators can identify attack methods, establish timelines, and trace the movements of attackers, helping to protect organizational networks from future intrusions.

# 6.2 Tools and Protocols for Packet Inspection.

Packet inspection is a key technique in network traffic analysis used to examine the data being transmitted across a network. By inspecting packets, cybersecurity professionals can identify malicious activity, unauthorized data exfiltration, and other signs of an attack. Packet inspection involves analyzing the metadata (header) and the actual content (payload) of network packets, helping forensic investigators understand how and why a breach or attack occurred. The tools and protocols used for packet inspection are critical in enabling investigators to gain a deep understanding of the traffic flow, detect vulnerabilities, and trace malicious activities across networks.

In this section, we will explore the main tools and protocols involved in packet inspection and discuss how they contribute to effective forensic analysis.

### 6.2.1 Tools for Packet Inspection

Packet inspection tools are essential in analyzing network traffic and detecting threats. These tools provide the functionality to capture, filter, and analyze packets, and some even offer deep inspection capabilities to look into the packet contents for more comprehensive analysis. Below are some of the most widely used packet inspection tools in forensic cybersecurity:

### 1. Wireshark

Wireshark is one of the most widely recognized and used open-source network protocol analyzers. It allows users to capture and interactively browse network traffic, making it a powerful tool for packet inspection and network troubleshooting.

### Features:

- Wireshark can capture network packets in real time, filtering them based on various parameters such as IP address, protocol, port, and more.
- It supports hundreds of protocols, providing in-depth analysis for each, including TCP, UDP, HTTP, DNS, SSL/TLS, and more.
- Provides detailed packet-level inspection, decoding the header and payload, and allowing users to view raw data.
- Offers features such as display filters to identify specific packet patterns and coloring rules for easier identification of suspicious traffic.
- Wireshark is often used in conjunction with other forensic tools to correlate packet-level data with other evidence.

### 2. tcpdump

tcpdump is a command-line packet analyzer that provides similar functionality to Wireshark but without a graphical interface. It's lightweight, fast, and widely used by network engineers and cybersecurity professionals for quick packet captures and analysis.

### Features
:

- tcpdump captures packets on the network and allows users to display them in real-time, providing the ability to analyze the contents of the packet.

- It supports a wide range of filters and capture options, enabling users to focus on specific network interfaces, IP addresses, or protocols.
- tcpdump also allows saving packet captures in pcap (packet capture) format, which can later be analyzed using other tools like Wireshark.

## 3. Suricata

Suricata is a high-performance, open-source Network IDS/IPS (Intrusion Detection/Prevention System) that also includes advanced packet inspection capabilities. It is designed to provide high-speed traffic analysis and detection of network-based attacks.

### Features:

- Suricata supports deep packet inspection (DPI) to examine the full content of packets, including the application layer.
- It can detect a wide range of attack signatures, including DDoS, buffer overflows, malware communication, and exploitation of network services.
- Suricata integrates well with other security monitoring systems and can be used in combination with tools like Elastic Stack for real-time analysis.
- It provides extensive logging and alerting features, helping cybersecurity teams respond promptly to threats.

## 4. Snort

Snort is another widely-used open-source network intrusion detection and prevention system. It is known for its ability to detect and prevent a wide range of attacks, and it also offers powerful packet inspection capabilities.

### Features:

- Snort inspects network traffic in real time, comparing packets against a database of known attack signatures.
- It supports Deep Packet Inspection (DPI), which examines the contents of each packet, including its header and payload, to detect suspicious patterns or anomalous behavior.
- Snort can be configured to log and generate alerts based on the detection of suspicious packets, and it supports integration with other monitoring tools for deeper analysis.

## 5. NetworkMiner

NetworkMiner is a network forensics tool that focuses on packet capture, analysis, and extracting information from network traffic. Unlike traditional packet sniffers, NetworkMiner focuses on the collection of network metadata and session reconstruction.

**Features:**

- NetworkMiner automatically extracts useful data from packet captures (pcap files), such as IP addresses, DNS queries, usernames, passwords, and files transferred over the network.
- It is particularly useful for recovering files and credentials from packet captures, which can aid in forensic investigations.
- NetworkMiner supports multiple protocols, including HTTP, FTP, and SMB, and can help reconstruct sessions or transactions during an attack

## 6. Xplico

Xplico is an open-source tool that specializes in the analysis of application layer protocols. It is used to extract useful data from packets captured from the network.

**Features:**

- Xplico supports a variety of protocols, such as HTTP, SIP (Session Initiation Protocol), SMTP, IMAP, and FTP, allowing investigators to reconstruct conversations and sessions from network traffic.
- It provides features for decoding and extracting email messages, voice communications, web pages, and other content from packets.

### 6.2.2 Protocols for Packet Inspection

Protocols play an essential role in packet inspection as they define how data is formatted and transmitted over the network. Understanding the structure and behavior of different protocols is crucial for effective packet analysis, as each protocol has its own way of encapsulating data. Below are some key protocols involved in packet inspection and their role in network traffic analysis:

## 1. Transmission Control Protocol (TCP)

TCP is one of the most common and important protocols used for packet-level communication on IP networks. It ensures reliable, ordered delivery of data between devices.

**Forensic Relevance**: TCP packets are used in a variety of applications, from web browsing to file transfers. Analyzing TCP streams helps investigators trace the flow of data between systems and detect potential data leaks, botnet communication, or abnormal traffic patterns.

## 2. User Datagram Protocol (UDP)

UDP is a connectionless protocol that sends packets without establishing a reliable connection. Unlike TCP, UDP does not guarantee packet order or delivery.

**Forensic Relevance**: While UDP is often used for real-time communication (e.g., VoIP, video streaming), it can also be exploited by attackers to transmit malware or DDoS attack traffic. Investigators often look for anomalous or unusually high UDP traffic to detect malicious activity.

## 3. Internet Protocol (IP)

IP defines the addressing system used to route packets between devices on a network. The two versions commonly used are IPv4 and IPv6.

**Forensic Relevance**: IP packets provide crucial information, such as source and destination addresses. Analyzing IP addresses can help forensic investigators track the origin of attacks or determine the external networks involved in data exfiltration.

## 4. HyperText Transfer Protocol (HTTP) and Secure HTTP (HTTPS)

HTTP is the protocol used for transferring web pages, while HTTPS is the encrypted version used to ensure data confidentiality between a web server and client.

**Forensic Relevance**: HTTP/HTTPS packets are often scrutinized in forensic analysis, particularly when investigating web-based attacks (e.g., Cross-Site Scripting, SQL injection) or tracing the movement of data to and from a compromised web server.

## 5. Domain Name System (DNS)

DNS is used to translate domain names (e.g., www.example.com) into IP addresses, which are necessary for devices to locate each other on the internet.

**Forensic Relevance**: DNS traffic is often analyzed to detect DNS tunneling, where attackers exfiltrate data using DNS queries and responses. Investigators may also examine DNS logs to identify malicious domains or control servers used by attackers.

### 6. Simple Mail Transfer Protocol (SMTP)

SMTP is the protocol used for sending email messages between servers.

**Forensic Relevance**: Investigating email traffic can reveal phishing attempts, spam, or malware propagation. SMTP packets often contain metadata and email content that can be analyzed for evidence of malicious activity.

Packet inspection is a fundamental process in network traffic analysis and plays a critical role in forensic investigations. By leveraging advanced tools like Wireshark, tcpdump, Suricata, and others, cybersecurity professionals can capture and analyze packets in real time, identify anomalies, and detect security threats. The ability to inspect the payload and headers of packets—along with an understanding of key protocols such as TCP, UDP, and DNS—enables investigators to uncover hidden threats and piece together a detailed picture of network activity during an attack. With a robust understanding of packet inspection tools and protocols, forensic experts can efficiently investigate, respond to, and mitigate cyber threats.

# 6.3 Responding to Breaches: Steps to Containment.

When a cyberattack occurs, time is of the essence. The longer the breach goes unchecked, the greater the potential for data exfiltration, system compromise, or further spread of malware within the network. Containment is the critical first step in limiting the damage caused by a breach and preventing the attacker from expanding their access or causing further harm. Effective containment requires a well-organized response strategy, precise technical actions, and a collaborative effort between cybersecurity teams, incident responders, and other stakeholders.

In this section, we will outline the essential steps in responding to a breach and implementing containment strategies. These steps will ensure that the threat is neutralized, the impact is minimized, and the organization can begin the recovery process with minimal long-term consequences.

### 6.3.1 Detection and Identification of the Breach

The first and foremost step in responding to a breach is detection. Cyberattacks often occur without immediate detection, and early identification is essential to mitigate their impact. Detection involves recognizing abnormal activities or indicators of compromise (IOCs) that suggest a security breach is taking place.

**Indicators of Compromise (IOCs):** These are artifacts or patterns that point to a potential breach. They can include unusual network traffic, unauthorized access to systems, the appearance of unfamiliar files, or malware signatures. Examples include:

- Unusual outbound network traffic, possibly indicating data exfiltration.
- Multiple failed login attempts or successful logins from unfamiliar IP addresses.
- Uncommon processes or files being executed on systems.

**Detection Tools**: Many organizations use Intrusion Detection Systems (IDS), Security Information and Event Management (SIEM) tools, and network monitoring software to detect breaches. These tools can automatically generate alerts based on predefined patterns of malicious behavior.

**Action**: When IOCs are detected, cybersecurity professionals should initiate an incident response plan, immediately alerting the appropriate response teams to investigate further.

### 6.3.2 Initial Containment: Isolation of Affected Systems

Once a breach is detected, it is critical to contain the threat by isolating the affected systems from the rest of the network. Early containment helps prevent the attacker from moving laterally within the network or escalating the attack to other devices or systems. The affected systems should be quarantined as quickly as possible to limit their ability to communicate with other systems, propagate malware, or exfiltrate data.

**Disconnecting Compromised Devices**: The immediate action may involve physically disconnecting affected machines from the network (e.g., pulling network cables, disabling Wi-Fi). This prevents further communication with the external attacker and reduces the risk of additional systems being compromised.

**Network Segmentation**: In larger networks, isolating compromised systems within a specific network segment can be an effective containment strategy. By segmenting networks into subnets with strong access controls, organizations can prevent lateral movement by attackers. The network's segmentation also ensures that compromised systems don't impact other critical systems.

**Disabling Remote Access**: Many attacks exploit remote access protocols to gain control over systems (e.g., RDP, VPN). If an attack is linked to a remote access compromise, the immediate disabling of remote access protocols is essential. Additionally, reviewing and revoking any credentials or keys that could facilitate further access is crucial.

**Action**: After isolating affected systems, forensic investigators should begin their analysis to identify how the breach occurred, what systems were affected, and what data may have been compromised.

### 6.3.3 Eradication of Malware and Intruder Tools

Once the systems are contained, the next step is to eradicate the malware or tools that the attacker used to breach the network. Malware removal, including any backdoors, rootkits, or trojans installed by the attacker, is crucial to preventing the attacker from regaining access. Without this step, the attacker could return through the same exploit or method.

**Identifying the Malware**: Forensic investigators need to identify the exact nature of the malware used in the attack. This involves analyzing the malicious files, network traffic, and system logs to determine the type of malware involved. Common techniques for identifying malware include:

- Static and dynamic analysis of files.
- Analyzing communication between the compromised system and external C2 (Command and Control) servers.
- Examining memory dumps or forensic images of affected systems.

**Removing the Malware**: Once identified, malware should be completely removed from the affected system. This could involve:

- Running antivirus and anti-malware software to remove known threats.
- Manually removing malicious files or processes identified through forensic analysis.
- Reinstalling compromised systems or restoring them to clean, known good configurations (if necessary).

**Cleaning Up Intruder Tools**: Attackers may have used tools such as keyloggers, Trojan horses, or remote access software to gain control of systems. These tools need to be identified and eradicated from all affected systems.

Action: During eradication, it's essential to preserve any evidence that could be useful for the ongoing investigation, such as system images, logs, and traces left by the malware.

### 6.3.4 Strengthening Defenses: Patching and Vulnerability Management

After eradicating the malware and preventing the attacker from regaining access, the next containment step is to ensure that the vulnerabilities exploited by the attacker are patched and properly secured. This will prevent the same breach from occurring again or being exploited by other attackers.

**Patch Management**: The breach may have been the result of a known vulnerability in unpatched software or a misconfigured system. It is essential to apply patches to any software, operating systems, or network devices that were involved in the breach. Regular patching of all systems should be a key part of an organization's cybersecurity hygiene.

**Vulnerability Scanning**: Use vulnerability management tools to identify unpatched vulnerabilities across the network. This can include scanning for outdated software, unsecure configurations, or weak credentials that might have contributed to the attack.

**Reinforcing Access Controls**: Strengthen access controls to reduce the attack surface. This can include:

- Enforcing multi-factor authentication (MFA) for critical systems.
- Reviewing and tightening user permissions.
- Disabling unnecessary services or protocols that could serve as entry points for attackers.

**Action**: Patch all systems, implement enhanced access controls, and configure systems with the latest security measures to bolster defenses against future attacks.

### 6.3.5 Communication and Reporting

Effective communication is crucial during a breach response. Once containment is achieved, internal and external stakeholders need to be informed about the situation and the steps being taken to address it. Transparency helps ensure that the organization can recover swiftly and that any required legal or regulatory actions are taken.

**Internal Communication**: Key stakeholders such as IT teams, executive leadership, and departments that may be impacted (e.g., HR, legal, compliance) should be notified about the breach. Detailed incident reports should be prepared, outlining the scope of the breach, the systems affected, and the actions taken.

**External Reporting**: Depending on the nature of the breach, external parties may need to be notified. These could include:

- **Law enforcement agencies**: Particularly in cases of large-scale data breaches or attacks that may involve criminal activity.
- **Regulatory bodies**: Depending on the sector, organizations may need to report data breaches to regulatory authorities, especially if sensitive personal or financial data has been exposed (e.g., GDPR in the EU, CCPA in California).
- **Customers and Partners**: If customer data was compromised, appropriate steps should be taken to notify affected parties, along with providing guidance on how they can protect themselves (e.g., changing passwords, monitoring accounts).

**Action**: Maintain clear communication with internal and external stakeholders while following legal and regulatory guidelines for breach notification.

### 6.3.6 Post-Breach Review and Recovery

Containment is not the end of the process. After securing the environment, a post-breach review is essential to understand the full scope of the breach and learn from the incident to improve future defenses.

**Root Cause Analysis**: Perform a detailed investigation into how the breach occurred. Analyze logs, network traffic, and forensic data to identify vulnerabilities or human errors that contributed to the breach.

**Recovery**: Once containment is complete, organizations can move into the recovery phase. This includes restoring affected systems from clean backups, rebuilding trust with stakeholders, and implementing lessons learned to strengthen future defenses.

**Action**: Perform a thorough post-breach analysis, update incident response protocols, and incorporate new cybersecurity measures to prevent future attacks.

Responding to a cybersecurity breach is a high-stakes process that requires swift action, technical expertise, and a well-coordinated approach. Containment is the first line of defense against an active attack, and by isolating compromised systems, eradicating malicious tools, and strengthening defenses, organizations can minimize the damage caused by the breach. Effective containment requires not only technical tools but also strong communication, collaboration, and continual improvement to protect the organization from future threats.

# 6.4 Building a Collaborative Incident Response Team.

An effective Incident Response Team (IRT) is essential to any cybersecurity strategy, as it ensures a coordinated, efficient, and effective response to security breaches, cyberattacks, and data compromises. Cybersecurity incidents are increasingly complex, and a fragmented or poorly coordinated team can make a bad situation worse. Building a collaborative Incident Response Team (IRT) is key to minimizing the damage, swiftly containing the attack, and restoring normal business operations. By uniting experts from different areas of the organization, a collaborative team can leverage diverse skills and knowledge, ultimately improving the organization's security posture and resilience.

In this section, we'll outline the steps for building a collaborative Incident Response Team, the roles and responsibilities of team members, and strategies for fostering teamwork and effective communication during a security incident.

### 6.4.1 Defining the Incident Response Team's Core Structure

An incident response team needs a well-defined structure to ensure that everyone knows their role and responsibilities during a security incident. The team should be composed of a mix of technical experts, management, legal advisors, and communication professionals to handle all aspects of a breach. Some of the core roles that should be part of the Incident Response Team include:

**1. Incident Response Manager:**

- The Incident Response Manager is responsible for leading the team, coordinating efforts across departments, and making critical decisions about how the incident will be handled.
- They oversee the incident response plan, prioritize actions, and ensure that communication is clear and efficient.
- The manager also serves as the main point of contact for executive leadership.

**2. Technical Experts:**

- These are professionals with deep technical knowledge of networks, systems, and security tools. They are responsible for identifying the root cause of the incident, analyzing malicious activity, isolating affected systems, and preventing further damage.
- Depending on the complexity of the breach, this could include system administrators, network engineers, malware analysts, and digital forensics experts.

## 3. Legal and Compliance Team:

- The legal team ensures that the organization complies with relevant laws and regulations in the aftermath of a breach. This may include data breach notification laws, privacy regulations (such as GDPR or CCPA), and industry-specific compliance standards.
- They are responsible for liaising with external authorities, managing legal risks, and advising the response team on the legal ramifications of the incident.

## 4. Communication Specialists:

- Clear and consistent communication is crucial during a cybersecurity incident. Communication specialists are responsible for drafting internal and external communications, including press releases, emails to customers, or social media updates.
- They also ensure that employees are informed of the incident and any actions they need to take to protect themselves or the company's assets.

## 5. Management and Executive Leadership:

- While not typically involved in the day-to-day response, management and executives play a critical role in decision-making, resource allocation, and overall oversight. They ensure the response plan aligns with business priorities and compliance requirements.
- They also manage external communications with stakeholders, including customers, investors, and the media.
- A multi-disciplinary approach ensures that all aspects of the incident—from technical analysis to legal considerations—are addressed in a comprehensive, coordinated manner.

## 6.4.2 Establishing Clear Roles and Responsibilities

Once the core team is established, defining the roles and responsibilities of each member is crucial for clarity and efficiency during an incident. Without clear roles, the team may struggle to act quickly, and some areas of response may be neglected.

- **Incident Response Manager**: Leads the team, makes key decisions, and liaises with senior management and other departments.
- **Technical Experts**: Provide expertise in identifying the nature of the attack, mitigating its impact, and restoring affected systems.
- **Legal and Compliance Team**: Advises on regulatory requirements, risk mitigation strategies, and manages legal notifications and breach reporting.
- **Communications**: Drafts and disseminates internal and external communications, ensuring messages are consistent and transparent.
- **Human Resources (HR):** Coordinates communication with employees and provides support to individuals who may be affected by the breach (e.g., employees whose data may have been exposed).
- **External Consultants**: In some cases, organizations may engage external experts, such as digital forensics firms, incident response providers, or third-party cybersecurity experts. These consultants can bring specialized knowledge to the team.

Each team member should be trained on their responsibilities and equipped with the tools and knowledge needed to perform their role effectively.

### 6.4.3 Building Cross-Department Collaboration

Cybersecurity breaches can affect all parts of an organization, from technical systems to human resources and legal compliance. For an incident response to be truly effective, it's essential that the Incident Response Team works collaboratively across departments. A siloed response can lead to confusion, delays, and missed opportunities for containment and recovery.

### 1. Regular Cross-Departmental Training:

- A successful collaborative team is built on ongoing training and familiarization with each department's roles and functions. By conducting regular joint training exercises, team members can better understand the scope of their colleagues' responsibilities.
- Training should include tabletop exercises that simulate various types of cybersecurity incidents. These exercises should be realistic and involve

representatives from each department, helping everyone practice working together under pressure.

## 2. Clear Communication Channels:

- During an incident, effective communication is essential. Team members should have direct and dedicated communication channels (such as encrypted email, phone lines, and internal messaging systems) that allow for fast, secure, and clear updates.
- Use a centralized incident management platform (such as ServiceNow, Jira, or a custom tool) to log and track incident response activities in real-time, ensuring that all team members are informed and up-to-date on the latest developments.

## 3. Collaboration Tools and Platforms:

- Collaborative tools like Slack, Microsoft Teams, or Trello can be effective in organizing the response efforts, ensuring that tasks are assigned, monitored, and completed promptly.
- Cloud-based document-sharing platforms (e.g., Google Drive or SharePoint) can enable real-time sharing of critical files, reports, and logs between team members, regardless of their physical location.

## 4. External Partners:

Collaborating with third-party vendors, such as cloud service providers, external security firms, or Managed Security Service Providers (MSSPs), can be critical in addressing incidents that involve third-party systems. Establish pre-established relationships with external partners to speed up the engagement process when needed.

### 6.4.4 Testing and Drills for Continuous Improvement

A successful incident response capability requires continuous improvement. Building a collaborative team doesn't stop once the team is established; it requires ongoing testing, drills, and post-incident reviews to identify areas for improvement and ensure the team remains agile and prepared.

**Tabletop Exercises**: Conduct periodic tabletop exercises where the team simulates real-world cybersecurity incidents. These exercises should be varied and include different attack vectors, such as ransomware attacks, insider threats, or DDoS attacks.

**Red Team vs. Blue Team Exercises**: These exercises involve two distinct teams—the Red Team (attackers) and the Blue Team (defenders). The Red Team simulates real-world attacks, while the Blue Team works to defend the systems. This helps strengthen defensive strategies and test team communication and response under pressure.

**Post-Incident Reviews**: After an incident has been fully resolved, conduct a post-mortem analysis to review the response process. Assess how well the team worked together, identify any gaps in communication or response, and improve the incident response plan accordingly.

**Documentation and Reporting**: Following each drill or actual incident, ensure that all actions taken, lessons learned, and improvements are documented. This creates a valuable resource for training new team members and refining the incident response plan.

### 6.4.5 Building Trust and Collaboration within the Team

Building a collaborative Incident Response Team goes beyond technical expertise and clear roles—it's also about fostering a culture of trust and teamwork. A collaborative, cohesive team can respond more effectively to incidents and adapt quickly to changing circumstances.

- **Foster Trust and Communication**: Encourage an environment where team members feel comfortable sharing information, asking for help, and working together to solve problems. Trusting each other's expertise and judgment can lead to faster, more effective responses during crises.
- **Mutual Respect and Recognition**: Recognize the contributions of each team member, whether they're working on technical analysis, legal compliance, or communications. Regularly acknowledge individual and team successes to motivate the group and maintain high morale.

Building a collaborative Incident Response Team is crucial for handling the ever-growing complexity of cybersecurity threats. A well-coordinated team that includes technical experts, legal advisors, communication specialists, and management can effectively minimize the impact of a breach and restore normal operations quickly. By fostering cross-department collaboration, ensuring continuous training and improvement, and promoting clear communication, organizations can create a highly effective incident response capability. Ultimately, the key to success lies in preparing ahead of time—so when a cybersecurity incident occurs, the team is ready to act swiftly, decisively, and collaboratively.

# 7. Malware Forensics

Malware forensics is essential for understanding and mitigating the impact of malicious software that infiltrates systems and networks. This chapter dives into the different types of malware, from viruses and worms to ransomware and spyware, explaining how each functions and spreads. It explores the techniques used to dissect and analyze malware, including static and dynamic analysis, reverse engineering, and sandboxing. By studying real-world malware cases and leveraging advanced forensic tools, readers will learn how to identify, isolate, and neutralize threats, while uncovering the motivations and methods behind cybercriminal activities.

## 7.1 Understanding Malware: Types and Threats.

Malware (short for "malicious software") is any software intentionally designed to cause damage to a computer system, network, or device. It is one of the most common threats in the cybersecurity landscape and is responsible for a wide range of attacks, from data breaches and system compromises to financial theft and espionage. Malware can target individuals, corporations, government agencies, and critical infrastructure systems, making it a significant concern for cybersecurity professionals.

In this section, we will explore the different types of malware, how they function, and the threats they pose to both individuals and organizations. Understanding the diverse range of malware and its tactics is essential for building effective defense mechanisms and responding to cyberattacks in a timely manner.

### 7.1.1 Types of Malware

Malware comes in many forms, each designed with specific objectives in mind. Below are some of the most common types of malware that organizations and individuals must be aware of:

### 1. Viruses

A virus is a type of malware that attaches itself to a legitimate file or program and spreads to other files or programs when executed. It can damage files, corrupt data, slow down system performance, and cause system crashes. Viruses often require user interaction (such as opening an infected attachment or running an infected program) to spread.

- **Infection Methods**: Viruses typically spread through infected emails, file sharing, or malicious websites.
- **Dangerous Effects**: File corruption, loss of data, system instability.

## 2. Worms

Unlike viruses, worms are self-replicating programs that can spread across networks without needing to attach themselves to a host file. Worms exploit vulnerabilities in operating systems or software to propagate, often without any direct user interaction.

- **Infection Methods**: Worms spread through network vulnerabilities, email attachments, or infected websites.
- **Dangerous Effects**: Network congestion, system crashes, widespread infections.

## 3. Trojans (Trojan Horses)

A Trojan horse is malware disguised as legitimate software. It often tricks users into installing it by appearing as harmless programs or files. Once executed, it can perform a variety of malicious activities, including stealing sensitive data, creating backdoors, or installing other malware.

- **Infection Methods**: Trojans are typically delivered via email attachments, social engineering, or infected software downloads.
- **Dangerous Effects**: Data theft, unauthorized access to systems, backdoor installations, espionage.

## 4. Ransomware

Ransomware is a particularly destructive type of malware that encrypts the victim's files or locks them out of their system, then demands payment (usually in cryptocurrency) in exchange for the decryption key. Ransomware attacks have grown significantly in recent years, targeting organizations of all sizes and even critical infrastructure.

- **Infection Methods**: Phishing emails, malicious attachments, compromised websites, or software vulnerabilities.
- **Dangerous Effects**: Data encryption, financial loss, reputational damage, operational disruption.

## 5. Adware

Adware is software designed to display unwanted advertisements on a user's device. While adware is not typically designed to be harmful, it can be invasive and lead to a poor user experience. Some adware programs can also track user activity, contributing to privacy issues.

- **Infection Methods**: Typically bundled with free software, downloaded from untrusted websites.
- **Dangerous Effects**: Slow system performance, privacy concerns, excessive pop-up ads.

## 6. Spyware

Spyware is a type of malware designed to secretly monitor and collect information from a user's device without their consent. It can capture keystrokes, record browsing habits, and steal sensitive data like passwords and financial information.

- **Infection Methods**: Downloaded via compromised websites, malicious ads, or bundled with legitimate software.
- **Dangerous Effects**: Privacy violations, identity theft, data theft.

## 7. Keyloggers

A keylogger is a specific type of spyware that records every keystroke a user makes on their device. This can include passwords, credit card numbers, emails, and other sensitive data. Keyloggers are commonly used for credential theft.

- **Infection Methods**: Often delivered via Trojans, phishing campaigns, or malicious websites.
- **Dangerous Effects**: Credential theft, identity theft, financial fraud.

## 8. Rootkits

A rootkit is a set of tools used by attackers to gain and maintain privileged access to a system without detection. Rootkits often hide their presence by modifying system files and processes, making it difficult for traditional antivirus software to detect them.

- **Infection Methods**: Rootkits can be installed via Trojans, vulnerabilities, or physical access to a device.
- **Dangerous Effects**: Escalation of privileges, stealthy system manipulation, persistence of malware.

## 9. Botnets

A botnet is a network of infected computers, or "bots," that are controlled remotely by an attacker. These networks are often used for Distributed Denial of Service (DDoS) attacks, data theft, or to send out large-scale spam emails. The user of an infected machine is usually unaware that their device is part of a botnet.

- **Infection Methods**: Malware infections, phishing emails, exploit kits.
- **Dangerous Effects**: DDoS attacks, data theft, distributed spam campaigns.

## 10. Fileless Malware

Fileless malware is a type of malicious software that doesn't write its code to disk but instead operates directly in the memory of a system. It is more difficult to detect because it doesn't rely on traditional files or executables.

- **Infection Methods**: Fileless malware often uses malicious scripts, exploits software vulnerabilities, or takes advantage of legitimate system tools (such as PowerShell) to execute its payload.
- **Dangerous Effects**: Stealthy attacks, long-term persistence, bypasses antivirus detection.

## 7.1.2 How Malware Works

Malware typically operates in a series of steps, from initial infection to spreading across networks and executing malicious payloads. Here's a basic breakdown of how most malware works:

1. **Delivery**: Malware is delivered through various vectors such as phishing emails, infected websites, compromised software downloads, or physical media like USB drives. Once the malware has been introduced to the system, it typically exploits vulnerabilities to gain a foothold.

2. **Installation**: Once on a system, malware may install itself in memory, modify existing system files, or create new files that allow it to persist. Some types of malware, such as rootkits, work silently to maintain privileged access without the user's knowledge.

3. **Execution**: After installation, the malware begins executing its payload, which could involve stealing data, encrypting files, or launching a DDoS attack. Malware may also

make attempts to connect to remote servers to receive commands, install additional malware, or exfiltrate data.

4. **Propagation**: Many types of malware, such as worms, are self-replicating, meaning they can spread automatically across a network without requiring user interaction. They exploit vulnerabilities in operating systems or software to propagate from one machine to another.

5. **Payload Activation**: In some cases, the full malicious impact of malware is not triggered immediately. Instead, the attacker may wait until certain conditions are met (e.g., a specific date, user behavior, or external command) before activating the payload.

### 7.1.3 Threats Posed by Malware

The threat posed by malware is multifaceted, with the potential to cause significant harm in various ways:

- **Data Theft**: Malware is often used to steal sensitive data, including personal information, financial records, intellectual property, and credentials.
- **Financial Loss**: Ransomware can lead to direct financial loss by demanding payment for decryption keys. In other cases, malware may facilitate fraud, leading to unauthorized transactions or stealing funds.
- **System Damage**: Malware can corrupt files, damage hardware, or disrupt system operations, leading to downtime and lost productivity. In severe cases, it may cause permanent system damage.
- **Reputational Damage**: A successful malware attack, especially one involving data breaches or customer data exposure, can lead to significant reputational harm for organizations. This can erode customer trust and result in a loss of business.
- **Regulatory Penalties**: Organizations that fail to prevent or respond to malware attacks, especially those involving personal data breaches, can face legal consequences, including fines and penalties under regulations like GDPR, HIPAA, or CCPA.

Malware remains one of the most prevalent and damaging threats in the cybersecurity landscape. With many different types of malware, each designed for specific purposes, organizations need to understand the unique characteristics and behaviors of these threats to effectively defend against them. By staying informed about the latest malware trends and investing in the right defense mechanisms, organizations can reduce the risk of infection and minimize the impact of successful attacks.

# 7.2 Methods of Reverse Engineering Malicious Code.

Reverse engineering is the process of analyzing and deconstructing a piece of software to understand its functionality, behavior, and underlying structure. In the context of cybersecurity, reverse engineering is often employed to examine malicious code (malware) to understand how it operates, identify vulnerabilities it exploits, and develop countermeasures to detect, mitigate, or neutralize its effects.

Reverse engineering malicious code is a critical skill in cyber forensics, as it allows analysts to dissect the workings of malware, uncover hidden payloads, and understand how the code compromises a system. By reverse engineering malware, cybersecurity professionals can gain insights into attack methods, improve detection mechanisms, and protect against future threats.

In this section, we will explore various techniques used for reverse engineering malicious code, the tools employed in the process, and the challenges analysts face when attempting to reverse-engineer sophisticated malware.

## 7.2.1 The Reverse Engineering Process

Reverse engineering malicious code involves a series of methodical steps to unpack the malware, understand its behavior, and gather intelligence that can help neutralize the threat. These steps can vary depending on the complexity of the malware, but they generally follow the same core process:

### 1. Initial Analysis and Acquisition of Sample

The first step in reverse engineering malware is obtaining a sample. This could come from a variety of sources, such as infected systems, honeypots, malware-sharing platforms, or network traffic analysis. Analysts often acquire the malware in its raw form—whether executable binaries, scripts, or file containers (e.g., .exe, .dll, .pdf).

### 2. Static Analysis

Static analysis involves studying the malware without actually executing it. This step is crucial as it allows analysts to gain insights into the code without triggering malicious behavior. Static analysis focuses on examining the structure of the file, extracting metadata, and identifying key components of the code.

Common static analysis techniques include:

- **Disassembly**: Converting machine code into assembly language, which provides a human-readable representation of the program's instructions.
- **Hexdump Analysis**: Inspecting the raw bytes of the malware to detect patterns, strings, and embedded resources.
- **String Analysis**: Extracting readable strings within the binary code, such as file paths, registry keys, IP addresses, and domain names, which may provide clues about the malware's functions and targets.

## 3. Dynamic Analysis

Dynamic analysis involves running the malware in a controlled environment to observe its behavior in real-time. This process typically occurs within a sandbox, an isolated virtual environment that mimics a real operating system but prevents the malware from spreading or causing damage to the actual system.

Analysts can observe how the malware interacts with the system, including file system changes, network activity, registry modifications, and processes initiated by the malware.

**Key steps in dynamic analysis include:**

- **Behavioral Monitoring**: Analyzing how the malware behaves when executed, such as the creation of files, the establishment of network connections, and system modifications.
- **Network Traffic Analysis**: Capturing and analyzing network traffic to identify any communication with remote servers (command and control servers), data exfiltration, or malicious payloads.
- **Debugger Usage**: Using debuggers (such as OllyDbg, x64dbg, or Immunity Debugger) to step through the malware's execution line by line to understand how it operates.

## 4. Code Modification and Emulation

After understanding the basic functionality of the malware, analysts may attempt to modify or emulate parts of the code to test their hypotheses about the malware's behavior. This can include deactivating certain parts of the code, such as payload delivery or self-replication, to see how the malware responds under different conditions.

Emulation involves running the malware on a software emulator that mimics the behavior of the target operating system, hardware, or network environment.

## 5. Documentation and Reporting

Once the malware's functions and behavior are understood, analysts document the findings in a report, detailing how the malware works, its objectives, and any indicators of compromise (IoC) that can be used for detection and mitigation.

This report may include:

- A description of the malware's functions and goals.
- Indicators such as file names, registry keys, IP addresses, domain names, and other identifying features.
- Recommendations for defensive measures and removal techniques.

## 7.2.2 Key Techniques and Approaches in Reverse Engineering

Several techniques are commonly used in reverse engineering malware. These approaches help analysts break down the structure and functionality of the malicious code to uncover hidden components and counteract its effects.

## 1. Code Obfuscation and Anti-Reverse Engineering Techniques

Malware authors often use techniques to hide their code's true purpose and make it difficult to reverse-engineer. This includes:

- **Code Obfuscation**: The use of complex and confusing programming techniques that make the code harder to read and analyze. Obfuscation can involve renaming functions and variables with meaningless names, using control flow obfuscation (such as encrypted instructions), and hiding or encrypting critical code.
- **Packing**: Malware may be packed, meaning that the executable code is compressed or encrypted, requiring unpacking before analysis. Unpacking tools are used to decompress or decrypt the malware code so it can be analyzed in its original form.
- **Anti-Debugging**: Malware may include checks for debugging tools or virtual machines, preventing the analysis environment from operating correctly. Techniques such as checking for specific debugger processes or using time delays can help malware evade detection.

## 2. Polymorphism and Metamorphism

Polymorphic malware changes its code each time it is executed, making detection based on signature matching more difficult. It may encrypt or mutate its own code, producing different versions with the same core functionality.

Metamorphic malware goes a step further, completely rewriting its code on each execution to avoid detection by traditional signature-based tools. This creates a challenge for reverse engineers, as they must reverse the core functionality without relying on previously identified signatures.

### 3. Rootkit Detection

Rootkits are often embedded deeply into a system to hide their presence and the actions they perform. Reverse engineers use techniques like kernel-mode analysis and memory dumps to uncover rootkits hiding in system processes, files, or even hardware-level components. Rootkit detection is particularly difficult due to their ability to alter system structures.

### 4. Heuristics and Pattern Recognition

Heuristic analysis involves detecting malware based on its behavior rather than its signature. This method involves identifying suspicious patterns or techniques commonly used in malware, such as attempts to overwrite system files, establish hidden network connections, or disable security software.

Reverse engineers use static heuristic methods, such as recognizing specific instructions or algorithms in the code, and dynamic heuristics, such as observing malicious actions during runtime.

### 7.2.3 Tools for Reverse Engineering Malware

Several tools are commonly used by cybersecurity experts when reverse engineering malicious code. These tools allow analysts to examine the malware's inner workings, observe its interactions with the system, and extract important information.

- **Disassemblers**: Programs like IDA Pro and Ghidra allow analysts to disassemble compiled code into human-readable assembly language. This helps analysts understand the basic structure and logic of the malware.
- **Debuggers**: Debugging tools like OllyDbg, x64dbg, and Immunity Debugger allow analysts to step through the execution of malware, observing its behavior and

identifying key actions, such as calls to malicious functions or changes in system state.

- **Sandboxes**: Tools like Cuckoo Sandbox or Any.Run provide a controlled environment where malware can be executed safely and its behavior analyzed without posing a risk to the host system.
- **Hex Editors**: Programs like HxD or 010 Editor allow analysts to examine the raw bytes of a file, helping to identify patterns, strings, or hidden sections of code that may reveal the nature of the malware.

### 7.2.4 Challenges in Reverse Engineering Malware

Reverse engineering malware is a complex and time-consuming process that requires a high level of expertise. Some of the key challenges that reverse engineers face include:

- **Complex and Sophisticated Malware**: Modern malware often incorporates advanced techniques such as encryption, obfuscation, polymorphism, and anti-reverse engineering measures, making it much harder to analyze.
- **Large Volume of Malware**: The volume of new malware strains being developed and deployed on a daily basis can overwhelm analysts. Keeping up with the sheer number of threats and new techniques requires continuous training and resource allocation.
- **Legal and Ethical Issues:** In some cases, reverse engineering may involve legal or ethical concerns, especially when dealing with intellectual property, proprietary software, or malware with unknown origins.

Reverse engineering malicious code is a critical skill for cybersecurity professionals tasked with understanding, mitigating, and preventing malware attacks. By dissecting the code and behavior of malware, analysts can identify its objectives, discover vulnerabilities it exploits, and create defenses to protect against similar threats in the future. While the process of reverse engineering malware is challenging, it is essential for improving detection techniques, analyzing sophisticated threats, and enhancing the overall cybersecurity posture of organizations.

# 7.3 Behavioral Analysis of Malware in Controlled Environments.

Behavioral analysis is a crucial technique in the field of cyber forensics, especially when dealing with malware. Unlike static analysis, which focuses on the structure and code of the malware, behavioral analysis involves studying the dynamic actions that the malware takes once executed in a controlled environment. The goal is to observe how malware interacts with the system, what changes it makes, and the specific effects it has on the operating system, network, and connected devices. This analysis helps cybersecurity professionals identify indicators of compromise (IoCs), uncover hidden capabilities, and gain insights into the attack's objectives.

In this section, we will explore the key concepts of behavioral analysis, the tools and techniques used to perform it in controlled environments, and the challenges involved in analyzing malware in such settings.

### 7.3.1 The Concept of Behavioral Analysis

Behavioral analysis involves examining the actions of a malware sample after it has been executed in an isolated environment. The key objective of this type of analysis is to identify malicious activities that occur in the system, as well as any attempts to hide or obfuscate the malware's presence.

Malware behavior can vary widely depending on the type of attack, but common actions observed during behavioral analysis include:

- **File System Modifications**: Malware may create, modify, or delete files, alter file attributes, or move files to specific locations. Understanding these behaviors helps analysts identify files that are part of the attack.
- **Registry Changes**: Many types of malware make modifications to the Windows registry, often adding new keys or altering existing ones to maintain persistence, disable security features, or configure other attack-related settings.
- **Network Communication**: Malware often communicates with external servers (Command and Control, or C&C servers) for further instructions or to exfiltrate data. By monitoring network traffic, analysts can identify IP addresses, domain names, and communication protocols used by the malware.
- **Process Creation**: Malware may create new processes, run in the background, or disguise itself by mimicking legitimate system processes. Behavioral analysis helps detect unusual or unexpected processes that may indicate malicious activity.
- **Keylogging and Data Exfiltration**: Some malware engages in activities such as logging keystrokes, stealing credentials, or scraping sensitive data. Behavioral analysis identifies these actions and helps trace the flow of stolen data.
- **Persistence Mechanisms**: Malware often tries to survive reboot cycles or reinfection attempts by establishing persistence mechanisms, such as altering startup programs, installing new services, or modifying system configurations.

### 7.3.2 Controlled Environments for Malware Analysis

To safely conduct behavioral analysis, malware must be run in an environment where it cannot cause harm to real systems or networks. A controlled environment is typically used for this purpose. These environments isolate the malware and prevent it from interacting with critical infrastructure, allowing analysts to observe its behavior without risk.

Key components of a controlled analysis environment include:

### 1. Sandboxing

A sandbox is a virtualized or isolated environment where malware can be safely executed and monitored. It is designed to simulate a real operating system and software environment, but it is contained so that the malware cannot affect external systems. Common sandbox solutions include Cuckoo Sandbox, Any.Run, and FireEye's Malware Analysis platform. These environments allow analysts to observe and interact with malware while protecting the underlying host system.

- **Advantages**: Sandboxes provide a safe, isolated environment for testing malware. They enable dynamic analysis without the risk of infecting production systems.
- **Limitations**: Some advanced malware may detect the sandbox environment and modify its behavior to avoid detection. In these cases, advanced techniques are required to bypass sandbox evasion strategies.

### 2. Virtual Machines (VMs)

Virtual machines are another popular method for analyzing malware. VMs allow analysts to create an isolated environment by emulating an entire computer system, complete with its own operating system and hardware resources. VMs can be easily snapshot, reverted, or reset after analysis, reducing the risk of permanent damage or contamination.

- **Advantages**: Virtual machines allow analysts to create multiple isolated environments for testing different malware samples and provide a flexible environment for experimentation. Snapshots and rollbacks enable easy restoration of the VM after malware execution.
- **Limitations**: Similar to sandboxes, some malware is capable of detecting VM environments and may adjust its behavior to avoid detection.

### 3. Dedicated Forensic Workstations

In addition to virtualized environments, some cybersecurity professionals use dedicated forensic workstations for malware analysis. These are physical systems set up with isolation techniques, such as disconnected network interfaces and secure operating systems, to prevent malware from escaping the test environment.

- **Advantages**: Dedicated workstations may provide greater control over the testing environment compared to virtualized solutions, with hardware-level isolation preventing malware from bypassing protections.
- **Limitations**: Maintaining and setting up dedicated systems for malware analysis is resource-intensive, and it may not be as flexible or scalable as virtualized solutions.

### 7.3.3 Tools and Techniques for Behavioral Analysis

A variety of tools and techniques are employed to facilitate behavioral analysis in controlled environments. These tools are designed to monitor and record the activities of malware, providing insight into its actions and intentions.

### 1. Monitoring Tools

- **Process Monitors**: Tools like Process Monitor (ProcMon) from Sysinternals allow analysts to observe real-time changes in file systems, registry, and processes. It logs detailed information about file reads, writes, and registry changes.
- **File System Monitors**: These tools help track files created or modified by malware. OSSEC, Antivirus software, and Sysmon are some common tools used to track changes to files during an analysis.
- **Registry Monitors**: RegShot and Process Monitor can capture registry key modifications made by malware, such as the creation of new keys or changes to existing values.

### 2. Network Monitoring Tools

- **Wireshark**: This network protocol analyzer allows analysts to capture and examine network traffic between the malware and external servers. It helps detect communication patterns, data exfiltration, and C&C server interaction.
- **NetFlow Analyzers**: Tools like ntopng and SolarWinds help monitor traffic flow, identifying abnormal or suspicious communications initiated by malware.

### 3. System Performance Monitoring

Resource Monitors: Tools like Task Manager, Process Explorer, and Resource Monitor provide insight into system resource consumption, such as CPU, memory, disk I/O, and network usage. Malware often consumes excessive resources or initiates unusual system behavior that can be detected using these tools.

## 4. Malware Analysis Platforms

- **Cuckoo Sandbox**: This open-source automated malware analysis system provides detailed reports about the behavior of malware, including file system and registry modifications, network activity, and executed processes. It can also generate static analysis reports to supplement the behavioral findings.
- **Any.Run**: Another interactive malware sandbox that allows analysts to observe malware behavior in real-time, including network traffic, system modifications, and file manipulations.

### 7.3.4 Challenges in Behavioral Analysis

Behavioral analysis, while powerful, presents several challenges, particularly as malware evolves and becomes more sophisticated.

## 1. Evasion Techniques

Many malware samples are designed to detect the environment in which they are running and modify their behavior to avoid detection. They may attempt to detect virtual machines or sandbox environments by checking for specific artifacts (e.g., VM-related processes or file names). If such evasion is detected, the malware might change its behavior to avoid revealing its true nature during analysis.

## 2. Anti-Analysis Features

Some malware is equipped with anti-analysis features that make it difficult to study its behavior. These can include:

- **Delay Mechanisms**: Malware may delay execution or activate only after a certain period, making it difficult to observe its actions in real time.
- **Self-Destruction**: Certain malware is designed to delete itself after execution or in the presence of analysis tools, making it difficult to capture and study.

## 3. Complex Multi-Stage Attacks

Modern malware often involves multi-stage attacks, where one piece of malware downloads or activates another after the initial infection. Behavioral analysis may need to be extended over multiple stages, which can complicate the analysis process and increase the time required to understand the attack fully.

**4. Large Data Volumes**

Malware analysis in controlled environments generates vast amounts of data, including logs, network traffic captures, and system changes. Sifting through this data and identifying relevant actions can be time-consuming and challenging, especially for analysts who need to identify critical IoCs quickly.

Behavioral analysis of malware in controlled environments is a powerful technique for understanding how malicious code operates and identifying its key indicators. By studying malware's dynamic actions, cybersecurity professionals can develop better detection tools, response strategies, and mitigation techniques. While challenges such as evasion tactics and the complexity of multi-stage attacks exist, behavioral analysis remains a vital part of the malware analysis process, helping to protect systems and networks from evolving cyber threats.

# 7.4 Real-World Malware Investigations and Lessons Learned.

Malware investigations play a crucial role in the broader context of cybersecurity. By analyzing real-world cases of malware attacks, security professionals gain valuable insights that help them develop better detection methods, enhance defensive strategies, and understand evolving cyber threats. The lessons learned from these investigations not only improve current defenses but also provide a roadmap for handling future incidents. In this section, we will explore some significant real-world malware investigations, the lessons learned from these cases, and how forensic cybersecurity practices can evolve as a result.

### 7.4.1 Notable Malware Cases and Investigations

### 1. The WannaCry Ransomware Attack (2017)

One of the most infamous malware attacks in recent history, the WannaCry ransomware attack exploited a vulnerability in Windows SMB (Server Message Block) protocol. The vulnerability, known as EternalBlue, was originally discovered by the U.S. National

Security Agency (NSA) and later leaked by a hacking group called Shadow Brokers. WannaCry spread rapidly across organizations worldwide, encrypting critical files and demanding ransom payments in Bitcoin.

**Investigation:**

The WannaCry attack initially spread quickly, infecting hundreds of thousands of systems across the globe. Researchers at Kaspersky Lab and Symantec played key roles in tracking the malware's spread and identifying its origin. The malware's behavior was traced to the SMB vulnerability, and within days, security experts were able to reverse-engineer the code and identify the ransomware's cryptographic methods.

Interestingly, a kill switch was discovered—an unregistered domain that, when activated, would stop the ransomware from propagating. The attack highlighted the vulnerabilities in outdated systems and the importance of patching critical software

**Lessons Learned:**

- **The Importance of Patching**: The WannaCry attack underscored the critical need for regular updates and patch management. Systems that were not patched with Microsoft's security updates were the primary targets of the attack.
- **Rapid Response Mechanisms**: The discovery of the kill switch demonstrated the importance of collaboration between security researchers and forensic experts in real-time to mitigate the spread of malware.
- **Awareness and Training**: The attack reinforced the need for organizations to continually train their employees on safe cyber hygiene practices, such as not clicking on suspicious links and maintaining up-to-date systems.

**2. NotPetya (2017)**

NotPetya was a destructive malware attack that primarily targeted organizations in Ukraine but spread globally, causing widespread disruption. Unlike traditional ransomware, which encrypts files and demands payment, NotPetya was a wiper malware designed to cause damage rather than make a profit. Initially appearing to be a variant of the Petya ransomware, NotPetya used similar techniques to spread, but its ultimate goal was to destroy data, not encrypt it for ransom.

**Investigation:**

- The attack's origins were traced to a compromised update in a Ukrainian tax software, MeDoc, which allowed the malware to spread through corporate networks. NotPetya leveraged a variety of tools, including EternalBlue, to propagate across systems. The attack caused billions of dollars in damage, affecting major organizations like Maersk, Merck, and FedEx.
- Cybersecurity experts from companies like CrowdStrike and Cisco analyzed the malware and identified its key features, including its fast-moving nature and ability to use multiple attack vectors to propagate.

**Lessons Learned:**

- **Importance of Supply Chain Security**: NotPetya demonstrated the vulnerability of software supply chains. The attack exploited a trusted update mechanism, emphasizing the need for security measures to ensure the integrity of third-party software.
- **Backup and Recovery Plans**: Unlike traditional ransomware, NotPetya's goal was data destruction. This highlighted the importance of regular, secure backups and tested recovery strategies.
- **Visibility and Network Segmentation**: The spread of the malware within organizations showed the need for improved network monitoring and segmentation. Isolating critical systems from less secure parts of the network can slow down the spread of such attacks.

### 3. The SolarWinds Supply Chain Attack (2020)

The SolarWinds attack was one of the most sophisticated and damaging cyberattacks in recent years, targeting U.S. government agencies, private companies, and critical infrastructure. The attack, which was attributed to a nation-state actor (likely Russia), involved the insertion of malicious code into the software updates of the popular IT management software SolarWinds Orion. This backdoor allowed attackers to gain unauthorized access to thousands of organizations and maintain stealthy surveillance over a long period.

### Investigation:

The attack was discovered when FireEye—a cybersecurity firm—noticed that it had been breached through a compromised SolarWinds update. Investigators found that the malware, dubbed SUNBURST, had been embedded in SolarWinds updates for months before being detected. The attackers had exploited the trusted software update process to compromise high-profile targets without being detected. The sophistication of the attack led many experts to believe that it was carried out by a nation-state actor.

**Lessons Learned:**

- **Supply Chain Risk Management**: The SolarWinds attack highlighted the vulnerabilities in supply chain security, particularly with software updates. Organizations need to ensure that all third-party software updates are rigorously tested and monitored for any signs of compromise.
- **Advanced Threat Detection**: SolarWinds demonstrated the need for advanced threat detection techniques, including behavioral analysis, network traffic monitoring, and anomaly detection. Attackers remained hidden within the network for months, making traditional signature-based detection ineffective.
- **Collaboration and Information Sharing**: The SolarWinds incident underscored the importance of collaboration between private cybersecurity firms, government agencies, and industry groups. Rapid information sharing enabled organizations to detect and mitigate the attack faster.

### 7.4.2 Lessons from Real-World Malware Investigations

While every malware attack presents unique challenges, several key lessons can be applied universally to improve future investigations and response efforts. Here are some of the overarching lessons from these and other high-profile incidents:

### 1. The Need for Proactive Cyber Defense

In all three cases, it became clear that waiting for a breach to occur before reacting is no longer a viable option. A proactive cybersecurity posture—focused on early detection, rapid response, and threat hunting—can significantly reduce the impact of a cyberattack. This includes continuous monitoring of networks, regular security assessments, and ensuring that all software is up to date.

### 2. The Importance of Incident Response Planning

Both WannaCry and NotPetya highlighted the necessity of having a robust incident response (IR) plan in place. Forensics investigators play a crucial role in containing, mitigating, and analyzing cyber incidents. By practicing response protocols and maintaining well-documented recovery strategies, organizations can minimize the downtime and damage caused by attacks.

## 3. Understanding the Evolving Nature of Cyber Threats

Cyberattacks are becoming increasingly sophisticated, with malware constantly evolving in its capabilities and methods of propagation. The SolarWinds attack, in particular, demonstrated how advanced persistent threats (APTs) can infiltrate organizations through subtle means and remain undetected for extended periods. As a result, cybersecurity experts must be prepared for new, evolving threats that may not follow traditional attack patterns.

## 4. Collaboration Across the Cybersecurity Ecosystem

The WannaCry, NotPetya, and SolarWinds incidents demonstrated the power of collaboration between various stakeholders in the cybersecurity ecosystem. From government agencies and private security firms to software vendors and researchers, information sharing and collective efforts are essential for tackling complex malware threats. Collaboration helps improve detection tools, share insights, and provide quicker responses to emerging threats.

## 5. Continuous Improvement of Forensic Capabilities

Forensic cybersecurity professionals must continuously refine their investigative techniques to keep pace with the sophistication of modern malware. This includes staying current with the latest tools and methodologies for malware analysis, reverse engineering, network forensics, and digital evidence handling. Furthermore, forensic experts need to adapt their practices to new challenges, such as cloud environments, IoT devices, and mobile platforms.

Real-world malware investigations offer invaluable insights into the tactics, techniques, and procedures used by cybercriminals. By learning from high-profile attacks like WannaCry, NotPetya, and SolarWinds, organizations can strengthen their defenses, improve response protocols, and better prepare for future threats. The lessons learned emphasize the need for proactive defense strategies, rapid incident response, and continuous collaboration within the cybersecurity community to stay ahead of evolving malware and cyber threats. Forensic cybersecurity practices will continue to play a central role in uncovering the full scope of attacks, protecting valuable data, and preserving the integrity of digital systems.

# 8. Cloud Forensics Challenges and Strategies

As more organizations move to cloud environments, the need for effective cloud forensics has become increasingly important. This chapter explores the unique challenges cloud forensics presents, including issues of data jurisdiction, multi-tenant environments, and the dynamic nature of cloud storage. It delves into strategies for collecting and analyzing cloud-based evidence, such as leveraging cloud service provider logs, API calls, and virtual machine snapshots. By examining best practices and forensic tools tailored for cloud environments, readers will gain the knowledge to tackle cloud-specific investigative hurdles and ensure robust evidence preservation in the cloud.

## 8.1 Unique Challenges in Cloud-Based Evidence Collection.

As businesses and individuals increasingly rely on cloud services for data storage, computing, and communication, the role of cloud computing in forensic investigations has become more prominent. Cloud environments, which offer scalability, flexibility, and cost-effectiveness, have transformed the way data is stored and accessed. However, these same characteristics introduce a range of challenges when it comes to collecting and preserving evidence in a forensic context. Unlike traditional on-premise systems, where investigators can physically seize and analyze data, cloud-based evidence collection involves navigating a more complex and dynamic environment, where data may not be stored in a single location and could be subject to frequent changes, multiple jurisdictions, and diverse service providers.

This section explores the unique challenges associated with collecting forensic evidence from cloud environments and the strategies that forensic investigators need to adopt to overcome these obstacles. From legal and technical difficulties to issues related to data volatility and vendor cooperation, these challenges require careful consideration to ensure that the evidence remains admissible and reliable in court.

### 8.1.1 Volatility and Transience of Cloud Data

One of the most significant challenges in cloud-based evidence collection is the volatility and transience of data stored in the cloud. In traditional environments, investigators can often rely on snapshots or physical copies of data. However, in cloud environments, data is frequently dynamic, constantly changing, and distributed across multiple servers and data centers.

- **Ephemeral Nature of Cloud Resources**: Cloud providers often use virtualized resources (such as virtual machines, containers, or serverless computing) that can be spun up or down on demand. This makes it challenging to capture a consistent, complete snapshot of data at a specific point in time. For example, if evidence needs to be collected from a virtual machine that is deallocated or terminated during the investigation, the data may no longer be available, unless proper logging and data retention policies are in place.
- **Auto-Scaling and Data Movement**: Cloud systems are designed to automatically scale and distribute workloads across multiple locations to optimize performance and reduce costs. This can result in data being moved from one server to another, potentially leaving investigators with incomplete or fragmented evidence. Without precise tracking of where the data is being stored and processed, collecting forensic evidence can become an unpredictable task.
- **Solution**: To mitigate these challenges, forensic investigators must work with cloud providers to understand the cloud architecture and data storage policies. Many cloud providers offer audit logs and data access history tools that allow investigators to trace where data is located and when it was accessed. Furthermore, cloud service agreements should clearly specify how long data will be retained and how to preserve evidence in compliance with legal standards.

### 8.1.2 Jurisdictional and Legal Issues

Cloud services often store data in multiple locations across different jurisdictions, which can complicate legal procedures and the collection of evidence. Different countries have varying data privacy laws, data retention requirements, and standards for evidence admissibility, which can impact the ability to collect, preserve, and use cloud-based evidence.

- **Cross-Border Data**: Cloud service providers often distribute data across multiple countries and regions, which may subject it to varying legal frameworks. For instance, data stored in the European Union (EU) may be subject to the General Data Protection Regulation (GDPR), while data stored in the U.S. may be governed by the Stored Communications Act (SCA) and other U.S. laws. The issue becomes even more complicated when countries with conflicting privacy laws are involved.
- **Cloud Provider Cooperation**: Cloud service providers may have different policies and levels of cooperation with law enforcement, depending on the country in which they are based. In some instances, obtaining the necessary data may require legal orders or subpoenas from foreign governments, which can introduce delays and complications in evidence collection.

- **Solution**: Forensic investigators must work closely with legal experts to understand the relevant laws and regulations governing data access and evidence collection in cloud environments. Investigators should also ensure they obtain the correct legal orders or warrants that are specific to the cloud provider's location and the relevant jurisdiction. When possible, a mutual legal assistance treaty (MLAT) may be used to facilitate cross-border cooperation and data access.

### 8.1.3 Data Integrity and Chain of Custody

Maintaining the integrity of cloud-based evidence and establishing an unbroken chain of custody is another critical challenge. In traditional forensics, investigators can physically seize hard drives or servers, which can then be analyzed in a controlled environment. However, in cloud environments, the evidence is often stored remotely, and investigators may not have direct physical control over the data.

- **Data Alteration Risks**: Since cloud providers manage and maintain the infrastructure, there is an inherent risk that data could be altered, moved, or even deleted without the knowledge of the investigator. Cloud providers may also perform routine maintenance, backups, or deletions that can impact the evidence before investigators have a chance to collect it.
- **Remote Evidence Collection**: Collecting digital evidence remotely increases the risk of unauthorized access, tampering, or accidental deletion. Without proper measures in place, the evidence may be compromised during collection or transmission.
- **Solution**: To preserve the integrity of cloud-based evidence, forensic investigators need to work with cloud service providers to create evidence collection agreements that ensure proper access and retention of data during the investigation. Implementing hashing techniques and timestamping during the collection process can help confirm the integrity of the evidence. Additionally, establishing strict protocols for documenting every action taken during the collection process is essential for maintaining the chain of custody.

### 8.1.4 Multi-Tenancy and Data Segregation

Cloud service providers typically use a multi-tenant model, meaning that multiple customers share the same physical resources. This introduces challenges when it comes to ensuring that evidence from a specific tenant can be isolated and extracted without interference from other customers' data.

- **Data Isolation**: Since cloud providers store data for many different customers on the same physical hardware, it is crucial to ensure that evidence from one customer's data does not get mixed up with data from another tenant. This can be a particular challenge when collecting logs or data that span across multiple services, as the forensic investigator must be certain that they are retrieving the correct, relevant data from a specific tenant's environment.
- **Access Control**: Cloud environments rely heavily on access control mechanisms to restrict who can view or modify data. Without proper access credentials, investigators may not be able to retrieve the data necessary for the investigation, particularly if it's encrypted or otherwise protected.
- **Solution**: Ensuring proper data segmentation and access control is critical when conducting forensic investigations in cloud environments. Forensic investigators must collaborate closely with cloud providers to ensure that the correct data is being collected, and that no other tenants' data is inadvertently accessed. Additionally, cloud access logs should be carefully reviewed to confirm that only authorized personnel are interacting with the data.

### 8.1.5 Lack of Standardized Forensic Procedures for the Cloud

Unlike traditional computing environments, cloud-based forensic practices are still evolving, and there is no universal, standardized process for collecting and analyzing evidence across all cloud platforms. Different cloud service models (IaaS, PaaS, SaaS) and providers (Amazon Web Services, Microsoft Azure, Google Cloud) may have different tools, interfaces, and methods for managing data, which complicates forensic procedures.

- **Fragmentation**: The variety of cloud providers and the range of services they offer can make it difficult to implement a consistent forensic methodology. Investigators must familiarize themselves with the specific tools and techniques required for each cloud environment.
- **Lack of Best Practices**: As cloud computing continues to evolve, many cloud service providers have not yet developed comprehensive forensic capabilities or documented procedures for handling incidents or assisting with investigations.
- **Solution**: It is essential for forensic investigators to stay updated with the evolving landscape of cloud computing and forensic best practices. As the industry matures, standardized guidelines and frameworks for cloud forensics are likely to emerge, but in the meantime, investigators must tailor their approach based on the specific cloud provider and service model being used.

Cloud computing offers a host of benefits, but it also introduces unique challenges when it comes to collecting and preserving forensic evidence. Volatility, jurisdictional complexities, data integrity concerns, and multi-tenancy issues require careful attention from both forensic investigators and cloud service providers. By understanding these challenges and implementing the right strategies, investigators can effectively collect, preserve, and analyze cloud-based evidence while ensuring compliance with legal and regulatory requirements. As cloud technology continues to evolve, forensic practices must also adapt to address new challenges and safeguard the integrity of digital investigations.

# 8.2 Tools and Techniques for Cloud Data Acquisition.

The rise of cloud computing has reshaped how data is stored, accessed, and managed. This transformation presents unique challenges for forensic investigators tasked with acquiring and analyzing digital evidence in cloud environments. Unlike traditional on-premise systems, cloud data is decentralized, often distributed across multiple geographic regions, and subject to frequent changes. Despite these complexities, forensic investigators have developed specialized tools and techniques for cloud data acquisition that enable the collection of evidence in a manner that ensures its integrity, reliability, and legal admissibility.

This section explores the tools and techniques commonly used in cloud-based forensic investigations, highlighting how they can be effectively employed to collect evidence while addressing the distinct challenges of the cloud environment.

### 8.2.1 Tools for Cloud Data Acquisition

The tools available for cloud data acquisition range from specialized software and hardware to cloud provider-specific solutions. These tools are designed to help investigators access, capture, and preserve evidence from cloud storage systems, applications, and logs. The most common tools for cloud data acquisition can be categorized into several types:

### 1. Cloud Service Provider Tools

Many cloud service providers (CSPs) offer native tools and interfaces that assist forensic investigators in accessing and acquiring data from their platforms. These tools are tailored to the specific cloud environment and often include robust logging and auditing features.

**Amazon Web Services (AWS) CloudTrail**: AWS CloudTrail is a service that provides detailed logs of API calls made within the AWS environment. Forensic investigators can use these logs to trace access to cloud resources, monitor user activity, and identify potential security breaches. CloudTrail is useful for gathering evidence related to unauthorized access, changes to data, and account activities.

**Microsoft Azure Security Center**: Azure provides several tools that assist investigators in capturing data from cloud-based systems. The Azure Security Center monitors cloud activity and generates alerts based on suspicious behavior, while Azure Monitor collects logs and metrics for analysis. These tools enable investigators to track user actions, detect anomalies, and ensure that evidence collection aligns with compliance and security policies.

**Google Cloud Platform (GCP) Stackdriver**: GCP's Stackdriver provides logging, monitoring, and diagnostics tools for cloud infrastructure. Stackdriver enables forensic investigators to access logs related to authentication, system access, and network activities, providing insights into any suspicious or unauthorized actions within the GCP environment.

These native tools from CSPs allow forensic investigators to collect data directly from cloud environments while ensuring that evidence is maintained in compliance with the provider's standards.

## 2. Third-Party Forensic Tools

Several third-party tools are available to assist forensic investigators in acquiring cloud-based data, even when the cloud service provider does not offer native tools or if additional functionality is required. These tools are designed to work across multiple cloud environments, providing a more unified solution for cloud forensics.

**FTK Imager**: AccessData's FTK Imager is a widely used tool for creating forensic images of cloud data. FTK Imager can acquire cloud-based data such as images, documents, and metadata, allowing investigators to create bit-by-bit copies of cloud storage for analysis. The tool supports a variety of file formats and can perform hash verification to ensure the integrity of the acquired data.

**EnCase**: EnCase is a comprehensive forensic tool that supports data acquisition from cloud environments. It enables investigators to collect and analyze cloud-based data, including email, documents, and logs. EnCase's built-in hashing and metadata features ensure that evidence remains untampered and admissible in court.

**X1 Social Discovery**: For forensic investigators focused on cloud-based social media and communication evidence, X1 Social Discovery provides specialized capabilities for acquiring and analyzing data from popular platforms like Facebook, Twitter, and LinkedIn. The tool enables investigators to collect social media posts, messages, and metadata while maintaining chain-of-custody integrity.

### 3. Cloud Storage Forensics Tools

Specific tools are designed to acquire and analyze data from cloud storage services like Dropbox, Google Drive, OneDrive, and iCloud. These tools are crucial when the cloud-based data being investigated is not hosted on a large enterprise platform but instead resides within individual cloud storage services used for personal or small-scale business storage.

**Cloud Forensics (Cloud Extractor):** Cloud Extractor is a tool that helps investigators acquire data from popular cloud storage services. It supports platforms like Dropbox, Google Drive, and OneDrive, allowing for the extraction of files, documents, and metadata from user accounts. The tool facilitates the retrieval of data directly from the cloud storage environment, ensuring proper forensic procedures during the acquisition process.

**ElcomSoft Cloud Explorer**: ElcomSoft Cloud Explorer is designed for extracting and analyzing data from cloud storage services like Google Drive, OneDrive, and iCloud. The tool can recover and analyze files, photos, documents, and other data, along with logs and timestamps, providing investigators with the necessary evidence for legal purposes.

### 8.2.2 Techniques for Cloud Data Acquisition

While having the right tools is essential, forensic investigators must also understand the techniques and strategies for acquiring cloud data effectively while maintaining data integrity. Here are the key techniques for cloud data acquisition:

### 1. Cloud Data Imaging

In traditional digital forensics, disk imaging (creating a bit-by-bit copy of a hard drive or storage device) is a standard method of preserving data. In cloud forensics, data imaging can be more challenging due to the distributed nature of cloud environments and the ephemeral nature of cloud resources.

**Cloud Imaging:** When dealing with cloud-based data, investigators must use specialized tools to create a copy of the cloud storage data, logs, or applications they need to analyze. Cloud imaging involves capturing data from cloud storage buckets or virtual machines, preserving the data's integrity and allowing investigators to analyze it offline.

**Data Integrity Verification**: Just as with physical data acquisition, forensic investigators must use hashing techniques to verify the integrity of the cloud data acquired. Hashing algorithms like MD5, SHA-1, or SHA-256 can generate a unique fingerprint of the cloud data, ensuring that no data has been altered during acquisition. The hash values can also be used for later comparison to verify that the evidence remains unchanged.

## 2. Data Acquisition from Cloud Backups

Cloud service providers often implement backup systems to ensure data recovery in case of system failure or disaster. These backups can also be a rich source of forensic evidence. Investigators need to consider accessing cloud backup systems to acquire historical versions of files, logs, or communications that may be crucial to an investigation.

**Versioned Data**: Cloud platforms like AWS, Azure, and GCP offer versioned storage, where earlier versions of data can be retrieved even after modifications or deletions. Forensic investigators can use this feature to recover previous versions of files or track the history of data changes.

**Backup Snapshots**: Many cloud platforms allow users to create snapshot copies of their cloud environments, including file systems, databases, and virtual machines. These snapshots contain a frozen image of the system at a specific time and can be used to preserve evidence without disrupting ongoing operations.

## 3. Acquisition of Cloud Application Data

In addition to storage data, many organizations rely on cloud-based applications such as email, project management tools, and CRM systems to manage their business operations. These applications store vast amounts of data that may be critical in an investigation.

**API Access**: Many cloud-based applications provide APIs (Application Programming Interfaces) that allow forensic investigators to extract data programmatically. By using these APIs, investigators can retrieve data such as email messages, chat logs, transaction records, and other relevant information without directly accessing the cloud provider's infrastructure.

**Log Analysis**: In many cases, cloud applications maintain detailed logs of user interactions and activities, which can be crucial in an investigation. Tools like Splunk, LogRhythm, and Elastic Stack can be used to analyze logs from cloud applications, identifying potential evidence of unauthorized access or malicious activity.

### 4. Legal Compliance and Chain of Custody

To ensure that cloud data can be used in legal proceedings, investigators must maintain a strict chain of custody and comply with the legal requirements of the jurisdiction in which the investigation is taking place.

**Preserving Evidence**: Investigators must ensure that all data collected from the cloud is properly documented, including timestamps, access logs, and any relevant metadata. This documentation helps preserve the chain of custody and demonstrates that the evidence has not been altered or tampered with.

**Collaboration with Cloud Providers**: For legal reasons, investigators often need to collaborate with the cloud provider to ensure that evidence is handled in compliance with the law. Cloud providers may require subpoenas or legal orders before releasing certain types of data. Investigators must follow the proper legal procedures to obtain access to cloud-based evidence.

Cloud-based data acquisition presents unique challenges, but modern forensic tools and techniques have evolved to meet these challenges. By leveraging native cloud provider tools, third-party forensic solutions, and techniques such as cloud data imaging, backup acquisition, and API access, investigators can collect crucial evidence from cloud environments while ensuring data integrity and legal compliance. As cloud computing continues to grow in popularity, cloud forensics will remain a key area of focus for cybersecurity professionals and law enforcement, requiring continued innovation in tools and techniques for effective evidence collection.

# 8.3 Jurisdictional and Legal Issues in Cross-Border Investigations.

As the world becomes increasingly interconnected through cloud computing and digital technologies, cross-border investigations in forensic cybersecurity have become more complex. The globalization of data storage and processing across multiple countries, combined with differing legal frameworks, creates significant challenges when investigators need to access, collect, or analyze digital evidence that spans across jurisdictions. These challenges often involve navigating varying data privacy laws, differing legal standards for evidence, and complex international agreements that govern the collection of digital evidence. This section explores the jurisdictional and legal issues investigators face in cross-border cloud forensics and offers guidance on how to address these issues effectively.

### 8.3.1 Jurisdictional Challenges in Cloud Forensics

The primary jurisdictional challenge in cloud forensics stems from the fact that cloud data is often stored in multiple, geographically dispersed data centers. A single file or application may be distributed across several countries or regions, subjecting the data to different local laws and regulatory frameworks.

### 1. Multi-Tenant Cloud Environments

Cloud environments are typically designed to be multi-tenant, where multiple customers' data can be stored on the same physical infrastructure. This is particularly problematic for investigators who may need to access data from one user or tenant in a cloud provider's system, but the data resides alongside other customers' data. Investigators must ensure they only access relevant data while preserving the privacy and security of other users' information. This requires a deep understanding of the cloud provider's architecture, access controls, and data segregation mechanisms.

### 2. Data Location and Global Distribution

Cloud providers often use content delivery networks (CDNs) and global infrastructure that dynamically distributes data across several data centers to ensure faster access and higher availability. This results in data fragmentation, where portions of data may be stored in different countries. For example, an email sent in one country might be stored temporarily on servers in a different country, with parts of it residing in multiple jurisdictions. When investigators need to access this data, it becomes unclear which country's laws apply and whether the data can be obtained without violating the privacy rights of individuals in other jurisdictions.

**Solution**: To address these challenges, forensic investigators need to have a clear understanding of the cloud architecture used by service providers. When conducting cross-border investigations, investigators must also work with legal professionals to determine the appropriate jurisdiction for data access, making sure to respect international agreements and avoid conflicts with local laws.

### 8.3.2 Legal Frameworks for Cross-Border Data Access

The lack of global consistency in digital evidence collection laws creates complications when collecting evidence stored in foreign countries. National and international legal frameworks often conflict with each other, especially when it comes to accessing data stored in cloud environments across borders.

### 1. Data Privacy Laws

Data privacy laws vary widely between jurisdictions and often place restrictions on how and when data can be accessed by foreign governments or investigators. For example, in the European Union, the General Data Protection Regulation (GDPR) imposes strict rules on data access, storage, and movement. GDPR requires that data concerning EU citizens be processed and stored within the EU, limiting cross-border data flows unless specific conditions are met. This creates barriers for U.S.-based investigators who may need to access data stored in the EU.

**GDPR**: GDPR imposes restrictions on transferring personal data outside the EU unless certain conditions are met, such as ensuring that the recipient country provides an adequate level of protection. If investigators wish to acquire data stored in the EU, they may need to follow a set of procedural requirements, including obtaining consent or ensuring data protection standards are met.

**U.S. Law**: In the U.S., the Stored Communications Act (SCA) and the Cloud Act govern the ability of U.S. authorities to request data stored overseas by cloud providers. Under the Cloud Act, U.S. law enforcement can compel providers to hand over data stored on servers located outside of the U.S., even if those servers are in countries with strict privacy laws. This has led to diplomatic tensions, as foreign governments may view the Cloud Act as an overreach of U.S. jurisdiction.

### 2. The Role of Mutual Legal Assistance Treaties (MLATs)

The Mutual Legal Assistance Treaty (MLAT) is a key legal instrument used to facilitate the cross-border exchange of criminal evidence. MLATs are agreements between two or more countries that enable them to request and provide assistance in criminal investigations, including digital forensics. However, MLATs often come with delays, especially when dealing with complex international cases. For example, in high-stakes investigations, the process of obtaining evidence through MLATs may take months, by which time crucial digital evidence may have been lost or overwritten.

**Solution**: Forensic investigators must work closely with legal experts to navigate the process of obtaining data through MLATs or other international cooperation mechanisms. In some cases, leveraging direct cooperation with cloud service providers may be a faster option if they have local teams or operations in the region of the investigation.

### 3. The Cloud Act and Its Implications

The Clarifying Lawful Overseas Use of Data (Cloud Act), enacted in 2018, attempts to simplify cross-border access to digital evidence by allowing U.S. law enforcement to compel U.S.-based cloud providers to provide access to data stored abroad. The act, however, has been controversial, as it allows U.S. authorities to bypass foreign legal processes for data access, raising concerns about sovereignty and international privacy standards.

The Cloud Act has caused friction between the U.S. and other countries, especially those that have stringent data protection laws, such as the EU, which has challenged the extraterritorial reach of the Act. In response, some countries have negotiated agreements with the U.S. to establish procedures for lawful data sharing, but these agreements are not always comprehensive or universally accepted.

**Solution**: Investigators need to be aware of the legal implications of the Cloud Act, including its limitations and potential conflicts with local laws. They should also understand how the Cloud Act can be used to expedite evidence collection from U.S.-based cloud providers, particularly when foreign jurisdictional issues arise.

### 8.3.3 Investigative Strategies for Cross-Border Forensics

Given the jurisdictional and legal hurdles in cross-border investigations, forensic investigators must adopt a strategic approach to ensure they comply with local laws while still gathering the necessary evidence for their investigation.

### 1. Collaboration with Local Authorities

Collaboration with local law enforcement agencies and legal authorities in the country where the data is stored is often critical. In many cases, investigators will need to involve local authorities in the process of data acquisition, especially when accessing encrypted data or proprietary cloud storage systems. Building strong relationships with local authorities can help investigators navigate the complex legal landscape and gain access to data more efficiently.

## 2. Cloud Service Provider Cooperation

Forensic investigators should work closely with cloud service providers, who often have global data centers and are well-versed in handling international investigations. Most cloud providers have designated teams that deal with law enforcement and government requests, and they are typically more familiar with the legal requirements in various jurisdictions. By cooperating with the cloud provider's legal team, investigators can ensure that evidence collection complies with the relevant laws and is handled in a way that maintains data integrity.

## 3. Data Minimization and Preservation

In cross-border investigations, data minimization is a critical principle. Investigators should only collect data that is necessary for the investigation and ensure that it is preserved in a way that meets both legal and forensic standards. Data preservation techniques, such as hashing and encryption, should be employed to maintain the integrity of the evidence.

Jurisdictional and legal issues in cross-border cloud forensics are significant challenges for forensic investigators. Navigating these challenges requires an understanding of the complexities surrounding data privacy laws, international agreements like MLATs, and the varying legal frameworks that govern digital evidence. By collaborating with local authorities, cloud providers, and legal experts, forensic investigators can overcome these obstacles and ensure that they collect and preserve evidence in a manner that is both legally compliant and admissible in court. As the global landscape of digital forensics evolves, the need for international cooperation and the development of clearer legal frameworks will be crucial in overcoming jurisdictional hurdles in cloud investigations.

# 8.4 Security Implications of Cloud Storage Providers.

As businesses and individuals increasingly migrate to cloud-based solutions for data storage, the security of cloud services has become one of the most significant concerns in the realm of forensic cybersecurity. Cloud storage providers offer various advantages, such as scalability, cost-effectiveness, and accessibility, but these benefits also introduce unique security risks and challenges that can impact the integrity of digital evidence. Investigators must understand these security implications to effectively collect, analyze, and preserve digital evidence while ensuring the protection of sensitive data in cloud environments. This section explores the key security risks associated with cloud storage providers and the measures that can be taken to mitigate these risks during forensic investigations.

### 8.4.1 Shared Responsibility Model in Cloud Security

One of the most important concepts in cloud security is the shared responsibility model. Cloud storage providers typically divide security responsibilities between themselves and their customers. While the cloud provider is responsible for the security of the infrastructure, including physical security, network security, and availability of the service, the customer (typically the organization using the service) is responsible for securing data, applications, and user access within the cloud environment.

This model creates security challenges for forensic investigators, as they must account for the division of responsibilities between the provider and the customer. It is crucial for investigators to understand which aspects of security fall under the provider's purview and which ones are the responsibility of the customer when dealing with evidence from cloud storage.

**For example:**

**Cloud Provider's Responsibilities**: The cloud provider is responsible for securing the underlying infrastructure—such as the physical servers, data centers, network infrastructure, and overall availability of the cloud service. Providers implement basic security controls, such as encryption, firewalls, and intrusion detection systems, to protect their infrastructure.

**Customer's Responsibilities**: The customer is responsible for securing their data, configuring access controls, encrypting sensitive information, and monitoring user behavior. This includes configuring cloud storage and services securely, applying proper authentication protocols, and ensuring compliance with security policies.

For forensic investigators, understanding this shared responsibility model is essential because any security failure—whether due to misconfigured cloud storage settings, inadequate encryption, or weak access controls—could compromise the integrity of digital evidence.

### 8.4.2 Data Breaches and Insider Threats

Data breaches are one of the most significant security risks associated with cloud storage. Cloud providers house massive amounts of data across their global networks, making them lucrative targets for cybercriminals. Attackers who gain unauthorized access to cloud storage environments can steal or alter sensitive data, including personal information, financial records, and intellectual property. Additionally, the multi-tenant nature of cloud storage means that data from different customers resides on the same physical servers, increasing the risk of a cross-tenant breach.

**External Attacks**: Attackers may exploit vulnerabilities in cloud infrastructure or cloud-based applications to gain unauthorized access to data. This could involve exploiting weak security controls, misconfigurations, or unpatched software vulnerabilities. Once an attacker gains access to a cloud environment, they may be able to exfiltrate large amounts of data or manipulate evidence.

**Insider Threats**: Insider threats—either through malicious intent or negligent behavior—are another major concern in cloud security. Employees, contractors, or anyone with privileged access to cloud resources can potentially misuse their access to steal or compromise data. Misconfigurations in access control settings or improper handling of credentials can also lead to unintentional exposure of sensitive information.

For forensic investigators, the risk of data breaches complicates the process of evidence collection. When conducting an investigation involving cloud storage, investigators must determine whether the evidence has been compromised by a breach, and if so, assess the extent of the breach and its impact on the integrity of the evidence.

**Solution**: Investigators should verify the integrity of the evidence by cross-referencing it with other records, such as access logs, to identify potential data tampering or unauthorized access. It is also important to ensure that proper forensic methods, such as imaging and hashing, are applied to preserve the authenticity of the evidence.

### 8.4.3 Data Encryption Risks and Challenges

Cloud storage providers typically offer data encryption both in transit and at rest to protect data from unauthorized access. However, encryption itself can introduce both advantages and challenges from a forensic perspective.

**Encryption at Rest and in Transit**: When data is stored in the cloud, it is often encrypted to prevent unauthorized access in case of a breach. Similarly, encryption is applied to data being transmitted between users and cloud servers to ensure that it remains secure during transfer. While encryption adds a layer of security, it can also complicate forensic investigations if investigators do not have access to the decryption keys.

**End-to-End Encryption**: Some cloud services implement end-to-end encryption, where only the customer holds the encryption keys. While this approach enhances the confidentiality of the data, it also creates a challenge for investigators if they require access to encrypted data for analysis. Without the decryption keys or the cooperation of the cloud customer, it may be impossible to access the data.

**Key Management**: The management of encryption keys is crucial. If the encryption keys are lost, misplaced, or improperly managed, it can prevent forensic investigators from accessing encrypted evidence. Furthermore, forensic investigators must ensure that cloud providers use strong encryption algorithms and that the encryption keys are stored securely.

**Solution**: Forensic investigators need to coordinate with cloud service providers to understand the encryption methods used and ensure that they can gain access to the necessary decryption keys. Collaboration with the customer (data owner) is often required to obtain decryption keys, especially in end-to-end encrypted environments. Legal instruments, such as warrants, may be needed to compel data decryption in certain cases.

### 8.4.4 Vendor Lock-In and Data Portability

Cloud customers face the risk of vendor lock-in, which can affect their ability to transfer data between providers or retrieve evidence in a usable form. When data is stored in proprietary formats or tied to a particular cloud service, it can be difficult to migrate it to another provider or to retrieve it for forensic analysis.

**Proprietary Formats**: Many cloud providers use proprietary formats for storing data or have specific APIs that are required for accessing the data. If investigators need to access data that is stored in a proprietary format, they may be limited to using the provider's tools, which may not be available or effective for forensic analysis.

**Data Portability Issues**: When data is stored across multiple cloud providers or in multi-cloud environments, moving data between providers or obtaining it for investigation can become a logistical challenge. Investigators may need to work with the cloud provider to retrieve evidence, but this process can be slow and may result in delays.

**Solution**: To address these challenges, investigators should ensure that the cloud service provider's tools are compatible with forensic standards and can support the collection of evidence in universally accepted formats. Additionally, when investigating cloud-based evidence, it is important to identify data portability issues and ensure that evidence is preserved in a format that can be analyzed independently of the cloud service.

### 8.4.5 Cloud Security Best Practices for Forensic Investigations

Despite the challenges cloud storage security presents, there are several best practices that can help mitigate these risks and facilitate effective forensic investigations:

**Access Control**: Implement strict access control mechanisms, including role-based access controls (RBAC), multi-factor authentication (MFA), and encryption keys management to limit unauthorized access to cloud resources.

**Monitoring and Logging**: Enable continuous monitoring and maintain comprehensive logs of all user and system activity within the cloud environment. Forensic investigators can use these logs to trace activity, identify suspicious actions, and validate the integrity of evidence.

**Data Segregation**: Ensure that data is properly segregated between tenants in the cloud environment to reduce the risk of unauthorized access to other users' data.

**Regular Security Audits**: Conduct regular security audits and vulnerability assessments to identify potential weaknesses in the cloud storage infrastructure and to ensure that security policies are up-to-date.

**Collaboration with Cloud Providers**: Maintain a strong relationship with cloud service providers to ensure they understand forensic requirements and can assist with data retrieval and preservation when necessary.

The security implications of cloud storage providers are significant and can have a major impact on forensic investigations. From issues like data breaches and insider threats to encryption and data portability challenges, investigators must navigate a complex landscape to ensure the integrity of digital evidence. By understanding the shared responsibility model, leveraging best practices for cloud security, and collaborating closely with cloud providers, forensic investigators can overcome these security challenges and collect evidence that is both accurate and legally admissible.

# 9. Mobile Device Forensics

With the proliferation of smartphones and tablets, mobile device forensics has become a critical component of modern cyber investigations. This chapter focuses on the unique challenges and techniques involved in extracting and analyzing data from mobile devices. It covers the methods for acquiring data from different mobile platforms (iOS, Android, etc.), including bypassing encryption and dealing with locked devices. The chapter also explores the analysis of mobile applications, location data, and messaging systems, as well as the growing role of IoT and wearables in mobile forensics. By mastering these methods, readers will be equipped to recover crucial evidence from mobile devices in the context of cybercrime investigations.

## 9.1 Data Acquisition Techniques for Mobile Devices.

Mobile devices, such as smartphones and tablets, have become integral parts of modern life, storing a wealth of personal, professional, and sensitive data. From text messages and emails to location history and app data, mobile devices are a treasure trove of digital evidence. For forensic investigators, acquiring this data is a critical part of the investigation process. However, due to the complexity of mobile device operating systems, encryption, and storage mechanisms, acquiring data from these devices presents unique challenges. This section outlines the key techniques for acquiring data from mobile devices, emphasizing the importance of following proper forensic protocols to ensure the integrity and admissibility of evidence.

### 9.1.1 Understanding Mobile Device Storage and Security

Before diving into data acquisition techniques, it is essential to understand how data is stored on mobile devices and the security mechanisms employed to protect it. Mobile devices typically use flash storage, which is non-volatile and retains data even when the device is powered off. Additionally, modern mobile operating systems (such as iOS and Android) employ a range of security features, including encryption, lock screens, password protection, and secure boot mechanisms to protect user data.

**iOS Devices**: Apple's iOS uses hardware encryption and a secure enclave for key management. Each device has a unique key that is required to decrypt data. In addition, iOS employs a variety of safeguards, such as App Sandbox (isolating apps from each other) and file system encryption that protects the device's data.

**Android Devices**: Android devices use a combination of file-based encryption and hardware-backed security mechanisms. Depending on the device manufacturer, the version of Android, and the security settings, Android can offer varying levels of encryption protection.

Understanding these security features is crucial for forensic investigators, as they must adapt their data acquisition strategies accordingly.

### 9.1.2 Logical Acquisition

Logical acquisition involves extracting data from a mobile device without bypassing its security mechanisms. It is the most straightforward and non-invasive method for data acquisition, typically performed when the device is unlocked, or when investigators have the necessary credentials (such as PINs or passwords) to access the device.

### 1. Using Built-In Tools and Software

Many mobile operating systems provide built-in tools for logical data extraction. For example, Apple's iTunes and Apple Configurator can be used for logical acquisitions from iOS devices. These tools allow investigators to back up the device's data, including contacts, messages, app data, and media files.

Android devices often allow investigators to extract data using tools like Android Debug Bridge (ADB) or specific device management software, which provides access to the device's file system and applications.

### 2. Data Types Retrieved via Logical Acquisition

Logical acquisition can retrieve data such as:

- Text messages (SMS) and multimedia messages (MMS)
- Emails and contacts
- Call logs
- App data, including settings, logs, and files from third-party apps
- Media files (photos, videos, etc.)
- Documents (PDFs, Word files, etc.)
- Location data, if available (e.g., GPS logs or location history)

This method is relatively quick, but it does not provide access to encrypted data that may reside within the device's secure enclave or encrypted storage.

### 9.1.3 Physical Acquisition

Physical acquisition allows forensic investigators to create a complete bit-by-bit copy of a mobile device's storage. This technique is more invasive than logical acquisition but can yield a more comprehensive data set, especially when dealing with encrypted devices or locked screens. Physical acquisition can extract data from areas of the device's storage that are inaccessible through logical acquisition, including deleted files and system files that are not typically visible to the user.

### 1. Using Specialized Forensic Tools

Physical acquisition is typically performed using specialized forensic tools that are designed to bypass security mechanisms and access raw data from the device's storage. Some commonly used tools include:

- **Cellebrite UFED**: One of the most widely used tools for mobile device data extraction, UFED is capable of performing physical, logical, and file system extractions on a variety of mobile devices.
- **XRY by MSAB**: Another leading tool that provides physical and logical acquisition capabilities for Android and iOS devices, including the ability to recover deleted data.
- **Oxygen Forensics**: This tool allows for physical, logical, and cloud data extraction, providing detailed reports on mobile device activity.

### 2. Accessing Encrypted Data

When using physical acquisition, investigators may be able to access encrypted data or data protected by a password or PIN, assuming they have the necessary credentials or the device has been jailbroken or rooted. In cases where investigators cannot bypass encryption or passwords, they may still be able to retrieve residual or partially encrypted data from the device's storage.

Physical acquisition often requires a higher level of expertise, as well as specialized hardware, such as dongles or write-blockers, which ensure that the device's storage is not altered during the acquisition process. Forensic tools like Cellebrite and XRY are equipped with these capabilities to ensure that the integrity of the evidence is maintained.

### 3. Forensic Imaging

Once the physical data extraction is completed, a forensic image (or bit-for-bit copy) of the device is created. This image can be analyzed in a controlled environment to retrieve data, recover deleted files, or perform other forensic processes. Creating a forensic image ensures that investigators can work with an exact replica of the device, minimizing the risk of tampering or data loss during the investigation.

### 9.1.4 File System Extraction

File system extraction is a hybrid technique between logical and physical acquisition. This method allows forensic investigators to access a mobile device's file system directly, extracting files in a readable format. It enables investigators to analyze the structure of the data, locate hidden or deleted files, and uncover evidence that might not be accessible using a logical acquisition.

Tools that facilitate file system extraction include Cellebrite UFED, XRY, and Oxygen Forensics, which support both logical and file system extraction from a wide range of devices, including those running encrypted operating systems like iOS and Android.

### 1. Accessing File System and Deleted Data

**File system extraction can uncover:**

- Deleted files, as many files are not completely wiped from the device's storage but are marked as deleted. Specialized forensic software can often recover these files.
- System files, including logs and application data that may not be part of a logical backup.
- App-specific data, which might include location information, browser history, and media files created or accessed by applications.

By accessing the file system directly, forensic investigators gain deeper insight into the device's activity, uncovering hidden or residual data that could be critical to the investigation.

### 9.1.5 Overcoming Mobile Device Security Protections

Mobile devices are equipped with numerous security mechanisms, including password protection, biometric authentication (such as fingerprint or facial recognition), and full disk encryption. Forensic investigators must be prepared to deal with these protections during data acquisition.

## 1. Unlocking Devices

If a device is locked, investigators may need to use various methods to unlock it, including:

- Brute-force methods (for example, attempting every combination of PINs or passwords)
- Bypassing lock screens using forensic tools that can unlock the device (often used in conjunction with vulnerabilities or exploits)
- Using jailbreaking or rooting techniques (for Android or iOS devices) to bypass security features, though this can risk compromising the integrity of the device or evidence.

## 2. Legal and Ethical Considerations

It is critical to ensure that any attempt to bypass mobile device security protections is done in a legally compliant manner. Investigators must obtain the necessary legal authority, such as a search warrant, before attempting to unlock a device. Additionally, care must be taken to maintain the chain of custody and preserve the integrity of the evidence throughout the acquisition process.

Mobile device data acquisition is a critical skill for forensic investigators, given the volume and importance of the data stored on these devices. By using the appropriate techniques—whether logical acquisition, physical acquisition, or file system extraction—investigators can ensure that they gather comprehensive, legally admissible evidence. Understanding the unique challenges posed by encryption, security features, and the variety of devices in use is essential for any mobile forensic investigation. With the right tools and techniques, investigators can overcome these obstacles, ensuring the integrity of their evidence and the success of their investigations.

# 9.2 Extracting and Analyzing Application Data.

In the realm of forensic cybersecurity, mobile devices are not just carriers of basic data like messages and call logs; they are also repositories of complex and potentially incriminating application data. From social media apps to messaging platforms, fitness trackers, and financial apps, mobile devices store vast amounts of personal, sensitive, and sometimes criminal data within the apps that users interact with daily. Forensic investigators must have the tools and techniques to extract and analyze this data effectively, as it can play a pivotal role in criminal investigations, corporate disputes, or other legal matters. This section explores the various techniques for extracting and analyzing application data from mobile devices.

### 9.2.1 Understanding the Role of Application Data

Mobile applications store a variety of data that can provide key insights into user activity, interactions, and personal habits. App data generally falls into the following categories:

- **User-generated content**: Messages, photos, videos, and files uploaded or created by the user within the app.
- **User activity logs**: History of interactions, such as browsing logs, searches, likes, and check-ins.
- **Authentication data**: Login credentials, session tokens, and security information like two-factor authentication (2FA) keys.
- **Configuration settings**: Preferences set by the user within the app, which could include privacy settings, device configurations, and account preferences.
- **Metadata**: Information related to the user's activity, such as timestamps, geolocation data, and device information.

Due to the highly sensitive nature of application data, extracting it requires careful consideration of technical challenges and legal ramifications. Improper extraction or analysis may lead to tampered evidence, which can significantly impact an investigation.

### 9.2.2 Techniques for Extracting Application Data

### 1. Logical Acquisition of App Data

Logical acquisition is the simplest form of data extraction and involves obtaining the app data that is readily accessible through the device's operating system. This can be done using various software tools, including built-in services and forensic toolkits.

**iOS Devices**: On iOS devices, logical extraction can be done using tools like iTunes or Apple Configurator, which allow investigators to back up the device data, including app data, to a computer. The backup file, often in the form of an .ipsw or .mobilebackup file, can then be parsed using forensic tools to retrieve app-specific data.

**Android Devices**: For Android devices, logical data extraction can be performed using Android Debug Bridge (ADB) or commercial forensic tools like Cellebrite UFED or Oxygen Forensics. These tools allow investigators to access app data and back it up in a readable format. Many apps store data in SQLite databases, which can be extracted using tools that can read and export this data.

## 2. Physical Acquisition for App Data

Physical acquisition involves extracting a complete, bit-by-bit copy of the device's storage. This allows investigators to obtain not only the visible app data but also deleted or hidden data that is still present on the device.

**Device Imaging**: Tools such as Cellebrite UFED, XRY, and Oxygen Forensics can perform physical data extractions, capturing the entire file system of the mobile device. This includes app data stored in system directories, temporary files, and cache storage that may not be accessible through logical acquisition.

**Data Recovery**: In cases where app data has been deleted or overwritten, physical acquisition increases the likelihood of recovering residual app data using forensic recovery techniques. Many forensic tools can locate unallocated space and deleted partitions to uncover traces of app data that were previously erased by the user.

## 3. File System Extraction

File system extraction is a hybrid method between logical and physical acquisitions. In this method, the forensic tool accesses the mobile device's file system to retrieve the app's data files directly. Many mobile apps store their data in SQLite databases, XML files, JSON files, and other data structures. File system extraction tools are often able to uncover these data files and provide investigators with access to app-specific data that would not be visible in a simple logical extraction.

**SQLite Databases**: Many mobile apps store their data in SQLite databases, which are small, lightweight databases that can store structured data. SQLite files are often found in the /data/data/ directory on Android devices or in /var/mobile/Containers/Data/Application/ on iOS. These files can contain vital information such as chat logs, user preferences, and metadata associated with app usage.

**Data Carving**: Forensic investigators use specialized software for data carving to locate fragmented pieces of deleted data from app databases. This process involves searching for residual data and reassembling it into usable formats.

## 9.2.3 Analysis of Application Data

Once application data has been extracted from a mobile device, the next critical step is to analyze it to determine its relevance to the investigation. Analyzing app data is often challenging because of the sheer volume of data, the diversity of formats in which it is stored, and the need to understand the app's internal structure.

## 1. Parsing App Data

Forensic tools often include specific modules for parsing and interpreting app data. These modules are designed to handle various file formats used by mobile apps, such as SQLite databases, JSON, XML, and plain text files.

**SQLite Database Analysis**: Tools like DB Browser for SQLite or Forensic Explorer can parse SQLite databases to retrieve stored information, such as chat logs, user preferences, and location history. These tools allow investigators to view and export specific tables and fields, making it easier to extract the relevant data.

**JSON and XML Parsing**: Many mobile apps use JSON or XML to store data. Forensic investigators can use parsers designed to read these formats, extracting useful information such as messages, user activity logs, and app-generated files.

## 2. Data Decryption and Accessing Encrypted App Data

Modern mobile apps often use encryption to protect sensitive data, such as messages, photos, or documents. Some apps, such as WhatsApp and Telegram, use end-to-end encryption, which ensures that only the sender and receiver can decrypt messages. Forensic investigators must account for encryption when accessing app data and may need specialized tools or cooperation from the app provider to gain access to encrypted information.

**Decryption Tools**: Tools like ElcomSoft iOS Forensic Toolkit and Cellebrite UFED can sometimes decrypt encrypted app data if investigators have the proper credentials, such as PINs, passwords, or decryption keys. However, if the data is encrypted using advanced algorithms or end-to-end encryption, decryption might not be possible without the appropriate key or authentication.

## 3. Timeline Reconstruction

One of the most valuable insights investigators can derive from app data is the ability to reconstruct timelines of user activity. Apps store detailed metadata—such as timestamps and geolocation information—that can be used to track a user's movements, interactions, and behavior.

**For example:**

- **Social Media Apps**: Investigators can analyze metadata from platforms like Facebook, Instagram, or Twitter to identify when certain posts were made, who was tagged, and where the post was uploaded. This information can help build a timeline of events related to the case.
- **Messaging Apps**: Forensic analysis of apps like WhatsApp, Signal, or Messenger can uncover the exact times messages were sent and received, as well as location data attached to media files.

### 4. Geolocation Analysis

Many mobile apps, particularly those related to social media and messaging, store geolocation data that can be analyzed to track a user's location history. By examining GPS coordinates and location metadata, investigators can determine where the device was at specific times and potentially link app activity to physical events.

Geolocation analysis can also provide insights into patterns of movement, such as:

- A suspect's travel routes
- Visits to specific locations (e.g., crime scenes)
- Connections with other individuals or devices at certain locations

### 9.2.4 Legal and Ethical Considerations in Extracting and Analyzing App Data

When extracting and analyzing application data, forensic investigators must be mindful of the legal and ethical issues that can arise. Improper handling of app data could result in violations of privacy, chain of custody issues, or challenges to the admissibility of evidence in court.

**Consent and Authorization**: Investigators should ensure they have the proper legal authorization (e.g., search warrants or consent forms) to access app data. Many apps require users to agree to terms of service, and accessing data without consent could violate privacy rights.

**Chain of Custody:** As with all digital evidence, forensic investigators must maintain a strict chain of custody when handling app data. This involves documenting the collection, transfer, and analysis processes to ensure that the evidence is not tampered with or altered.

Extracting and analyzing application data from mobile devices is a critical aspect of modern forensic investigations. With mobile apps storing vast amounts of sensitive data, investigators must employ a combination of logical, physical, and file system acquisition methods to gather app data effectively. Analyzing this data requires specialized tools to parse various file formats, decrypt encrypted information, and reconstruct timelines of user activity. Given the complexity of mobile app data, forensic experts must stay updated on new tools and techniques to ensure they can handle the evolving challenges in mobile device forensics. By following proper legal and ethical guidelines, forensic investigators can ensure that the evidence extracted from mobile apps is reliable, accurate, and admissible in court.

# 9.3 Overcoming Encryption and Lock Mechanisms.

Mobile devices, by their nature, contain highly sensitive personal data, making encryption and lock mechanisms essential for safeguarding user privacy and security. However, these security measures also present significant challenges for forensic investigators attempting to retrieve and analyze digital evidence from mobile devices. This section explores the complexities surrounding encryption and lock mechanisms on mobile devices, as well as the techniques and tools that forensic professionals use to overcome these obstacles.

### 9.3.1 The Importance of Encryption on Mobile Devices

Encryption is a process that transforms data into an unreadable format to protect it from unauthorized access. With mobile devices storing a wide range of sensitive information, such as text messages, emails, banking details, photos, videos, and location history, encryption plays a critical role in safeguarding privacy. Common forms of encryption on mobile devices include:

**Full Disk Encryption (FDE):** This encryption method encrypts the entire storage of a mobile device, including app data, system files, and user data. FDE is commonly used by Android and iOS devices to protect data when the device is powered off or locked.

**File-Level Encryption**: Instead of encrypting the entire disk, some apps encrypt their specific files. For example, messaging apps like WhatsApp, Signal, and Telegram often encrypt messages and multimedia files sent by users.

**End-to-End Encryption (E2EE)**: This encryption ensures that only the sender and recipient of a message can read its contents. E2EE is commonly used in messaging apps, making it much harder for forensic investigators to access the data unless they can acquire the necessary decryption keys.

Encryption is a crucial tool for protecting user data from theft and unauthorized access. However, for forensic investigators, this encrypted data presents significant challenges during criminal investigations, as access to it often requires overcoming multiple security barriers.

### 9.3.2 Types of Lock Mechanisms on Mobile Devices

In addition to encryption, mobile devices are often secured by various lock mechanisms that prevent unauthorized users from accessing the device. These include:

**PINs and Passwords**: Users often secure their devices with numeric PIN codes, alphanumeric passwords, or pattern locks. While these mechanisms provide a basic level of protection, investigators may attempt to bypass them during an investigation.

**Biometric Locks**: More modern devices utilize biometric security features such as fingerprint scanners, facial recognition, or iris scanners to unlock the device. These methods provide a higher level of security and are often more difficult to bypass, although forensic tools and techniques have been developed to assist in extracting data from these devices.

**Device-Specific Locks**: Certain manufacturers, such as Apple and Samsung, use device-specific security mechanisms to lock the device, such as Apple's Face ID and Samsung's Knox. These locks can be more resistant to bypass methods, requiring specialized knowledge and tools to overcome.

While these security features are designed to protect the user's data, they present obstacles for forensic investigators who need access to the device's contents to retrieve critical evidence. By understanding how these mechanisms work, forensic experts can identify the appropriate techniques for overcoming them.

### 9.3.3 Techniques for Overcoming Encryption and Lock Mechanisms

Overcoming encryption and lock mechanisms requires a combination of legal permissions, technical expertise, and specialized forensic tools. While no technique is universally applicable to all devices or situations, investigators can use several methods to attempt to access encrypted data and bypass lock mechanisms.

## 1. Brute Force Attacks

Brute force is one of the most common methods for bypassing PINs, passwords, and pattern locks. In this technique, forensic tools systematically try every possible combination of characters or numbers until the correct one is found.

**Password Cracking Tools**: Tools like ElcomSoft iOS Forensic Toolkit and Cellebrite UFED can perform brute-force attacks on encrypted mobile devices. These tools use powerful algorithms to attempt every combination within a defined set of criteria, such as the length and character type (numeric, alphabetic, or alphanumeric).

**Limitations**: Brute force attacks can be time-consuming and computationally intensive. Additionally, modern mobile devices often include mechanisms such as rate-limiting or wipe functions after a certain number of incorrect attempts, making brute force more challenging.

## 2. Chip-Off Forensics

Chip-off forensics involves physically removing the memory chip from the mobile device and directly accessing its data. This technique can bypass the need for PINs, passwords, and other lock mechanisms. By removing the flash memory from the device's motherboard and connecting it to a forensic workstation, investigators can perform a bit-by-bit copy of the storage.

**Data Extraction**: After extracting the chip, forensic investigators use specialized equipment to read the chip's data, which may include encrypted files, app data, and other system files. The data can then be analyzed using forensic tools to recover information, even if the device is locked or encrypted.

**Limitations**: Chip-off forensics is an invasive procedure that requires advanced technical knowledge and tools, and there is a risk of damaging the device's hardware during the extraction. Furthermore, it is often more time-consuming and expensive than other methods.

## 3. JTAG and UART Forensics

JTAG (Joint Test Action Group) and UART (Universal Asynchronous Receiver-Transmitter) are specialized techniques that involve connecting to a mobile device's internal test ports to extract data directly from the memory. These ports allow forensic investigators to bypass lock mechanisms and obtain a complete image of the device's storage.

**JTAG**: This technique enables access to the device's memory without needing to unlock the operating system. By connecting the JTAG interface to a forensic workstation, investigators can retrieve raw data from the device's storage chip.

**UART**: UART interfaces allow access to the device's low-level data, enabling investigators to bypass security mechanisms and extract data from the mobile device's internal memory.

While JTAG and UART can be highly effective, they require specialized knowledge, equipment, and technical expertise to implement successfully. Additionally, these methods are often device-specific and may not be applicable to all mobile devices.

## 4. Exploiting Vulnerabilities

Exploiting software vulnerabilities is another method used to bypass encryption and unlock devices. Many devices have vulnerabilities in their firmware or operating systems that can be leveraged to gain unauthorized access to the device.

**Exploiting Known Vulnerabilities**: Forensic investigators may use public or private zero-day exploits to bypass lock mechanisms or unlock encrypted devices. These exploits take advantage of vulnerabilities that have not been patched by the manufacturer, allowing forensic experts to gain access to locked or encrypted data.

**Rooting and Jailbreaking**: Rooting (for Android) and jailbreaking (for iOS) are processes that bypass the manufacturer's restrictions on the device, allowing forensic investigators to install custom software that can access locked or encrypted data. While these methods may provide valuable access to a device's data, they can also alter the integrity of the evidence, making them controversial in certain legal contexts.

## 5. Using Manufacturer Backdoors or Tools

In certain cases, mobile device manufacturers may provide forensic investigators with specialized tools or backdoors to help them access locked or encrypted devices.

**Apple's Advanced Forensics**: Apple, for instance, has historically worked with law enforcement agencies to provide assistance in unlocking devices under certain circumstances. This might involve providing the investigators with special access to an Apple server or device-specific recovery keys.

**Other Manufacturers**: Other manufacturers, such as Samsung and Huawei, may also provide special tools for forensic investigations, although these are typically limited to law enforcement and may require legal approval or cooperation.

### 9.3.4 Legal and Ethical Considerations

Bypassing encryption and lock mechanisms must always be done within the bounds of the law. Legal and ethical considerations are paramount, as any violation of privacy rights or mishandling of evidence can jeopardize an investigation or lead to the inadmissibility of evidence in court. Investigators must ensure they have proper warrants or consent before attempting to access a locked or encrypted device, and they must follow established procedures to maintain the chain of custody for the evidence.

Overcoming encryption and lock mechanisms is one of the most challenging aspects of mobile device forensics. Forensic investigators must use a combination of brute force techniques, hardware-based methods like chip-off forensics, and software exploits to gain access to locked or encrypted data. Despite the complexity, advancements in forensic tools and methodologies continue to evolve, offering investigators more effective ways to access and analyze mobile device data while adhering to legal and ethical standards. By overcoming encryption and lock barriers, forensic experts can ensure that critical evidence is preserved and made available for legal proceedings.


# 9.4 Investigating Emerging Mobile Technologies: IoT and Wearables.

In recent years, the proliferation of Internet of Things (IoT) devices and wearable technologies has reshaped the landscape of digital forensics, presenting new challenges and opportunities for forensic investigators. Unlike traditional mobile devices, IoT and wearables often serve as interconnected nodes in a larger ecosystem of data exchange and communication, creating complex, multi-source evidence chains that can be critical in criminal investigations. This section explores the investigation of emerging mobile technologies such as IoT and wearables, with a focus on the forensic challenges they pose and the techniques used to collect, preserve, and analyze data from these devices.

### 9.4.1 The Rise of IoT and Wearables in Digital Forensics

IoT devices are everyday objects embedded with sensors, software, and network connectivity, allowing them to collect and exchange data with other devices and systems. These include smart home devices (e.g., thermostats, security cameras, and smart speakers), wearable health monitors (e.g., fitness trackers and smartwatches), and connected vehicles, among others. Wearables, such as smartwatches and fitness trackers, have become ubiquitous, offering real-time data on a user's physical activity, health metrics, and location.

In addition to providing valuable insights into a person's activities, habits, and movements, IoT devices and wearables can serve as key sources of evidence in criminal investigations, whether in the context of a health-related case, a missing person investigation, or a broader criminal enterprise.

As these technologies continue to evolve, they introduce new avenues for evidence collection. However, the very nature of these devices—always-on, connected, and cloud-dependent—complicates the investigation process. Forensic investigators must adapt their approaches to handle these unique data sources effectively.

### 9.4.2 Forensic Challenges in Investigating IoT Devices

IoT devices present unique forensic challenges that differ from traditional mobile devices in several key ways:

**Data Fragmentation**

Unlike mobile phones, which store data locally on the device, IoT devices often store data in multiple locations: on the device itself, in cloud storage, or on other connected devices. For example, a smart thermostat may collect and store temperature data locally while simultaneously syncing this data to cloud-based servers for remote monitoring and analysis. This distributed nature of data requires investigators to access multiple sources to gather a complete picture of the evidence.

**Data Volatility**

Many IoT devices, especially those designed for real-time monitoring (e.g., security cameras or smart doorbells), store data in volatile memory or may overwrite old data automatically when storage is full. This can complicate the task of preserving evidence, as investigators may need to act quickly to capture relevant data before it is overwritten or erased.

## Interoperability

IoT devices often rely on multiple communication protocols (Wi-Fi, Bluetooth, Zigbee, etc.) to interact with other devices or cloud-based systems. Each device may use a different communication standard or API, making it difficult to standardize the extraction process. Investigators must have knowledge of these various communication protocols and the ways in which devices exchange and store data.

## Legal and Privacy Concerns

Given that IoT devices can collect extensive personal data (e.g., health metrics, location history, and even audio or video recordings), there are significant privacy concerns. Investigators need to ensure they have the proper legal authorization, such as a warrant or subpoena, before accessing personal data stored on IoT devices. In some jurisdictions, accessing certain types of data without consent may lead to legal challenges, especially when data is stored in the cloud or across multiple countries with different data protection laws.

### 9.4.3 Techniques for Investigating IoT Devices

To successfully investigate IoT devices, forensic investigators employ a combination of traditional forensic techniques and specialized tools tailored for IoT environments:

## Cloud Forensics

Since many IoT devices rely on cloud storage for data backup and analysis, cloud forensics plays an important role in IoT investigations. Investigators may need to access cloud accounts linked to the IoT device to retrieve data. This could involve data acquisition from cloud platforms like Amazon Web Services (AWS), Google Cloud, or private server farms. Techniques like data carving, file system analysis, and examining cloud logs can help reconstruct timelines of activities or communications related to the device.

## Network Traffic Analysis

IoT devices often communicate over various networks, making network forensics a valuable method for investigating them. By capturing network traffic, investigators can analyze the interactions between IoT devices and other components (e.g., smart homes, smartphones, or cloud servers). Tools like Wireshark, TCPdump, and NetFlow analyzers allow investigators to monitor traffic patterns, detect suspicious behavior, and potentially identify unauthorized data transmissions.

### Device Imaging

When possible, creating a full image of the IoT device's storage (e.g., memory, firmware, or SD card) can be invaluable. This is especially true for devices that don't rely on cloud storage but store data locally. Tools like Forensic Disk Imagers or specialized hardware acquisition tools may be used to obtain a complete bit-for-bit copy of the device's data, which can then be analyzed for traces of digital evidence.

### Firmware Analysis

Some IoT devices run on custom firmware or software that could contain valuable evidence. Forensic investigators may analyze the device's firmware to detect vulnerabilities, understand its data collection methods, and potentially uncover hidden data. Reverse engineering firmware can help identify backdoors, default passwords, or hidden logs that could be used as evidence in an investigation.

### 9.4.4 Investigating Wearables: Unique Challenges and Approaches

Wearables, including fitness trackers, smartwatches, and health monitors, also represent an important category of IoT devices. They collect a wide variety of personal data, including physical activity, sleep patterns, GPS location, and biometric information such as heart rate, oxygen levels, and stress indicators. This data can provide critical insights into a person's whereabouts, habits, and overall health, making them key targets in investigations.

Challenges in wearable forensics include:

### Data Accessibility

Wearable devices often sync data to paired smartphones or cloud accounts. While smartphones can be seized and analyzed for data, retrieving data from the wearable itself can be more complicated due to the device's limited interface and security mechanisms (e.g., PIN codes, biometrics). Wearable devices may not have built-in forensic tools or export capabilities, requiring investigators to find alternative methods of access.

### Health and Privacy Concerns

The data stored on wearables is deeply personal and sensitive, often related to an individual's health or medical conditions. There are ethical and legal considerations when accessing this data, especially when it involves confidential health information under laws like HIPAA (Health Insurance Portability and Accountability Act) in the U.S. or similar data protection laws in other regions. Investigators must ensure that they comply with privacy regulations while accessing and handling this data.

Techniques for investigating wearables include:

### Device Pairing Forensics

Many wearables communicate with smartphones or other devices via Bluetooth or Wi-Fi. Forensic investigators may examine these paired devices to extract synced data from wearables. Tools such as Cellebrite or X1 Social Discovery can facilitate the extraction of data from paired mobile devices, allowing investigators to obtain data that originated from wearables.

### Cloud and Health Data Services

Wearables often sync data to cloud platforms (e.g., Fitbit, Apple Health, Google Fit). Investigators can use cloud forensic techniques to access and analyze this data. In cases where wearables store health-related information, investigators may also contact health service providers or access medical databases to obtain relevant records for an investigation.

### Direct Data Extraction

In some cases, direct extraction of data from the wearable may be possible. If the device supports USB or other direct connections, forensic tools can be used to access the device's internal storage. This can be particularly useful for fitness trackers that store logs of physical activity, location history, or biometric data directly on the device.

### The Future of Forensic Investigations in the Era of IoT and Wearables

The rapid growth of IoT devices and wearables presents both exciting opportunities and significant challenges for digital forensics. As these devices continue to evolve and become more integrated into daily life, they will likely provide increasingly detailed data that could be crucial for criminal investigations. However, the unique features of these devices—distributed data storage, constant connectivity, real-time data transmission, and privacy concerns—require investigators to adapt their forensic strategies and develop new tools and techniques.

Investigating IoT and wearables is an emerging field within forensic cybersecurity, one that will continue to evolve in response to technological advances. By staying ahead of these developments and refining their expertise, forensic investigators can ensure that they are equipped to handle the complexities of digital evidence in this new era.

# 10. The Role of Artificial Intelligence in Forensic Cybersecurity

Artificial Intelligence (AI) is revolutionizing forensic cybersecurity by enhancing the speed, accuracy, and efficiency of cyber threat detection and investigation. This chapter explores how AI and machine learning algorithms are being leveraged to identify patterns in vast amounts of digital data, detect anomalies in network traffic, and automate the analysis of malware. It also examines AI's role in predictive analytics for preventing future attacks and improving incident response times. By understanding the integration of AI into forensic processes, readers will gain insights into how emerging technologies are shaping the future of cyber defense and forensic investigations.

## 10.1 AI Applications in Threat Detection and Forensics.

The rise of artificial intelligence (AI) has fundamentally transformed various industries, and cybersecurity is no exception. AI technologies, such as machine learning (ML) and deep learning, have found powerful applications in the detection, prevention, and investigation of cybercrimes. In the field of forensic cybersecurity, AI plays a critical role in streamlining the often time-consuming and resource-intensive process of identifying, analyzing, and mitigating cyber threats.

AI-powered tools can process and analyze vast amounts of data at speeds and accuracies far beyond human capabilities, allowing for real-time threat detection and more effective forensic investigations. This section explores how AI is applied in threat detection and forensic investigations, highlighting the tools and techniques that benefit from this technological advancement.

### 10.1.1 AI-Driven Threat Detection

AI has revolutionized the approach to detecting cyber threats by enabling systems to recognize suspicious activities, detect vulnerabilities, and respond to anomalies in real-time. Traditional security systems often rely on predefined signatures or rules to identify threats, which can be effective but is limited when faced with new, sophisticated, or previously unseen attack techniques. AI-based systems, on the other hand, leverage the power of machine learning and data-driven models to detect threats that evolve over time, making them more adaptable to modern cyberattacks.

Key applications of AI in threat detection include:

**Anomaly Detection:**

AI systems use machine learning algorithms to identify deviations from normal patterns of behavior across network traffic, user activity, or system processes. By training models on large datasets, these AI systems can distinguish between legitimate actions and malicious behavior. For example, an AI algorithm can detect unusual login patterns, such as a user logging in from an unusual geographical location or a sudden spike in data access, both of which could signal an account compromise.

**Behavioral Analytics:**

Through behavioral analytics, AI systems can monitor the actions of users or entities over time to create a baseline of normal behavior. When an action deviates from this baseline, the system triggers an alert for further investigation. This technique is particularly useful in detecting insider threats, where an attacker might already have access to the system but attempts to escalate privileges or perform unauthorized actions.

**Predictive Analytics and Threat Intelligence:**

AI can also leverage predictive analytics to forecast potential threats before they occur. By analyzing historical data, patterns, and trends, AI systems can predict and preemptively block attacks. These systems can be fed with cyber threat intelligence feeds that use AI to analyze and correlate data from multiple sources, such as known threat actor behaviors, emerging vulnerabilities, and malware signatures. The result is more proactive and dynamic defense mechanisms.

**Automated Malware Detection:**

Traditional malware detection often depends on signatures or known characteristics of malware strains. However, sophisticated malware frequently evolves to evade detection. AI-based malware detection tools can analyze file behavior, code structure, and other dynamic characteristics in real-time. This is especially valuable in detecting zero-day attacks, where the malware's signatures have never been seen before.

### 10.1.2 AI in Digital Forensic Investigations

In addition to improving threat detection, AI has become an invaluable tool in digital forensic investigations, particularly when investigators are dealing with large amounts of data or complex attack scenarios. The use of AI in forensics helps streamline the analysis process and enhances the ability to uncover evidence that might otherwise be overlooked.

**Data Mining and Evidence Collection:**

Cyber forensic investigations often involve sifting through vast quantities of data across multiple systems—emails, documents, files, logs, and network traffic. AI-powered data mining techniques can be used to quickly analyze and categorize large volumes of unstructured data. For example, AI algorithms can sift through logs, emails, and messages to identify key phrases, keywords, or patterns that are relevant to the investigation. This can greatly speed up the evidence collection process.

**Automated Log Analysis:**

Logs are a critical part of any forensic investigation as they provide a detailed record of system activity, including successful and unsuccessful access attempts, network connections, file transfers, and system changes. However, the sheer volume of log data generated by modern systems can overwhelm investigators. AI can automate the process of log analysis by using natural language processing (NLP) and pattern recognition to identify anomalies, correlate events, and flag relevant log entries. This automation reduces the workload of forensic experts and helps uncover evidence faster.

**Image and Video Analysis:**

Investigations involving digital devices, particularly mobile devices, often yield large amounts of multimedia data. AI can be used to analyze images and videos, automatically recognizing faces, objects, and locations within the content. This can help investigators identify crucial pieces of evidence quickly, such as identifying a suspect in a video or cross-referencing an object in a photo with other records or known data points.

**File Carving and Data Recovery:**

When data is deleted, it is not always fully erased. Digital forensics investigators often use file carving techniques to recover deleted files from storage media. AI can assist in this process by identifying fragments of data that are scattered across a storage device, intelligently piecing them together, and recovering incomplete or damaged files. AI-based tools improve the accuracy and efficiency of file carving, which can significantly enhance the investigation.

**Natural Language Processing (NLP) for Textual Analysis:**

Investigators often need to analyze large volumes of text-based data, such as emails, instant messages, and documents. NLP algorithms allow AI systems to process and analyze written language, detecting patterns, sentiment, and anomalies. For example, AI can help identify communication patterns in email chains, flag suspicious messages, or recognize coded language that might indicate criminal intent. It can also automatically categorize and tag text-based evidence, making it easier for investigators to access relevant information.

**Facilitating Peer-to-Peer (P2P) and Dark Web Investigations:**

The dark web is a notorious space for criminal activity, including illegal data exchanges, malware distribution, and illicit transactions. Investigating activities in these areas can be complex due to the use of encryption and anonymous browsing technologies. AI can assist by continuously monitoring dark web forums, peer-to-peer (P2P) networks, and other encrypted communication channels for emerging threats or evidence of cybercrime. By analyzing data from these sources, AI can help identify potential suspects, detect criminal patterns, and track illicit transactions.

### 10.1.3 The Challenges of Integrating AI in Cyber Forensics

While AI offers significant advantages in threat detection and digital forensics, its implementation comes with a few challenges that need to be addressed:

**Data Quality and Bias:**

AI systems rely heavily on data, and if the data used to train AI models is incomplete, biased, or unrepresentative, the performance of these models can be compromised. In the case of cyber forensics, where precision and accuracy are crucial, poor-quality data or biased models can lead to false positives or missed evidence.

**Complexity and Cost of Implementation:**

AI tools can be complex to set up and require significant computational resources. Additionally, organizations may face high costs related to acquiring, training, and maintaining AI-powered forensic tools. Small organizations or teams with limited budgets might find it difficult to access these resources.

**Interpretability of AI Decisions:**

Many AI systems, particularly those based on deep learning, operate as "black boxes," making it difficult to interpret how a specific decision or conclusion was reached. In a forensic investigation, where the chain of evidence and methodology must be transparent, the lack of interpretability can be problematic. This may present challenges in legal contexts where clear, understandable reasoning is needed to support forensic conclusions.

Artificial intelligence is transforming the landscape of cybersecurity and digital forensics, providing investigators with powerful tools to detect threats and uncover critical evidence more effectively. AI's capabilities in anomaly detection, behavioral analysis, and data mining are making forensic investigations faster, more accurate, and more comprehensive. However, as AI technologies continue to evolve, it is essential to be mindful of the challenges associated with their use, such as data bias, system complexity, and interpretability. As AI matures, its role in cybersecurity and forensics is only expected to grow, further enhancing the ability to combat cyber threats and provide justice in the digital age.

# 10.2 Machine Learning for Pattern Recognition in Digital Evidence.

Machine learning (ML), a subset of artificial intelligence (AI), has revolutionized many fields, including cybersecurity and digital forensics. One of the most valuable applications of machine learning in forensic cybersecurity is its ability to perform pattern recognition on vast amounts of digital evidence. In a world where cybercrime is becoming increasingly sophisticated, investigators face the challenge of sifting through immense volumes of data from various sources, such as logs, network traffic, devices, and even cloud-based storage. Machine learning can significantly enhance this process by identifying hidden patterns and relationships in data that would otherwise go unnoticed.

This section explores how machine learning is applied to pattern recognition in the context of digital evidence collection and forensic investigations. It discusses the methods, tools, and challenges of integrating machine learning into forensic cybersecurity, with a focus on how pattern recognition can assist investigators in detecting anomalies, uncovering malicious activities, and accelerating the investigative process.

### 10.2.1 Introduction to Pattern Recognition in Digital Forensics

Pattern recognition refers to the ability to identify regularities, trends, or anomalies in a given dataset. In digital forensics, this typically involves finding patterns in large datasets like network traffic logs, system logs, email histories, and even device file systems. Machine learning plays a crucial role in automating this task, especially when dealing with unstructured data or when traditional forensic tools and human efforts are unable to keep up with the sheer volume and complexity of modern cyber environments.

Machine learning techniques—such as supervised learning, unsupervised learning, and reinforcement learning—can be applied to digital evidence to recognize patterns that indicate the presence of cyber threats or criminal activity. By training on labeled datasets or using unsupervised methods to learn from data without predefined labels, machine learning systems can identify previously unknown attack vectors, detect anomalous behaviors, and uncover hidden evidence that would be impossible or time-consuming for human investigators to find manually.

### 10.2.2 Types of Pattern Recognition Used in Digital Forensics

Machine learning leverages various pattern recognition techniques to process and analyze digital evidence. Some of the most commonly used methods in digital forensics include:

### Anomaly Detection:

One of the key applications of machine learning in pattern recognition is the identification of anomalies in digital evidence. By establishing a baseline of normal behavior from historical data, machine learning models can detect deviations from the norm. This is particularly useful for identifying advanced persistent threats (APTs), where attackers often operate stealthily over long periods and try to evade detection. For example, if a network normally shows a predictable pattern of data traffic, any sudden spike or unusual data flow could indicate the presence of a cyberattack. Machine learning algorithms can continuously monitor such behavior and automatically flag anomalies for further investigation.

### Classification of Data:

Classification is another fundamental machine learning task in which the system assigns categories or labels to data points. In a forensic investigation, data collected from various sources (emails, files, logs) can be classified into different categories based on their relevance to the case. For example, machine learning models can be trained to classify emails into malicious or benign categories, helping investigators prioritize which emails to examine based on their likelihood of being related to an attack. Similarly, files can be classified as either part of malware, evidence, or system files, allowing investigators to quickly isolate suspicious files during the analysis process.

**Clustering for Unknown Threats:**

In unsupervised learning, machine learning algorithms can identify patterns in data without needing predefined labels. This is especially useful in scenarios where investigators do not know exactly what they are looking for, such as when investigating a new type of malware or a previously unknown attack. Clustering algorithms group similar data points together based on shared characteristics. For example, clustering can be used to group related network traffic packets that are part of the same attack campaign, helping forensic investigators identify attack patterns even in the absence of prior knowledge. These clusters can reveal hidden connections between disparate pieces of evidence, allowing investigators to connect the dots and understand the bigger picture.

**Time-Series Analysis for Behavior Modeling:**

Many forensic investigations rely on the analysis of time-series data such as logs, network traffic, and event histories. Machine learning techniques are particularly effective at modeling and identifying patterns over time. Time-series analysis helps identify abnormal sequences of events that could suggest malicious activity. For instance, a sudden surge in failed login attempts over a short period might indicate a brute-force attack. Using machine learning algorithms such as Recurrent Neural Networks (RNNs), forensic experts can track patterns in time-series data and predict future malicious actions or behaviors.

**Natural Language Processing (NLP) for Textual Data:**

In cases involving digital communications, investigators may need to analyze vast amounts of text-based evidence such as emails, social media messages, and chat logs. Machine learning, particularly Natural Language Processing (NLP), is invaluable in recognizing patterns in textual data. NLP algorithms can identify keywords, phrases, and sentiment in the text, helping investigators filter out irrelevant communications and focus on those most likely to contain evidence of cybercrimes. NLP also helps in recognizing suspicious patterns in large volumes of text, such as identifying phishing attempts or social engineering tactics in email correspondence.

**10.2.3 Machine Learning Models and Tools for Pattern Recognition in Digital Evidence**

To implement pattern recognition effectively, forensic investigators employ various machine learning models and tools that are specifically designed for handling digital evidence. These tools help automate the detection and analysis of patterns, enabling faster and more accurate investigations.

**Supervised Learning Algorithms**: Supervised learning involves training the algorithm on labeled datasets where the outcome is already known. Common supervised learning algorithms used in digital forensics include:

- **Support Vector Machines (SVM)** – A classification technique used to categorize data into classes, such as distinguishing between normal and malicious activities.
- **Decision Trees** – A model that splits data into branches based on feature values to make decisions. It's particularly useful for classifying events like security incidents or system breaches.
- **Random Forests** – An ensemble method that combines multiple decision trees to increase accuracy. It's highly effective for anomaly detection in network traffic or identifying malicious files.

**Unsupervised Learning Algorithms**: In unsupervised learning, there are no predefined labels or categories. Instead, the algorithm identifies hidden patterns in the data. Common unsupervised learning techniques in digital forensics include:

- **K-Means Clustering** – A popular method for grouping similar items in large datasets. In forensics, this could help identify clusters of similar events or files that are related to a particular attack or campaign.
- **Principal Component Analysis (PCA)** – Used for dimensionality reduction, PCA can help simplify large datasets and identify the most significant features that might indicate suspicious activity.

**Deep Learning Algorithms**: Deep learning, particularly neural networks, can learn complex patterns in large datasets and is especially useful for unstructured data like images, videos, and logs. Models such as Convolutional Neural Networks (CNNs) and Recurrent Neural Networks (RNNs) are used to identify complex patterns in time-series data or detect anomalies in digital images, such as identifying hidden malware signatures in files or images.

**AI-Powered Forensic Tools**: Several AI-powered forensic tools are available that integrate machine learning techniques for pattern recognition. For example:

- **Cellebrite UFED** – A tool used for mobile device forensics that incorporates machine learning to identify patterns in data extracted from smartphones.
- **FTK Imager** – A forensic tool that includes machine learning capabilities for pattern recognition in disk images and can identify suspicious file activity or potential evidence.
- **X1 Social Discovery** – A tool used for social media forensic investigations, utilizing NLP and machine learning to detect patterns of criminal behavior within social media data.

### 10.2.4 Challenges and Limitations of Machine Learning in Forensic Cybersecurity

While machine learning holds immense promise for digital forensics, there are several challenges and limitations that investigators must be aware of:

**Data Quality and Labeling:**

For machine learning models to be effective, they need large, high-quality datasets for training. In many cases, digital evidence is incomplete, corrupted, or not well-labeled, which can reduce the accuracy and reliability of machine learning models. Properly labeled training data is especially critical for supervised learning methods, and obtaining such datasets can be time-consuming and difficult.

**False Positives and Negatives:**

Machine learning models are not infallible, and they can produce false positives (incorrectly flagging benign behavior as malicious) and false negatives (failing to identify actual threats). In forensic investigations, these errors can delay the investigation or lead investigators to miss crucial evidence. Fine-tuning the models and continuously updating them based on new data are essential practices to mitigate these issues.

**Complexity and Interpretability:**

Many machine learning models, especially deep learning algorithms, operate as "black boxes," meaning that it can be difficult to understand how they arrive at a particular decision. This lack of transparency can be problematic in legal contexts where forensic evidence must be clearly explainable. Investigators need tools that not only detect patterns but also provide an understandable rationale for their findings.

**Overfitting:**

Machine learning models can sometimes "overfit" to the data they are trained on, meaning they perform well on that specific dataset but fail to generalize to new, unseen data. This can lead to poor performance when the model is applied to live investigations with new types of attacks or novel data patterns.

Machine learning for pattern recognition in digital evidence represents a powerful advancement in forensic cybersecurity. Through the use of various ML algorithms, investigators can process vast amounts of data, uncover hidden patterns, and detect previously unknown threats. However, as with any technology, machine learning presents challenges such as data quality, model interpretability, and the risk of false positives and negatives. As these challenges are addressed, machine learning's role in cyber forensics will continue to grow, providing investigators with invaluable tools to tackle the evolving landscape of cybercrime.

# 10.3 Ethical and Legal Challenges of AI in Cyber Investigations.

The integration of Artificial Intelligence (AI) in cyber investigations has brought significant advancements, enabling investigators to process vast amounts of data efficiently, detect anomalies, and uncover hidden patterns that would otherwise be challenging to identify manually. However, alongside these technological benefits come a range of ethical and legal challenges that must be carefully considered. As AI becomes more prevalent in cyber forensics and digital investigations, it is essential to understand how its use intersects with legal frameworks and ethical considerations, ensuring that these powerful tools are used responsibly and effectively without infringing on privacy rights or due process.

This section explores the ethical and legal challenges faced by cyber investigators when using AI in digital forensic investigations, shedding light on concerns around data privacy, accountability, transparency, bias, and the potential for misuse.

### 10.3.1 Ethical Implications of AI in Cyber Investigations

AI in cyber investigations introduces various ethical concerns that need to be addressed to ensure responsible use. These concerns often revolve around issues like privacy, autonomy, and the potential for discrimination in automated decision-making.

**Privacy Violations and Data Handling:**

AI systems in digital forensics often require access to vast amounts of sensitive personal data, such as communication logs, browsing histories, financial records, and device data. The ethical challenge lies in balancing the need for thorough investigation with the protection of individuals' privacy rights. While AI can significantly enhance investigations by quickly scanning through this data, there is a risk that it may lead to unjustified invasions of privacy if not properly governed. For example, AI systems may overreach, scanning irrelevant data or accessing personal information that is not pertinent to the case. This could potentially infringe upon privacy rights and violate legal protections under laws such as the General Data Protection Regulation (GDPR) in Europe or the Fourth Amendment in the United States.

**Informed Consent and Transparency:**

The use of AI in cyber investigations raises concerns about informed consent, especially when AI is deployed in contexts that involve monitoring or analyzing personal communications. Investigators must ensure that individuals are aware of and consent to their data being used for investigation purposes. Furthermore, AI algorithms are often described as "black boxes," meaning their decision-making processes are not always transparent. This lack of transparency in how AI systems identify patterns or make decisions can lead to ethical dilemmas, particularly in legal proceedings where the rationale behind a decision must be explained clearly. Lack of transparency could undermine the trust in the investigative process and lead to questions regarding fairness and accountability.

**Bias and Discrimination:**

One of the critical ethical issues associated with AI is its potential for bias. AI systems are only as objective as the data on which they are trained. If the data used to train AI systems in cyber investigations is biased—reflecting past prejudices or disproportionately focusing on certain groups—it can lead to discriminatory outcomes. For example, an AI model trained on biased datasets might falsely flag certain behaviors or individuals as suspicious based on race, gender, or geographic location, leading to unfair targeting. Ensuring that AI models are trained on diverse and unbiased datasets is essential for minimizing this risk. Furthermore, investigators must regularly audit AI systems to ensure they do not perpetuate harmful stereotypes or biased decision-making.

**10.3.2 Legal Challenges in the Use of AI for Cyber Investigations**

The application of AI in cyber investigations must adhere to a strict legal framework to ensure that investigations are conducted within the bounds of the law. There are several legal challenges related to the use of AI tools in forensic cybersecurity, ranging from questions of evidence admissibility to the compliance with jurisdictional laws.

**Admissibility of AI-Generated Evidence:**

A key legal challenge of using AI in cyber investigations is the admissibility of AI-generated evidence in court. The rules of evidence often require that evidence be both reliable and relevant to the case. AI systems, particularly those based on machine learning algorithms, can sometimes produce results that are difficult to explain or understand, raising questions about whether the findings can be considered reliable enough for courtroom presentation. For example, if an AI system flags certain data as evidence of a cybercrime, it may be difficult to establish how the AI reached that conclusion, especially when the system operates as a "black box." Courts may require more transparency and explanation of how AI algorithms function and how evidence was processed to ensure that AI-generated findings are admissible and meet the legal standards for evidentiary reliability.

**Data Protection and Compliance with Privacy Laws:**

Legal challenges surrounding AI in cyber investigations are often connected to issues of data protection and privacy. In many countries, there are strict regulations governing how personal data can be collected, processed, and shared. For example, under the GDPR, individuals have the right to control how their personal data is used, and organizations must ensure that their AI systems comply with these regulations. Cyber investigators must navigate these legal requirements when using AI tools to process data, ensuring that the data is collected with proper consent, the scope of its usage is clearly defined, and that individuals' privacy rights are respected. Additionally, investigators must be cautious of cross-border data flow issues, especially when AI systems are used to process data from multiple jurisdictions with differing privacy laws.

**Jurisdictional Challenges and Cross-Border Investigations:**

The global nature of the internet creates complex jurisdictional issues when conducting cyber investigations. AI tools may be used to analyze data that crosses borders, creating potential conflicts between local laws and international regulations. For example, when investigating cybercrimes that involve data stored in different countries, investigators must contend with conflicting legal frameworks governing data access, privacy, and the use of AI. Jurisdictional challenges can arise when AI is used to collect and process digital evidence that exists across multiple countries, requiring careful coordination between law enforcement agencies from different jurisdictions. Some jurisdictions may impose restrictions on how their citizens' data is accessed, which could complicate investigations that rely on AI tools to analyze large datasets.

**Accountability and Liability:**

When AI is involved in a cyber investigation, the issue of accountability becomes crucial. Who is responsible if an AI system makes an error, such as falsely flagging an individual as a cybercriminal or missing critical evidence? If an AI system contributes to an unjust arrest, wrongful conviction, or failed investigation, legal questions arise regarding liability. Is it the responsibility of the forensic investigator who used the tool, the developers of the AI system, or the organization that deployed it? Legal frameworks must be updated to address these questions and establish clear guidelines for holding both individuals and AI systems accountable when things go wrong.

### 10.3.3 Balancing Innovation and Responsibility

As AI continues to evolve, the challenge for cyber investigators and policymakers is to strike a balance between leveraging the capabilities of AI to improve efficiency and accuracy in investigations and safeguarding individual rights and legal standards. Policymakers must develop legal frameworks that encourage innovation while also establishing clear guidelines for ethical AI use, ensuring that AI-based investigations do not violate privacy rights or perpetuate bias.

Additionally, organizations using AI for cyber forensics should ensure that they adopt best practices to address both ethical and legal challenges. These practices include ensuring transparency in how AI algorithms work, ensuring compliance with data protection regulations, implementing bias mitigation techniques, and conducting regular audits of AI tools to ensure fairness and accuracy.

The application of AI in cyber investigations offers transformative potential for the field of digital forensics, enabling investigators to uncover complex patterns and handle large volumes of data. However, as with any powerful technology, there are significant ethical and legal challenges that must be addressed. Striking a balance between technological innovation and responsible use is crucial to maintaining public trust and ensuring that AI-based investigations are conducted in a manner that respects individual rights, adheres to legal standards, and promotes fairness and accountability. As AI technologies evolve, it will be essential for law enforcement, legal experts, and policymakers to work together to create a framework that allows for the effective, ethical, and legal use of AI in forensic cybersecurity.

# 10.4 Future Trends: AI-Powered Forensic Tools.

The evolution of Artificial Intelligence (AI) is poised to revolutionize the field of cyber forensics, providing unprecedented opportunities for enhancing investigative capabilities. As AI continues to advance, its potential to automate complex tasks, analyze massive datasets, and identify subtle patterns of cybercriminal activity will transform how digital evidence is processed, analyzed, and presented in court. In this section, we will explore the future trends of AI-powered forensic tools, focusing on how these innovations are likely to shape the future of cybersecurity investigations, the emerging challenges, and the ways in which investigators will need to adapt.

### 10.4.1 The Integration of Machine Learning in Forensic Investigations

Machine learning (ML), a subset of AI, is expected to play an increasingly central role in the future of forensic investigations. By leveraging vast datasets, ML algorithms can be used to identify trends, anomalies, and behaviors that might otherwise be overlooked by traditional forensic methods. As forensic cybersecurity tools become more sophisticated, ML will be instrumental in enhancing pattern recognition, allowing for more accurate identification of malicious activities, such as advanced persistent threats (APTs), insider threats, and new forms of malware.

**Automated Threat Detection and Response:**

One of the most exciting future developments is the integration of AI-driven automated threat detection and response systems. These tools will be able to recognize attack patterns, predict the likelihood of future incidents, and even automate responses to neutralize threats in real time. For example, an AI tool might recognize a potential cyberattack in progress by analyzing network traffic, historical attack patterns, and system behavior, and then automatically isolate the affected systems to prevent further damage. As AI algorithms become more accurate, these systems could evolve into self-sustaining autonomous defense mechanisms that enhance the speed and efficacy of cyber responses, reducing the time to contain and mitigate a breach.

**Predictive Analytics for Cybercrime Prevention:**

Another emerging trend is the use of predictive analytics powered by AI. By analyzing historical data, ML models can forecast potential future cybercrimes before they occur. For example, AI systems could monitor cybercrime trends, identify vulnerabilities, and predict when and where attacks are most likely to happen. This proactive approach to cyber forensics could enable organizations and law enforcement agencies to anticipate and prevent cyberattacks before they escalate, ultimately improving overall cybersecurity posture and reducing the number of incidents.

### 10.4.2 Enhancing Digital Evidence Processing

AI-powered forensic tools will increasingly be used to enhance the processing and analysis of digital evidence. Traditional forensic investigations often require investigators to sift through vast amounts of data manually, a process that is not only time-consuming but also prone to human error. With the help of AI, investigators will be able to automate many of these tasks, significantly improving the efficiency and accuracy of digital evidence collection and analysis.

### Automated Data Classification and Indexing:

One of the key trends is the development of AI-driven tools that can automatically classify and index digital evidence, making it easier to search, retrieve, and analyze relevant information. For example, AI tools can be trained to recognize patterns in data—whether it's emails, text messages, metadata, or log files—and automatically categorize this information into predefined buckets. This would drastically reduce the time it takes to manually search through massive datasets and allow investigators to focus their efforts on the most critical evidence.

### Natural Language Processing (NLP) for Data Analysis:

AI tools incorporating natural language processing (NLP) will enable forensic investigators to understand and process large volumes of text-based data, such as emails, chat logs, and documents, more efficiently. NLP algorithms can be used to identify key topics, sentiment analysis, and potential threats in textual data. In the future, AI will assist investigators in recognizing hidden connections between entities, such as individuals, organizations, or geographical locations, by analyzing text data and identifying patterns and anomalies that might suggest malicious activity.

### Digital Evidence Triaging:

The AI-powered triage process will be another key advancement. Rather than reviewing all digital evidence manually, AI systems will be able to prioritize evidence based on its relevance to the investigation, helping investigators focus on the most critical pieces of evidence. For example, AI algorithms can evaluate the context, date, and metadata associated with files to rank them based on their potential value to the case, allowing investigators to spend less time sorting through irrelevant data and more time analyzing important findings.

### 10.4.3 AI-Enhanced Visual Forensics and Image Recognition

In the future, image recognition and visual forensics will be significantly enhanced through AI tools, transforming how investigators analyze digital images, videos, and other multimedia evidence. AI-driven computer vision algorithms will allow investigators to identify tampering, face recognition, scene reconstruction, and even forensic analysis of video footage. These advancements will be particularly useful in investigations involving online harassment, child exploitation, and terrorism, where image and video evidence often play a central role.

**Facial Recognition and Object Detection:**

As facial recognition technology continues to improve, AI-powered tools will help forensic investigators identify individuals in videos and photographs, even in challenging environments such as poor lighting or at angles that make traditional human recognition difficult. Additionally, AI algorithms will be able to identify specific objects within images or video footage, such as weapons, vehicles, or specific locations, making it easier to gather critical evidence from multimedia sources.

**Video Forensics and Deepfake Detection:**

With the rise of deepfakes—AI-generated videos that can manipulate the likeness of individuals or events—AI-powered forensic tools will be crucial in identifying tampered or manipulated videos. AI systems will become increasingly adept at detecting deepfake videos, flagging inconsistencies in lighting, movement, or pixel-level data that indicate the presence of synthetic media. These tools will play an important role in maintaining the integrity of video evidence, ensuring that investigators can rely on authentic video footage when building their cases.

### 10.4.4 AI-Driven Cyber Forensics in Real-Time Investigations

The future of AI in cyber forensics will also involve real-time analysis of ongoing cyber incidents. By integrating real-time monitoring systems powered by AI, forensic investigators will be able to conduct immediate analysis of attacks as they unfold, reducing the time required to contain and mitigate a threat.

**Real-Time Incident Response and Evidence Collection:**

AI-based tools will allow for live monitoring of network activity and system behavior, enabling real-time analysis of potential cyberattacks. This will provide investigators with immediate insights into the nature of the attack, its source, and its potential impact, allowing them to respond more swiftly. Moreover, AI will help automate the collection and preservation of evidence during these live investigations, ensuring that all digital evidence is captured in an admissible format, even as the attack is ongoing.

**Instantaneous Attribution and Threat Intelligence Sharing:**

As AI tools analyze the behavior of threat actors in real-time, they will also assist in attribution, helping to identify the origin of an attack. AI systems can compare attack patterns to global databases of known cybercriminal activities, providing investigators with potential leads. Additionally, AI can facilitate real-time threat intelligence sharing between organizations and law enforcement agencies, ensuring that critical data is communicated swiftly and effectively across jurisdictions.

### 10.4.5 Conclusion: Shaping the Future of Cyber Forensics

AI-powered forensic tools are set to transform the landscape of cyber forensics, bringing speed, efficiency, and accuracy to investigations that were once hindered by manual processes and resource limitations. As machine learning, computer vision, and predictive analytics continue to evolve, investigators will gain access to more powerful tools to analyze digital evidence, track cybercriminals, and prevent cyberattacks. However, as these technologies advance, it is crucial to address the ethical and legal challenges associated with their use, ensuring that AI remains a force for good in the fight against cybercrime. The future of cyber forensics lies in the synergy between human expertise and AI innovation, allowing investigators to stay ahead of evolving threats and to protect digital spaces with unprecedented precision.

# 11. Case Studies: Lessons from High-Profile Investigations

Real-world case studies offer invaluable insights into the challenges and strategies involved in forensic cybersecurity. This chapter examines high-profile cyber incidents, such as large-scale data breaches, ransomware attacks, and nation-state cyber espionage, to uncover the investigative techniques and tools used to solve them. By analyzing these cases, readers will learn critical lessons about the importance of thorough evidence collection, the role of collaboration in complex investigations, and the potential pitfalls that can hinder success. These lessons not only highlight the intricacies of digital forensics but also offer actionable takeaways to apply in future investigations.

## 11.1 Case Study: Solving a Global Ransomware Attack.

Ransomware attacks have become one of the most prevalent and devastating cybercrimes in recent years, causing significant financial damage to organizations, disrupting operations, and compromising sensitive data. One of the key challenges of responding to a ransomware attack is identifying the attackers, understanding their methods, and recovering from the breach while minimizing further harm. This case study will explore a real-world example of a global ransomware attack, the forensic investigative process used to solve the case, and the lessons learned from the incident that shaped future cybersecurity strategies.

### Background: The Attack

In this case, a multinational company operating in several industries, including finance, healthcare, and logistics, was targeted by a sophisticated ransomware group. The attackers deployed a variant of ransomware known as Conti, which had a reputation for exploiting vulnerabilities in widely used software and network protocols. The company discovered the attack when employees were suddenly locked out of critical systems, with ransom notes demanding payments in Bitcoin to unlock files and restore access to the affected systems.

The ransomware spread rapidly across the company's network, encrypting sensitive documents, emails, and database files. In some cases, the attackers even exfiltrated sensitive data before encrypting it, threatening to release this information publicly unless the ransom demands were met. The attack not only affected the company's operations but also put its reputation at risk, as customer data and financial transactions were exposed to potential breaches.

The company immediately activated its incident response team, but the scale and sophistication of the attack posed significant challenges. To solve the case and mitigate the impact, a collaborative forensic investigation involving cybersecurity experts, law enforcement agencies, and external forensic firms was initiated.

## Step 1: Incident Containment and Initial Analysis

The first step in responding to the ransomware attack was to contain the breach to prevent further encryption of data and spread of the ransomware. The organization's IT team, along with cybersecurity consultants, took immediate action by isolating affected systems from the network. Critical servers and endpoints were disconnected from the internet to prevent further data exfiltration and to stop the ransomware from spreading to other systems.

Simultaneously, the company's incident response team began performing an initial digital forensics analysis to identify the source of the attack and determine how the ransomware had infiltrated the network. The team used endpoint detection and response (EDR) tools to trace the origins of the attack, analyze logs, and identify the specific vulnerabilities that the attackers had exploited. Initial findings revealed that the attackers had gained access through a phishing email, which contained a malicious attachment. This was a common tactic used by the ransomware group to infiltrate organizations and escalate their attack from an initial point of access to full network compromise.

## Step 2: Forensic Investigation and Attribution

Once the containment was established, the forensic team turned its focus to understanding the scope of the attack and attributing it to a specific cybercriminal group. Using a combination of log analysis, network traffic analysis, and digital evidence recovery, investigators began piecing together how the attack unfolded.

## Log and Network Analysis:

The first forensic task involved analyzing network logs to determine how the ransomware moved laterally through the company's systems. The forensic team identified unusual traffic patterns, particularly outbound connections to foreign IP addresses that were associated with the ransomware's command-and-control (C&C) servers. By tracing this network traffic, investigators discovered the path the ransomware took to infiltrate the company's internal network.

### Reverse Engineering the Ransomware:

The next step in the investigation was to reverse-engineer the ransomware to understand its operation and identify any potential weaknesses that could be exploited for decryption. Using malware analysis tools, forensic investigators were able to break down the ransomware's code, revealing how it encrypted files and what methods the attackers used to hide their presence on the network. The forensic team found that the ransomware used asymmetric encryption, making it difficult to decrypt without the private key held by the attackers. This analysis also uncovered several vulnerabilities in the ransomware's design that could be exploited for future investigations.

### Attribution and Intelligence Sharing:

Using the clues collected from the digital evidence, the investigation was able to attribute the attack to a ransomware-as-a-service (RaaS) group known as Conti, which had been responsible for several high-profile attacks across various industries. The forensic team worked with law enforcement agencies and threat intelligence organizations to gather additional data about the group's operations and to share findings with other organizations that might be at risk.

### Step 3: Recovery and Mitigation

After the attribution was made, the forensic team worked with the affected company to determine the best course of action for data recovery and preventing future attacks. One of the main challenges in this stage was determining whether to pay the ransom or pursue alternative methods of data recovery. The company, advised by cybersecurity experts, chose not to pay the ransom, as doing so would incentivize further attacks and may not guarantee the return of the encrypted data.

### Data Recovery through Backups:

Fortunately, the company had a robust data backup strategy, and the forensic team was able to restore many of the affected systems using clean backup copies. However, some of the data had been encrypted without prior backups, and recovering this information required a combination of reverse engineering the ransomware and working with specialized decryption tools. In some cases, law enforcement provided access to decryption keys that had been obtained from previous successful takedowns of the Conti group's infrastructure.

## Forensic Evidence Preservation:

Throughout the entire recovery process, the forensic team ensured that evidence was preserved in a way that maintained its integrity for potential use in criminal proceedings. Chain of custody protocols were followed to ensure that all evidence related to the attack—ransomware binaries, logs, network traffic data, and any communication from the attackers—was documented and securely stored.

## Implementing Stronger Security Measures:

In addition to data recovery, the company worked with cybersecurity experts to implement a more comprehensive security strategy. This included installing next-generation firewalls, improving endpoint protection, conducting security awareness training for employees to prevent phishing attacks, and adopting more advanced intrusion detection systems (IDS) to identify suspicious activity in real time.

## Step 4: Legal Action and Post-Incident Analysis

Once the immediate response and recovery were completed, the investigation shifted to a legal and post-incident analysis phase. Law enforcement authorities, including international agencies such as Europol and FBI, became involved in tracking down the individuals behind the Conti ransomware group. This multi-jurisdictional effort focused on dismantling the ransomware operation, taking down C&C servers, and disrupting the group's ability to launch future attacks.

## Coordinating with International Authorities:

The collaborative nature of modern cybercrime investigations meant that authorities from various countries worked together to disrupt the global network supporting the ransomware group. By sharing intelligence across borders, law enforcement was able to freeze assets, seize servers, and take down key infrastructure used by the criminals.

## Lessons Learned and Industry-Wide Impact:

The case study demonstrated the importance of a comprehensive incident response plan, regular backups, and cybersecurity training for employees in combating ransomware attacks. The lessons learned from this attack had a broader impact on the industry, encouraging other organizations to adopt more robust cybersecurity practices and invest in advanced threat detection systems. The collaboration between the private sector, cybersecurity firms, and law enforcement also highlighted the importance of cross-sector cooperation in responding to global cyber threats.

**Conclusion: Key Takeaways**

This case study underscores the critical role of cyber forensics in understanding, mitigating, and recovering from ransomware attacks. Key takeaways from the investigation include the importance of rapid containment, leveraging digital evidence to trace the origin of attacks, and the necessity of collaboration between organizations, law enforcement, and cybersecurity experts. In the face of increasingly sophisticated ransomware campaigns, AI-powered forensics, threat intelligence sharing, and preventative measures will continue to evolve, ensuring that organizations are better equipped to defend against future attacks. The lessons learned from this case will help shape more resilient strategies for tackling ransomware and other forms of cybercrime in the years to come.

# 11.2 Case Study: Forensic Insights into a Nation-State Cyber Espionage.

Cyber espionage, particularly when perpetrated by nation-states, represents one of the most complex and challenging threats to national security, intellectual property, and global stability. These attacks often involve highly skilled threat actors, sophisticated tools, and the ability to conduct operations with stealth and precision over extended periods. This case study explores a nation-state cyber espionage operation targeting a defense contractor, shedding light on the forensic investigation methods used to uncover the attack, understand the motives, and attribute the attack to a state-sponsored group. The case also illustrates the long-term implications for organizations in defending against such threats and the importance of cyber forensics in countering nation-state activities.

**Background: The Attack**

In this case, a leading defense contractor that worked closely with military and intelligence agencies was targeted by a nation-state-backed hacker group. The organization had a significant amount of sensitive data, including military designs, intelligence reports, and proprietary technologies critical to national defense. The attack was first discovered when several employees reported anomalies in system performance, slow network speeds, and suspicious emails. Despite the early indicators, it took months before the full extent of the cyber espionage operation became apparent.

The attackers, who were later attributed to a state-sponsored hacking group, had successfully infiltrated the contractor's network through a spear-phishing campaign that targeted senior executives. Once inside, the attackers used a combination of advanced persistent threat (APT) techniques to exfiltrate confidential files, monitor communications, and evade detection. The attack was sophisticated enough to go unnoticed for months, with the attackers covering their tracks by using rootkits, backdoors, and data exfiltration tools designed to avoid detection by conventional security systems.

## Step 1: Discovery and Initial Response

The forensic investigation began after the anomalies in system performance were flagged by the internal security team. Initial efforts to contain the breach were challenging, as the attackers had already established deep access within the company's network. The first priority for the incident response team was to isolate affected systems and prevent further exfiltration of data. At the same time, security logs were collected and analyzed to look for any signs of lateral movement or command-and-control (C&C) communications that could point to the attackers' actions.

The initial phase of the forensic investigation involved network traffic analysis to identify any unusual connections or communication patterns. By examining the internal network logs, investigators were able to uncover evidence of unauthorized data access and movement. A critical breakthrough occurred when investigators discovered that the attackers had used encrypted communication channels to exfiltrate data, making it difficult to monitor the exfiltration in real-time.

## Step 2: In-Depth Forensic Analysis and Attribution

Once containment efforts had been initiated, the forensic team began a more in-depth investigation into the methods used by the attackers to infiltrate and maintain access to the network. Several forensic techniques were employed to identify the attack vector, uncover the tools and techniques used, and attribute the attack to a nation-state actor.

## Malware Analysis and Reverse Engineering:

One of the first steps in the forensic analysis was the reverse engineering of the malware used by the attackers. The malicious software used in the attack was identified as a custom-built remote access tool (RAT) designed to give the attackers persistent access to the victim's network. The malware was sophisticated, capable of evading traditional antivirus solutions, and included features such as keylogging, file exfiltration, and screen capture to monitor the activities of the target organization. By deconstructing the malware, the forensic team was able to identify specific indicators of compromise (IOCs) and unique signatures that helped in identifying the origin of the attack.

**Attribution to a Nation-State Actor:**

As the investigation progressed, digital forensics revealed that the attack exhibited characteristics associated with a specific nation-state hacking group. Analysis of the malware code revealed similarities to previously attributed attacks by the APT29 group, also known as Cozy Bear, which has been linked to Russian intelligence services. This attribution was further supported by examining TTPs (Tactics, Techniques, and Procedures) used during the attack, which aligned with known methods employed by APT29.

Forensic evidence collected from the C&C servers, network traffic patterns, and the use of stealthy exfiltration techniques pointed to a sophisticated, well-funded group with access to resources typically available to state-sponsored actors. The forensic team worked closely with national security agencies to cross-reference evidence and confirm the attribution to Russian state-backed hackers.

**Timeline Analysis and Evidence Correlation:**

Forensic investigators created a detailed attack timeline that mapped out the entire attack sequence, from the initial phishing email to the final stages of data exfiltration. This timeline was crucial in understanding how the attackers moved through the network, from compromising individual machines to gaining access to highly sensitive files. By correlating the evidence collected from various systems, investigators were able to determine the specific types of information targeted by the attackers, such as military contracts, strategic documents, and intellectual property related to defense technologies.

**Attribution through Digital Footprints:**

One of the final steps in the attribution process involved the examination of digital footprints left by the attackers during their operation. This included tracking IP addresses, analyzing the tools used in the attack, and correlating them with known patterns of attack from other APT groups. In this case, forensic investigators were able to trace back some of the IP addresses to Russian-controlled infrastructure, further strengthening the link to a nation-state actor.

## Step 3: Incident Recovery and Long-Term Mitigation

Once the forensic investigation confirmed that the attackers were part of a nation-state-backed group, the focus shifted to recovery and long-term mitigation. The organization, in coordination with national security agencies, took several measures to recover from the attack and implement stronger defenses.

### Data Recovery and Threat Intelligence Sharing:

Since the attackers had exfiltrated large amounts of sensitive data, a critical step was to ensure that the stolen information did not appear on the dark web or in the hands of adversaries. To help with this, the organization collaborated with law enforcement and cyber intelligence agencies to monitor data leaks and mitigate the potential impact. Additionally, they shared the indicators of compromise (IOCs), malware samples, and TTPs with industry partners, improving collective defenses against the same threat actor.

### Cybersecurity Posture Enhancement:

Following the incident, the organization took extensive steps to improve its cybersecurity posture. This included conducting a thorough security audit of all systems, improving email filtering systems to block spear-phishing attempts, and implementing multi-factor authentication (MFA) for all employees. The organization also employed advanced threat-hunting techniques to detect any residual traces of the attacker's presence on the network and ensure that no backdoors were left in place.

### Employee Training and Awareness:

Given that the attack was initiated through a spear-phishing campaign, the organization implemented a robust employee cybersecurity training program to raise awareness about the risks of phishing and social engineering. This training focused on recognizing suspicious emails, links, and attachments, and encouraged employees to report any suspicious activity immediately.

### Ongoing Monitoring and Incident Response:

The organization established a more proactive incident response capability, incorporating continuous network monitoring and real-time intrusion detection systems (IDS) to ensure early detection of future threats. The use of artificial intelligence (AI) and machine learning

(ML) tools for automated threat detection became a central component of the organization's long-term cybersecurity strategy.

## Step 4: Legal and Geopolitical Implications

The nation-state attack had not only cybersecurity and financial implications but also significant geopolitical consequences. The investigation was closely followed by international law enforcement and intelligence agencies. In the aftermath, diplomatic channels were used to address the incident, and the organization's government worked with international partners to confront the nation-state actor behind the cyber espionage.

### Diplomatic Action and Sanctions:

The attribution of the attack to a state-sponsored group led to diplomatic discussions between the affected nation and the aggressor state. The incident resulted in public condemnation and the implementation of sanctions aimed at deterring future cyber espionage activities. These actions highlighted the growing importance of cybersecurity in global diplomacy.

### International Cybersecurity Cooperation:

The case underscored the need for greater international cooperation in combating cyber espionage. The attack led to the formation of new coalitions between countries, cybersecurity firms, and global organizations to share intelligence, create cyber norms, and enhance the collective response to nation-state threats.

### Conclusion: Lessons Learned and Strategic Recommendations

This case study of a nation-state cyber espionage attack highlights the importance of digital forensics in identifying, mitigating, and recovering from sophisticated cyber threats. The key lessons learned from this investigation include the need for comprehensive incident response planning, advanced threat detection tools, and cybersecurity awareness across organizations. Additionally, it demonstrates the challenges of defending against nation-state actors, who possess significant resources and expertise. To mitigate the risk of similar attacks in the future, organizations must adopt a multi-layered security approach, collaborate with industry peers, and stay informed about emerging cyber threats and evolving tactics used by state-sponsored hackers.

# 11.3 Lessons Learned from Failed Forensic Investigations.

In the complex world of cybersecurity, forensic investigations are critical to uncovering the truth behind cyber incidents, but they are not always successful. Several high-profile cases have highlighted the difficulties and challenges that investigators face, resulting in incomplete or failed investigations. These failures often occur due to a variety of factors, including inadequate preparation, poor evidence handling, lack of expertise, or insufficient tools. This case study will explore some of the key lessons learned from failed forensic investigations and discuss how organizations can prevent similar failures in future investigations.

## 1. The Importance of Proper Evidence Handling

One of the most common reasons forensic investigations fail is improper handling of digital evidence. Evidence contamination, accidental deletion, or failure to preserve data can significantly hinder an investigation. A famous example of this occurred in a large-scale data breach at a major healthcare provider, where investigators failed to properly secure the compromised servers and cloud data. As a result, some of the most crucial evidence was either overwritten or lost during the investigation process.

**Lesson Learned**: A core lesson from this incident is the importance of establishing a robust chain of custody early in the investigation. Every step, from the moment evidence is collected to when it is analyzed and presented in court, must be meticulously documented and preserved. Failure to follow proper evidence handling protocols not only jeopardizes the investigation but can also lead to legal challenges when the evidence is presented in court.

**Best Practices:**

- Use write-blockers and data acquisition tools to ensure that evidence is not tampered with during the collection process.
- Implement a digital evidence management system to track and store data securely.
- Ensure that all personnel involved in evidence handling are trained in chain of custody principles.

## 2. Lack of Clear Incident Response Plans

Another common pitfall leading to failed forensic investigations is the absence of a clear and effective incident response plan. In several high-profile cases, organizations lacked an actionable response framework, resulting in slow detection of the breach and disorganized investigative efforts. For example, a retail company fell victim to a major data breach where sensitive customer data was exfiltrated by cybercriminals, but the incident response team failed to quickly identify the attackers' tactics and methods. As a result, the forensic investigation was delayed, and critical data that could have helped trace the attackers was lost.

**Lesson Learned**: A well-defined incident response plan is crucial for the timely and efficient collection of evidence. Without a proactive and organized response, investigators may miss important digital footprints or allow attackers to cover their tracks. Early detection and immediate action are key to minimizing the damage caused by cyber incidents.

## Best Practices:

- Develop an incident response playbook that outlines specific steps for identifying, containing, and investigating cyber incidents.
- Assign roles and responsibilities to ensure clear coordination between forensic experts, IT staff, and legal teams.
- Regularly test and update the plan through simulated cyberattack exercises.

### 3. Insufficient Expertise in Emerging Threats

Another factor that can lead to forensic investigation failures is a lack of expertise in dealing with new and emerging threats. Cyberattacks are constantly evolving, and investigators may not always be prepared to handle novel techniques used by threat actors. For instance, in a case involving an advanced persistent threat (APT) targeting an energy company, the attackers used a highly sophisticated form of malware that was previously unseen in the industry. The forensic team, lacking the experience to identify and dissect this specific type of malware, struggled to fully understand the attack method and the scope of the compromise.

**Lesson Learned**: Forensic investigations can fail when teams are not equipped with the specialized knowledge or cutting-edge tools needed to address emerging threats. Cybersecurity and forensic experts need to continually update their skill sets to stay ahead of evolving tactics used by attackers.

## Best Practices:

- Invest in continuous training and development for forensic professionals, ensuring they are familiar with the latest attack techniques and tools.

- Regularly update forensic tools and software to handle emerging threats like zero-day vulnerabilities or new malware types.
- Collaborate with other cybersecurity experts and organizations to exchange intelligence and best practices for handling new threats.

## 4. Inadequate Tooling and Technology

The failure to utilize the appropriate forensic tools and technology can significantly hinder an investigation. In one case, a large financial institution experienced a cyberattack that resulted in the exfiltration of sensitive financial data. The institution's forensic team used outdated tools, which were unable to fully analyze the data and metadata from the compromised systems. This lack of proper tools led to incomplete forensic findings and missed evidence that could have helped identify the attackers.

**Lesson Learned**: Having the right tools is essential for forensic investigations. Without appropriate forensic software, hardware, and systems for data analysis, investigators may not be able to fully uncover critical evidence. Organizations must continually assess and update their forensic toolsets to ensure they are equipped to handle new forms of digital evidence.

**Best Practices:**

- Regularly evaluate and upgrade forensic tools, especially for advanced data types like cloud storage and mobile devices.
- Ensure that forensic tools are integrated with incident detection systems to enable real-time data collection during an active investigation.
- Test tools in a controlled environment to ensure their functionality and reliability before deployment in real cases.

## 5. Difficulty in Attribution and Global Jurisdictional Challenges

Attribution, or determining the identity of the attacker, is often one of the most difficult tasks in a forensic investigation. In one failed investigation, a global organization was targeted by a cyberattack, and while the forensic team identified significant evidence of malicious activity, they could not conclusively attribute the attack to a specific hacker group or nation-state. The complexity was further compounded by jurisdictional issues, as the attack originated from a foreign country with different legal standards and cooperation protocols.

**Lesson Learned**: Forensic investigations can fail when attribution is complex or when legal barriers prevent investigators from accessing key evidence. In cases where attacks span multiple countries, cooperation with international law enforcement and cybersecurity agencies is essential for gathering the information needed to identify and apprehend the attackers.

**Best Practices:**

- Work closely with international law enforcement and legal experts to ensure that investigations comply with global laws and jurisdictional constraints.
- Use digital forensics frameworks that allow for cross-border evidence sharing and collaboration.
- Build strong relationships with cyber intelligence agencies and global security organizations to facilitate international cooperation in investigations.

## 6. Delays in Detection and Analysis

In some cases, forensic investigations fail because organizations fail to detect breaches in a timely manner. For example, a large online retailer was unaware of a data breach that had been occurring for several months. By the time the attack was detected, much of the stolen data had already been sold on the dark web. The delayed discovery led to a failed investigation, as there was not enough time to collect critical evidence and trace the attackers.

**Lesson Learned**: Delayed detection significantly reduces the effectiveness of a forensic investigation. The longer an attacker remains inside a system, the more difficult it becomes to gather relevant evidence and identify the full scope of the breach.

**Best Practices:**

- Implement continuous monitoring and real-time alerts to detect malicious activities as soon as they occur.
- Use machine learning and AI-powered tools for anomaly detection to identify potential threats early.
- Establish forensic-ready environments, where logs, data, and systems are prepared for investigation as soon as an attack is suspected.

## Conclusion: Key Takeaways

The failure of forensic investigations can be costly, both in terms of financial damage and loss of reputation. However, each failed investigation provides valuable lessons that can help improve future efforts. The key takeaways from these failures include the importance of proper evidence handling, the need for a clear incident response plan, the value of expertise and continuous training, the necessity of using the right tools, and the challenges associated with attribution and jurisdiction. By implementing best practices, maintaining preparedness, and continuously adapting to new challenges, organizations can improve their chances of conducting successful forensic investigations and mitigating the impact of cyberattacks.

# 11.4 Key Takeaways for Practitioners and Investigators.

In the field of forensic cybersecurity, successful investigations hinge on a combination of technical proficiency, legal understanding, and strategic foresight. As the cyber threat landscape evolves, practitioners and investigators must adapt their methods and approaches to stay ahead of increasingly sophisticated cybercriminals. The following key takeaways are essential for any forensic investigator, whether they are just starting out or are seasoned professionals, aiming to strengthen their investigative practices and ensure more effective outcomes.

## 1. Establish Robust Incident Response Protocols

One of the most critical components of a successful forensic investigation is the incident response plan. The earlier an investigation begins, the greater the chances of uncovering critical evidence. Incident response must be swift, organized, and proactive, with clear roles assigned to each team member. Practitioners should ensure that they have a structured plan in place that is tested regularly and updated to reflect new threats.

**Key Takeaway**: Develop, test, and refine an incident response plan to ensure rapid, organized responses to incidents, which maximizes the ability to collect relevant evidence and minimize damage.

## 2. Maintain Strict Evidence Handling Procedures

Forensic investigators must be rigorously trained in the principles of evidence handling to avoid contamination, loss, or mishandling of data. The integrity of the evidence collected, from the moment of discovery to the courtroom, is paramount. A well-documented chain of custody is critical for maintaining the admissibility of evidence in court and ensuring its validity during legal proceedings. Any lapse in this process can significantly compromise an investigation and potentially invalidate the entire case.

**Key Takeaway**: Prioritize evidence integrity by adhering to strict chain of custody protocols and using proper tools and methods to ensure that data remains untampered with and legally viable.

### 3. Invest in Specialized Training and Skill Development

Given the ever-changing nature of cybercrime, forensic investigators must keep their skills and knowledge up to date. Cybercriminals constantly evolve their tactics, leveraging new malware, attack vectors, and encryption methods. Professionals should invest in continuous training and specialize in emerging fields such as cloud forensics, mobile forensics, and AI-powered analysis to maintain a competitive edge.

**Key Takeaway**: Ongoing education and specialization in emerging areas of cybersecurity and digital forensics are essential for investigators to keep pace with new threats and technologies.

### 4. Select and Use the Right Tools for the Job

The tools used for digital forensics can significantly impact the efficiency and effectiveness of an investigation. From data acquisition tools and imaging software to log analysis and reverse engineering tools, it's essential to choose solutions that match the complexity of the case at hand. Relying on outdated or inappropriate tools can lead to incomplete investigations or missed evidence. It is crucial to assess new forensic tools regularly to ensure they meet the evolving challenges posed by cyber threats.

**Key Takeaway**: Regularly evaluate and update forensic tools to ensure they are capable of handling the latest types of cyberattacks, digital evidence formats, and legal requirements.

### 5. Understand Legal and Jurisdictional Complexities

Cybersecurity investigations often involve complex legal and jurisdictional considerations, particularly when the breach spans multiple countries. Data privacy laws, cross-border data transfers, and local regulations can all affect how evidence is collected, analyzed, and presented in court. Investigators must be familiar with the relevant digital evidence regulations and be prepared to collaborate with legal teams to ensure compliance with national and international laws.

**Key Takeaway**: Understand the legal landscape, including jurisdictional issues, when conducting digital forensic investigations to avoid legal pitfalls and ensure evidence is handled in compliance with applicable laws.

## 6. Collaboration and Cross-Agency Coordination Are Crucial

In many cases, successful forensic investigations require collaboration with other entities, such as law enforcement agencies, private sector partners, and cybersecurity vendors. Sharing knowledge, tools, and intelligence can provide valuable insights and help piece together a fuller picture of an attack. Collaborative efforts often lead to quicker identification of perpetrators and better response strategies.

**Key Takeaway**: Foster collaboration with law enforcement and other relevant stakeholders to share intelligence and strengthen investigative capabilities.

## 7. Focus on Prevention Alongside Investigation

While forensic investigators are typically called in after an incident has occurred, prevention should also be a part of the forensic mindset. By analyzing data from previous attacks, investigators can identify patterns, suggest improvements to security protocols, and help organizations better defend against future incidents. A preventive approach can significantly reduce the likelihood of recurring attacks and create a more resilient security posture.

**Key Takeaway**: Adopt a preventative approach by learning from past incidents and contributing to stronger cybersecurity defenses to reduce the likelihood of future breaches.

## 8. Be Prepared for Complex Cases

Forensic investigations often involve dealing with highly complex environments, such as cloud platforms, mobile devices, or multi-layered networks. Investigators should be prepared to face challenges posed by encrypted data, advanced malware, and obfuscated network traffic. Having the ability to think critically and adapt investigative methods for complex cases is crucial. In some cases, this may involve developing new approaches or techniques for data acquisition and analysis.

**Key Takeaway**: Be adaptable and flexible in your approach to complex investigations, especially when dealing with new technologies, encryption, and evolving attack methods.

## 9. Consider the Role of AI and Automation

Emerging technologies like artificial intelligence (AI) and machine learning are beginning to play an increasingly important role in forensic investigations. AI can be leveraged to identify patterns, detect anomalies, and even predict potential future attacks based on past behavior. Investigators who incorporate AI tools into their practice can accelerate their investigation processes, improve accuracy, and make sense of large volumes of digital data that would be otherwise unmanageable.

**Key Takeaway**: Stay ahead of the curve by integrating AI and machine learning into forensic practices to enhance speed, accuracy, and predictive capabilities in investigations.

## 10. Communicate Clearly and Effectively

Effective communication is essential throughout the forensic investigation process, from the initial response to the final report. Investigators need to be able to present complex technical findings in a clear, concise manner to stakeholders, including legal teams, executives, and law enforcement. This includes the ability to explain complex technical concepts to individuals without technical expertise, ensuring that all parties involved can make informed decisions based on the findings.

**Key Takeaway**: Clear communication is essential in forensic investigations to ensure that findings are accessible to all stakeholders and can be effectively used in legal or organizational decision-making.

## 11. Maintain an Ethical Approach

Ethics play a critical role in the field of forensic cybersecurity. Investigators must operate with a high level of integrity, ensuring that evidence is gathered and analyzed in accordance with legal and ethical standards. Additionally, investigators should be aware of potential conflicts of interest, biases, or other ethical dilemmas that may arise during the investigation, ensuring that their work remains objective and impartial.

**Key Takeaway**: Ethical conduct is paramount in maintaining the credibility and trustworthiness of forensic investigations. Always operate with integrity and impartiality, adhering to legal and ethical standards.

## Conclusion: Preparing for Future Challenges

Forensic investigators play a crucial role in defending against cybercrime, identifying perpetrators, and ensuring justice. By taking these key takeaways into account, forensic professionals can enhance their investigative practices and overcome common challenges that may arise in complex cases. As the cyber threat landscape continues to evolve, staying informed, adaptable, and equipped with the right tools will be essential for tackling the digital threats of tomorrow.

# 12. Building a Robust Cybersecurity and Forensics Ecosystem

Creating an effective cybersecurity and forensics ecosystem is essential for defending against and responding to cyber threats. This chapter explores how organizations can develop a cohesive strategy that integrates both proactive cybersecurity measures and reactive forensic capabilities. It covers the importance of collaboration between IT security teams, forensic investigators, legal departments, and external partners to create a unified defense against cybercrime. The chapter also delves into best practices for continuous monitoring, threat intelligence sharing, and building resilient infrastructures. By establishing a strong ecosystem, organizations can better detect, respond to, and recover from cyber incidents while minimizing future risks.

## 12.1 Creating a Unified Approach to Cybersecurity and Forensics.

In today's rapidly evolving digital landscape, cybersecurity and digital forensics are two closely intertwined fields that play complementary roles in protecting organizations and responding to cyber incidents. However, while these disciplines have traditionally operated as separate entities, their integration is becoming increasingly vital to effectively prevent, detect, and respond to cyberattacks. A unified approach to cybersecurity and forensics not only strengthens an organization's overall defense posture but also streamlines the investigative process, ensuring that all aspects of a breach are covered—from prevention to post-incident analysis.

Creating a unified approach requires strategic alignment of policies, tools, and expertise across the two domains. It also involves fostering collaboration between cybersecurity professionals, forensic experts, legal teams, and organizational leadership. This holistic approach ensures that incidents are swiftly detected, properly investigated, and mitigated, while also safeguarding the integrity of the data and evidence for future legal proceedings. Below are the key steps involved in creating a successful unified approach to cybersecurity and forensics:

### 1. Integrating Cybersecurity and Forensics Teams

Historically, cybersecurity and forensics teams have operated in silos, with the cybersecurity team focusing on threat prevention and defense, while the forensics team is called upon after a breach occurs. To create a unified approach, it is essential to encourage greater collaboration between these teams before, during, and after incidents.

**Pre-Incident Collaboration**: Cybersecurity professionals should involve forensic experts when designing systems and implementing security measures. By considering how evidence might be collected and preserved during potential incidents, security measures can be better aligned with forensic requirements.

**During an Incident**: When a cyberattack occurs, having both teams collaborate from the outset can improve the response. The cybersecurity team can implement containment measures while the forensics team begins gathering critical evidence, ensuring that digital footprints are preserved, and analysis can begin quickly.

**Post-Incident Analysis**: After a breach is contained, a unified team can analyze the collected data and evidence to determine the root cause of the attack, assess its scope, and identify the attackers. Collaborative efforts ensure that the cybersecurity team's findings are closely tied to the forensic investigation and that any lessons learned are fed back into preventive strategies.

**Key Takeaway**: Encourage cross-disciplinary collaboration between cybersecurity and forensics teams to ensure effective and cohesive responses to incidents and improve overall organizational security.

## 2. Establishing Clear Communication Channels

Clear and consistent communication between cybersecurity and forensic experts is critical in a unified approach. During an active investigation, maintaining open lines of communication ensures that critical information flows freely between team members, enabling swift decision-making. Additionally, fostering effective communication with other stakeholders—such as management, legal teams, and external agencies—is essential for providing updates and ensuring that all parties are aligned on actions and objectives.

For example, cybersecurity professionals may need to provide updates on the status of containment and remediation efforts, while forensic teams may need to communicate their progress in gathering and analyzing evidence. Legal teams should also be kept in the loop to ensure that any evidence handling or collection aligns with applicable laws and regulations.

**Key Takeaway**: Establish clear communication protocols across all involved teams to ensure that information is shared efficiently, enabling swift responses and coordinated actions during an investigation.

## 3. Standardizing Procedures and Tools Across Both Domains

A unified approach to cybersecurity and forensics requires the standardization of procedures and tools used by both teams. While cybersecurity professionals use a variety of tools for threat detection and mitigation, and forensic investigators rely on specialized tools for evidence collection and analysis, integrating these toolsets can lead to a more seamless investigation.

**Unified Procedures**: Develop standardized protocols for incident detection, evidence collection, analysis, and reporting. These protocols should define how data is captured, who is responsible for each phase of the process, and how evidence is preserved to ensure it is admissible in court. These shared procedures enable both teams to work in harmony during an investigation and ensure that they follow best practices.

**Integrated Tools**: Utilize tools that are capable of supporting both cybersecurity and forensic objectives. For example, log analysis tools that monitor system behavior can be used to detect anomalies (cybersecurity) and also serve as valuable sources of evidence during a forensic investigation. Ensuring that tools are compatible across both domains reduces friction and allows teams to work with the same data throughout the investigation.

**Key Takeaway**: Standardize procedures and tools across both cybersecurity and forensic teams to enable smoother collaboration and ensure consistency in the response and investigation processes.

## 4. Developing a Comprehensive Threat Intelligence Strategy

A unified approach to cybersecurity and forensics requires a comprehensive threat intelligence strategy that informs both proactive defense and reactive investigation. By sharing threat intelligence across both teams, organizations can improve their ability to anticipate cyberattacks and respond to breaches effectively.

**Proactive Defense**: Cybersecurity teams can leverage threat intelligence to improve preventive measures, detect vulnerabilities, and strengthen defenses against emerging threats. This can include intelligence on the latest attack vectors, malware variants, and known adversaries.

**Forensic Insights**: Forensic experts can analyze previous incidents, using threat intelligence data to better understand the attacker's methods, tools, and motives. This information helps forensic investigators trace attackers' movements across digital systems, identify targets, and uncover patterns that may link different incidents together.

**Key Takeaway**: Develop a robust threat intelligence framework that incorporates data from both cybersecurity and forensics teams, creating a proactive defense while also informing investigative efforts.

### 5. Implementing Forensic-Ready Security Architecture

A unified cybersecurity-forensics approach requires building a forensic-ready security architecture. This means embedding forensic capabilities into the organization's IT infrastructure from the outset. By doing so, organizations can ensure that all critical data and activities are continuously captured in a way that can support forensic investigations, should an attack occur.

**Data Collection**: Implement systems that continuously log relevant data, such as network traffic, user activity, and system changes. This data is invaluable for forensic investigators when analyzing an incident.

**Data Storage and Preservation**: Ensure that collected data is securely stored and easily accessible for future forensic investigations. It should be archived in a way that allows it to be retrieved without compromising its integrity.

**Security Measures**: Design security architecture that prevents tampering with evidence and allows for the identification of anomalies in real-time. For example, employing write-blockers and other data-preservation technologies during evidence collection can prevent any data modification.

**Key Takeaway**: Build a forensic-ready security architecture that integrates data collection, storage, and preservation into everyday operations, ensuring that data is available for analysis and secure from tampering.

### 6. Continuous Training and Cross-Disciplinary Education

A unified approach is not just about processes and tools—it also involves people. Professionals in both cybersecurity and forensics should be trained to understand each other's roles and responsibilities and to be aware of how their work impacts the other team's goals. Cross-disciplinary education can help build a shared understanding of the challenges faced by both teams and encourage collaboration.

For example, cybersecurity professionals should be familiar with forensic evidence handling, while forensic experts should understand the importance of real-time data protection and attack mitigation in the context of ongoing threats. Regular joint training exercises can simulate real-world attacks, allowing both teams to practice responding together in a coordinated and efficient manner.

**Key Takeaway**: Invest in cross-disciplinary training to foster mutual understanding and cooperation between cybersecurity and forensic professionals, strengthening the overall response and investigative capabilities of the organization.

### 7. Building a Cybersecurity and Forensics Culture

Finally, creating a unified approach to cybersecurity and forensics requires a shift in organizational culture. Leadership should encourage collaboration between departments, break down silos, and emphasize the importance of both proactive and reactive security measures. This cultural shift can improve overall security awareness and ensure that both cybersecurity and forensic teams understand the importance of their roles in protecting the organization.

**Key Takeaway**: Foster a security-first culture in which cybersecurity and forensics teams work collaboratively, aligned with the organization's overall cybersecurity strategy and goals.

### Conclusion: Achieving Resilience Through Integration

A unified approach to cybersecurity and forensics is essential in today's complex threat environment. By integrating teams, standardizing tools and procedures, sharing threat intelligence, and preparing the infrastructure to be forensic-ready, organizations can improve their ability to detect, investigate, and respond to cyber incidents efficiently. This integration not only strengthens the organization's overall security posture but also enhances its ability to mitigate risk, reduce the impact of incidents, and support post-incident legal actions. Through collaboration, shared knowledge, and continuous improvement, a unified approach ensures that both cybersecurity and forensics work in tandem to protect the organization from an ever-growing array of digital threats.

## 12.2 Training and Development for Forensic Teams.

In the rapidly evolving world of cyber threats and digital forensics, continuous training and development for forensic teams are not only essential but mandatory for ensuring effectiveness and staying ahead of increasingly sophisticated cyberattacks. As the complexity of cybercrimes grows, forensic experts must be equipped with both the technical skills and the legal knowledge to tackle these challenges efficiently. Cybercriminals continuously innovate with new tactics, making it crucial for forensic professionals to adapt by learning about new tools, techniques, and emerging technologies.

A well-rounded training and development program ensures that forensic teams are not only prepared for current threats but are also future-proofed against the evolving nature of cybercrime. Below are the key components of an effective training and development strategy for forensic teams.

### 1. Core Competencies in Digital Forensics

At the foundation of any forensic training program is the development of core competencies in digital forensics. These skills are critical for professionals working in this field and must be honed continuously to keep pace with new technological advances. Core competencies include:

**Data Acquisition**: The process of securely collecting digital evidence from computers, networks, mobile devices, cloud environments, and other sources. Training should focus on mastering both physical and logical acquisition techniques and ensuring the integrity of the data collected.

**Evidence Analysis**: Forensic experts must be adept at analyzing various forms of digital evidence, such as file systems, logs, memory, and network traffic. Specialized tools and techniques for analyzing encrypted data, hidden files, and malicious software are also important components of this skillset.

**Data Preservation and Chain of Custody**: Preserving the integrity of evidence is crucial for legal proceedings. Training must emphasize best practices for maintaining the chain of custody and ensuring that evidence is protected from tampering or loss.

**Key Takeaway**: Forensic teams must undergo foundational training in data acquisition, evidence analysis, and preservation to ensure that they can effectively collect, analyze, and protect digital evidence throughout the investigation.

## 2. Legal and Ethical Training

Digital forensics is not only a technical field but also one that requires deep understanding of legal frameworks and ethical standards. Forensic teams must be trained to operate within the boundaries of the law, ensuring that all evidence handling procedures are compliant with local, national, and international regulations.

**Evidence Admissibility**: Forensic experts should understand the requirements for evidence to be admissible in court, including how to handle, document, and present evidence to ensure it meets legal standards.

**Privacy and Compliance Laws**: Understanding privacy laws like GDPR (General Data Protection Regulation), HIPAA (Health Insurance Portability and Accountability Act), and other data protection regulations is essential. Forensic professionals must ensure that their actions respect privacy rights while gathering and analyzing evidence.

**Ethical Dilemmas**: Forensic investigators often face ethical challenges, such as potential conflicts of interest or handling sensitive data. Training programs should emphasize ethical decision-making and adherence to professional codes of conduct, ensuring that forensic teams always act with integrity.

**Key Takeaway**: Legal and ethical training is critical for forensic professionals to ensure they collect, analyze, and handle evidence in compliance with laws and regulations while maintaining the highest standards of integrity.

## 3. Specialized Training in Emerging Technologies

As the digital landscape evolves, so do the tools and technologies used by cybercriminals. A critical aspect of forensic team development is equipping professionals with the latest knowledge and skills regarding emerging technologies. These include:

**Cloud Forensics**: As more organizations migrate to the cloud, forensic experts must be familiar with the unique challenges of investigating cloud environments, including data storage, jurisdictional issues, and multi-tenancy concerns. Training should include the use of cloud forensics tools, and the protocols required to capture and preserve cloud-based evidence.

**Mobile Device Forensics**: The rise of mobile devices as primary computing platforms means that forensic teams must have specialized training to extract and analyze data from smartphones, tablets, and other mobile devices. Training should cover how to handle locked devices, recover deleted data, and investigate mobile applications.

**Internet of Things (IoT) Forensics**: As IoT devices proliferate, these devices can become critical sources of evidence. Forensic teams need to understand how to extract data from IoT devices, which may involve dealing with proprietary technologies and non-standard operating systems.

**Artificial Intelligence and Machine Learning in Cybersecurity**: As AI and machine learning become increasingly prevalent in both cyberattacks and cybersecurity tools, forensic teams need to understand how these technologies impact the threat landscape and how they can be leveraged in investigations to detect anomalies and predict threats.

**Key Takeaway**: Forensic teams must undergo specialized training in emerging technologies like cloud forensics, mobile device forensics, IoT forensics, and AI to remain equipped to handle modern threats and tools used by cybercriminals.

### 4. Hands-On Training and Simulation Exercises

One of the most effective ways to ensure that forensic professionals are ready for real-world incidents is through hands-on training and simulation exercises. These training exercises should replicate actual cyberattack scenarios and require forensic teams to work through the incident response and investigation process.

**Incident Response Drills**: Regular simulation of cyberattacks, such as ransomware incidents, insider threats, or data breaches, allows forensic teams to practice their response in a controlled environment. These exercises allow participants to refine their skills, identify weaknesses in their procedures, and improve their coordination with other teams (e.g., cybersecurity, legal, and management).

**Capture the Flag (CTF) Challenges**: Many organizations use CTF exercises that challenge forensic teams to solve a variety of digital forensic puzzles, such as analyzing data for clues, uncovering hidden files, or breaking passwords. These exercises help improve problem-solving skills and the ability to think critically under pressure.

**Red Team and Blue Team Exercises**: These exercises involve ethical hackers (Red Team) attempting to breach systems while forensic investigators (Blue Team) work to defend and investigate the breaches. This helps develop teamwork and understanding between offensive and defensive cybersecurity practices.

**Key Takeaway**: Hands-on training through real-world simulations, drills, and exercises is essential for forensic teams to hone their skills and stay prepared for actual incidents.

## 5. Certifications and Continuing Education

To ensure that forensic professionals remain at the cutting edge of their field, they should be encouraged to pursue certifications and engage in continuous education. Certifications not only validate expertise but also expose professionals to the latest developments in technology and best practices.

**Certifications**: Well-recognized certifications such as Certified Computer Examiner (CCE), Certified Forensic Computer Examiner (CFCE), EnCase Certified Examiner (EnCE), and Certified Information Systems Security Professional (CISSP) are critical for demonstrating competence in forensic practices and cybersecurity. These certifications often require candidates to pass rigorous exams and participate in continuing education.

**Conferences and Workshops**: Forensic professionals should attend industry conferences, workshops, and seminars to stay current on the latest trends in cyber threats, forensic techniques, and legal requirements. Networking with other professionals and learning from experts in the field is an essential part of professional development.

**Online Courses and Webinars**: With the availability of online learning platforms, forensic professionals can easily access courses on topics such as digital forensics, incident response, malware analysis, and legal issues. These platforms allow individuals to stay up to date on the latest tools and techniques without having to take time off from their regular duties.

**Key Takeaway**: Certifications, conferences, and continuing education are critical for ensuring that forensic teams are well-equipped with the latest skills, knowledge, and best practices.

## 6. Building a Culture of Continuous Improvement

Training and development should be an ongoing process. In addition to initial training, forensic teams must be encouraged to adopt a mindset of continuous learning and improvement. This involves seeking feedback after each investigation, reviewing successes and failures, and learning from mistakes to refine future processes.

**Post-Incident Reviews**: After an investigation or incident, forensic teams should conduct thorough reviews to identify areas for improvement. This should include evaluating the effectiveness of the tools and methods used, identifying any gaps in knowledge, and discussing what could be done differently in the future.

**Knowledge Sharing**: Foster a culture where forensic professionals regularly share their knowledge and experiences with their peers. This can be done through internal meetings, documentation of best practices, and collaboration on challenging cases.

**Key Takeaway**: A culture of continuous improvement encourages forensic professionals to regularly assess and improve their skills, tools, and techniques to stay effective in an ever-changing environment.

### Conclusion: The Importance of a Holistic Approach

Training and development for forensic teams are foundational to their ability to detect, investigate, and respond to cyberattacks effectively. As cyber threats continue to evolve, ongoing education, specialized knowledge, hands-on practice, and certifications become increasingly important. By adopting a comprehensive training and development strategy, organizations can ensure that their forensic teams are well-equipped to handle the challenges of modern cybersecurity investigations and continue to protect against and mitigate the impacts of cybercrime.

# 12.3 Leveraging Technology to Build Resilience.

In the age of sophisticated cyber threats and constantly evolving digital environments, building resilience within forensic teams and cybersecurity infrastructures is essential. Leveraging advanced technology to strengthen the resilience of organizations not only enhances their ability to respond to cyber incidents but also ensures they are better equipped to prevent, detect, and recover from attacks. The integration of cutting-edge tools, platforms, and strategies plays a pivotal role in enhancing the effectiveness of forensic investigations and cybersecurity measures. This section explores how leveraging technology can build resilience across both forensic and cybersecurity operations.

### 1. Automation and Artificial Intelligence for Enhanced Detection

One of the most powerful ways to enhance resilience is through the integration of automation and artificial intelligence (AI) into cybersecurity and forensic workflows. AI and machine learning (ML) can significantly improve the ability to detect threats faster, reduce human error, and increase the speed of investigations. These technologies can analyze vast amounts of data, identify anomalous patterns, and flag potential security incidents or breaches in real time.

**Threat Detection and Response**: Automated systems powered by AI and machine learning can quickly analyze network traffic, system logs, and user behavior to identify early signs of cyberattacks. These systems can then trigger alerts and, in some cases, take immediate action (such as blocking malicious IP addresses or isolating infected systems) to contain potential breaches. This immediate response helps limit the damage caused by cybercriminals and enables forensic teams to focus their efforts on the most critical areas.

**Automated Forensic Investigations**: AI-driven tools can automate the process of evidence collection, sorting, and initial analysis. By using machine learning models trained on vast datasets of known attack patterns and cybercrime techniques, these tools can help forensic experts quickly assess and prioritize evidence, reducing the time it takes to start an investigation.

**Predictive Capabilities**: With the help of AI and machine learning, organizations can predict potential threats based on historical data and threat intelligence. Forensic teams can then take proactive steps to investigate vulnerabilities before they are exploited, strengthening the overall resilience of the organization.

**Key Takeaway**: The use of automation and AI in threat detection and forensic investigations enables faster, more accurate responses to cyber incidents, enhancing an organization's ability to recover and learn from attacks.

## 2. Advanced Data Analytics and Big Data Processing

Data is at the heart of cybersecurity and forensic investigations, and advanced analytics plays a critical role in extracting valuable insights from large volumes of data. Big data technologies, such as Hadoop and cloud-based analytics platforms, enable forensic teams to process and analyze massive amounts of data in a fraction of the time it would take manually.

**Data Correlation**: Forensic investigations often involve sifting through vast quantities of logs, network traffic, and endpoint data to uncover critical evidence. By leveraging big data tools and analytics platforms, forensic professionals can correlate data from various sources more efficiently, identifying patterns and anomalies that might otherwise go unnoticed.

**Real-Time Monitoring and Analysis**: With real-time data analysis capabilities, organizations can continuously monitor their networks and systems for signs of unusual activity. Big data platforms allow forensic teams to analyze streams of data as they come in, enabling faster detection of incidents and reducing the window of opportunity for attackers.

**Enhanced Investigation Efficiency**: By automating the process of analyzing and correlating large data sets, organizations can streamline the investigation process. This reduces manual errors and allows forensic experts to focus on interpreting results rather than sorting through raw data.

**Key Takeaway**: Leveraging advanced data analytics and big data technologies enables forensic teams to analyze large datasets efficiently, identify threats faster, and improve investigative outcomes.

### 3. Cloud-Based Forensics and Distributed Storage Solutions

As businesses increasingly rely on cloud infrastructure, the need for cloud-based forensic tools and distributed storage solutions has grown significantly. Cloud forensics refers to the process of investigating digital evidence hosted in cloud environments, where traditional on-premises forensics may be insufficient or impractical.

**Cloud Storage for Scalability**: Cloud environments offer scalability and flexibility, allowing organizations to store vast amounts of forensic data without the constraints of physical infrastructure. In the event of a cyber incident, cloud-based storage solutions enable forensic teams to access data from multiple locations and devices, streamlining the collection and analysis of evidence.

**Centralized Evidence Repository**: Cloud solutions also enable the creation of centralized evidence repositories where forensic teams can securely store and share evidence collected during investigations. These centralized platforms ensure that data is always available for analysis and can be easily accessed by different stakeholders involved in an investigation, whether they are working remotely or from different geographical locations.

**Cross-Border and Cross-Platform Access**: Many cybercrimes span multiple jurisdictions, making it essential to have access to cloud-based tools that support cross-border investigations. Cloud forensic tools allow for evidence collection from various cloud providers and platforms, enabling forensic teams to maintain continuity during investigations that cross international boundaries.

**Security and Encryption**: Cloud-based forensic tools are also designed with advanced security features, including end-to-end encryption, which ensures that evidence remains protected during the collection, storage, and analysis phases. This reduces the risk of tampering or unauthorized access, further increasing the integrity of digital evidence.

**Key Takeaway**: Cloud-based forensic tools and distributed storage solutions provide scalability, flexibility, and security, enabling forensic teams to manage data and evidence more effectively while adapting to modern cloud infrastructures.

## 4. Blockchain for Evidence Integrity and Transparency

Blockchain technology, known for its role in cryptocurrencies, can also play a significant role in enhancing resilience in digital forensics by providing transparent, immutable records of digital evidence. Blockchain's decentralized and tamper-resistant nature makes it an ideal solution for ensuring the integrity of digital evidence throughout the forensic process.

**Immutable Evidence Logging**: By storing evidence-related information (such as timestamps, hash values, and metadata) on a blockchain, forensic teams can create a secure, tamper-proof record of the evidence collection and handling process. This ensures that the integrity of the evidence is maintained and can be verified at any point in the investigation.

**Transparency in the Chain of Custody**: Blockchain technology can streamline the management of the chain of custody by providing a transparent and auditable log of all actions taken on evidence, including who accessed it, when, and for what purpose. This helps ensure that all forensic actions are fully documented and can be verified in court.

**Collaboration Across Jurisdictions**: Blockchain's decentralized nature facilitates collaboration among international forensic teams, ensuring that evidence handling is transparent and verifiable across borders. This is particularly beneficial in cross-border investigations involving multiple jurisdictions with varying legal requirements.

**Key Takeaway**: Blockchain technology enhances the integrity and transparency of the evidence handling process, ensuring that forensic evidence is secure, verifiable, and tamper-resistant.

## 5. Incident Response Automation and Orchestration

One of the most effective ways to increase resilience is through the automation and orchestration of incident response processes. These tools help forensic teams respond more quickly to security incidents by automating routine tasks and coordinating the response across different teams and systems.

**Automated Incident Detection and Prioritization**: Incident response platforms can automatically detect security incidents and prioritize them based on severity. By automating initial triage, forensic teams can focus their efforts on the most critical incidents, reducing response time and minimizing the impact of a breach.

**Coordinating Multi-Stage Response**: Incident response often involves multiple stages, including containment, eradication, and recovery. Automated orchestration tools ensure that forensic teams follow predefined workflows and procedures during each phase of the response, improving efficiency and consistency.

**Post-Incident Reporting and Analysis**: Incident response automation platforms can also generate detailed reports after an incident, documenting all actions taken and their outcomes. These reports can be used for forensic investigations, legal proceedings, and post-incident reviews.

**Key Takeaway**: Incident response automation enhances resilience by streamlining workflows, enabling faster response times, and ensuring that forensic teams can address security incidents effectively.

### Conclusion: Building Resilience Through Technology

Leveraging technology is a crucial strategy for building resilience in both forensic and cybersecurity teams. Automation, AI, big data analytics, cloud forensics, blockchain, and incident response orchestration are just a few of the tools that enhance the speed, accuracy, and effectiveness of cyber investigations. By adopting these technologies, organizations can significantly improve their ability to detect, respond to, and recover from cyberattacks, thereby ensuring greater protection of digital assets, data integrity, and overall security posture. As the digital landscape continues to evolve, the ability to integrate advanced technologies will be the key to building lasting resilience in the face of growing cyber threats.

# 12.4 Best Practices for Proactive Threat Mitigation.

In the rapidly evolving world of cybersecurity, proactive threat mitigation is essential to safeguard organizational assets, maintain data integrity, and ensure continuity of operations. Reactive approaches, while necessary, are often too late to prevent significant damage from cyberattacks. By adopting proactive measures, organizations can detect potential threats before they cause harm, address vulnerabilities, and strengthen their defenses. This section outlines best practices for proactive threat mitigation, providing a roadmap for strengthening cybersecurity measures and ensuring a robust defense against potential cyber threats.

## 1. Continuous Risk Assessment and Vulnerability Management

One of the cornerstones of proactive threat mitigation is regular risk assessments and vulnerability management. Identifying vulnerabilities before they are exploited by attackers is essential for maintaining security resilience.

**Regular Risk Assessments**: Organizations should continuously assess potential risks by evaluating their digital assets, networks, and systems. This involves identifying critical assets, understanding the threat landscape, and evaluating the likelihood and potential impact of various threats. Regular risk assessments help prioritize security measures based on the highest-risk areas.

**Vulnerability Scanning and Patching**: Conducting routine vulnerability scans and promptly addressing identified weaknesses is crucial. Cybercriminals often exploit unpatched software vulnerabilities to gain access to systems, so regular patching of operating systems, applications, and network devices is essential for closing potential attack vectors.

**Penetration Testing**: Regular penetration testing (ethical hacking) allows organizations to identify vulnerabilities from an attacker's perspective. Simulated cyberattacks can reveal exploitable weaknesses in systems and processes that might otherwise be overlooked.

**Key Takeaway**: Regular risk assessments and vulnerability management allow organizations to identify and address security weaknesses before attackers can exploit them, providing an ongoing defense mechanism against potential threats.

## 2. Comprehensive Threat Intelligence and Monitoring

Effective threat intelligence provides organizations with insights into emerging threats, attack techniques, and vulnerabilities. A proactive approach to threat intelligence and continuous monitoring is essential to stay ahead of cybercriminals.

**Threat Intelligence Sharing**: Participating in threat intelligence sharing networks (e.g., Information Sharing and Analysis Centers or ISACs) enables organizations to learn about emerging threats from others in their industry. This collaboration helps identify common attack vectors and provides early warnings about global and regional threats.

**Real-Time Threat Monitoring**: Leveraging real-time monitoring tools, such as Security Information and Event Management (SIEM) systems, allows organizations to detect suspicious activities and indicators of compromise (IOCs) in real-time. Proactive monitoring enables the early detection of potential threats, such as abnormal user behavior, network traffic anomalies, or unauthorized access attempts.

**Threat Hunting**: Proactive threat hunting involves actively searching for signs of malicious activity within an organization's network and systems, even before a specific threat is identified. By continuously seeking out hidden threats, organizations can uncover sophisticated attacks that might evade traditional detection methods.

**Key Takeaway**: A proactive approach to threat intelligence sharing and real-time monitoring empowers organizations to detect emerging threats early, enabling them to take preventive action before an attack occurs.

### 3. Defense in Depth: Multi-Layered Security Architecture

The principle of "defense in depth" emphasizes using multiple layers of security controls to protect systems and data. A multi-layered security approach ensures that even if one layer is breached, other defenses are still in place to prevent or mitigate the attack.

**Network Segmentation**: Segmenting networks into isolated zones can prevent the lateral movement of attackers within an organization's infrastructure. If one segment is compromised, the attacker is limited in their ability to access other critical systems. Network segmentation also helps prioritize security efforts by isolating sensitive data and high-value assets.

**Firewalls and Intrusion Prevention Systems (IPS):** Firewalls and IPS devices are fundamental to blocking unauthorized access and detecting malicious activities. Firewalls should be configured to filter traffic based on the least-privilege principle, only allowing necessary traffic to pass through. Similarly, IPS systems should be used to detect and block suspicious activities in real-time.

**End-Point Protection**: Implementing endpoint security tools such as antivirus software, anti-malware programs, and device encryption is essential for safeguarding all endpoints (computers, smartphones, IoT devices). Given that many cyberattacks begin with endpoint compromise, ensuring these devices are secured is a key layer in defense-in-depth strategies.

**Zero Trust Security Model**: The Zero Trust model operates on the principle of "never trust, always verify." In this model, access to systems is granted based on strict identity and authentication checks, even for users within the internal network. This reduces the risk of insider threats and limits the damage that can be caused by a compromised account.

**Key Takeaway**: Implementing a defense-in-depth strategy with multi-layered security controls significantly enhances an organization's resilience, limiting the chances of a successful cyberattack by providing several layers of defense.

## 4. Employee Education and Awareness Training

One of the most common causes of cyber incidents is human error. Employees, being the first line of defense, play a vital role in mitigating threats. Proactively training staff on cybersecurity best practices, potential risks, and how to recognize threats helps reduce the likelihood of successful attacks, such as phishing or social engineering.

**Phishing Awareness Training**: Phishing remains one of the most prevalent attack methods. Regular training on how to recognize phishing emails, malicious attachments, and deceptive links is crucial. Employees should be taught to scrutinize emails from unfamiliar sources and to avoid clicking on links or downloading attachments without verifying the sender.

**Social Engineering Awareness**: Social engineering attacks exploit human psychology rather than technical vulnerabilities. Educating employees about tactics such as pretexting, baiting, and tailgating helps them recognize manipulative behaviors and avoid inadvertently assisting attackers.

**Simulated Cyberattack Drills**: Conducting mock cyberattacks or simulated phishing exercises allows organizations to test their employees' response to security threats.

These exercises help reinforce lessons learned in training and offer insights into where additional education may be needed.

**Clear Reporting Procedures**: Employees should be trained to report any suspicious activity immediately. Having a well-defined incident response plan that employees can follow ensures that security teams are alerted to potential threats quickly, minimizing the impact of a breach.

**Key Takeaway**: Employee education and awareness training are essential to reduce human errors and empower staff to recognize and respond to potential threats, strengthening an organization's security posture.

### 5. Incident Response Planning and Testing

Proactive threat mitigation includes preparing for incidents before they happen. By developing and testing incident response plans (IRPs), organizations can respond quickly and effectively to cybersecurity breaches, minimizing damage and downtime.

**Creating and Documenting an IRP**: An incident response plan outlines the steps to be taken when a cyberattack occurs. This plan should include identifying key personnel, defining roles and responsibilities, and detailing communication procedures. Having a pre-established plan helps ensure that the response is swift and organized, even in high-stress situations.

**Conducting Tabletop Exercises**: Regularly testing the IRP through tabletop exercises simulates real-world cyberattack scenarios. These exercises help identify gaps in the plan, improve coordination among team members, and ensure everyone knows their responsibilities during a security incident.

**Post-Incident Analysis**: After an attack or breach, conducting a post-mortem analysis to review the incident response and identify areas for improvement is essential. This analysis should include lessons learned and recommendations for improving security measures to prevent future attacks.

**Integrating Threat Intelligence into IRP**: Incorporating up-to-date threat intelligence into the incident response process ensures that response teams are prepared for the latest attack methods and techniques. Threat intelligence feeds can help identify emerging threats and inform how incidents should be handled.

**Key Takeaway**: Incident response planning ensures organizations are ready to act swiftly and effectively in the event of a cyberattack, minimizing impact and helping to prevent future incidents through continuous improvement.

## Conclusion: Proactive Threat Mitigation as a Strategic Imperative

Proactive threat mitigation is no longer optional in today's threat landscape—it is a strategic imperative for organizations of all sizes and industries. By continually assessing risks, implementing defense-in-depth strategies, educating employees, and preparing for incidents before they happen, organizations can significantly reduce the risk of successful cyberattacks and minimize potential damage. Building a proactive cybersecurity culture requires commitment, but the payoff is substantial: enhanced security, reduced breach frequency, and a more resilient organization in the face of evolving cyber threats.

# 13. Future Trends and Emerging Threats

As technology continues to evolve, so do the tactics of cybercriminals, making it essential to stay ahead of emerging threats. This chapter explores the future landscape of forensic cybersecurity, focusing on the impact of cutting-edge technologies like quantum computing, the rise of artificial intelligence in cyberattacks, and the increasing vulnerabilities in emerging fields such as the metaverse and IoT. It also addresses the growing concerns around cyber warfare and nation-state actors. By examining these trends, readers will gain a forward-looking perspective on the challenges and opportunities facing cybersecurity professionals, helping them prepare for the next generation of cyber threats and the future of digital forensics.

## 13.1 Quantum Computing and Its Impact on Cyber Forensics.

Quantum computing is poised to revolutionize the world of computing by enabling calculations that are exponentially faster than classical computers. While quantum technology promises numerous advancements, it also introduces significant challenges, particularly in the realm of cybersecurity and digital forensics. The advent of quantum computing could fundamentally alter the landscape of cryptography, data security, and forensic investigations. In this chapter, we explore the potential impact of quantum computing on cyber forensics, focusing on both the opportunities and risks it presents.

### 1. The Fundamentals of Quantum Computing

To understand the impact of quantum computing on cyber forensics, it is essential to first grasp the basics of quantum mechanics and how quantum computers work. Unlike classical computers that process information as binary data (0s and 1s), quantum computers utilize quantum bits, or qubits, which can exist in multiple states simultaneously due to quantum superposition. This allows quantum computers to process massive amounts of data in parallel, enabling them to solve complex problems much faster than traditional computers.

Quantum computers also leverage entanglement, a phenomenon where the state of one qubit is directly related to another, regardless of the distance between them. This characteristic enables quantum computers to perform certain types of calculations much more efficiently than classical systems, which will have profound implications for cryptography, data analysis, and forensic investigations.

## 2. The Impact on Cryptography and Digital Evidence Protection

Quantum computing poses a direct threat to traditional encryption methods used to protect digital data. Currently, public-key cryptography (e.g., RSA and ECC) forms the backbone of internet security, securing communications, financial transactions, and stored data. These systems rely on the computational difficulty of factoring large numbers or solving discrete logarithm problems, which classical computers find challenging. However, quantum computers could potentially break these encryption schemes in a matter of seconds using algorithms like Shor's algorithm, which can efficiently factor large integers.

For cyber forensics, this presents a major challenge. Many forensic investigations rely on the ability to access encrypted data, either from compromised systems or cloud services, to collect evidence. Quantum computing could render current cryptographic systems obsolete, allowing attackers to decrypt data with ease, and potentially hindering the ability of forensic experts to secure and analyze evidence. As quantum computing advances, forensic professionals may be required to find new ways to secure and access data while ensuring its integrity for legal and investigative purposes.

**Post-Quantum Cryptography**: In response to this threat, the field of post-quantum cryptography (PQC) has emerged. PQC focuses on developing encryption algorithms that are resistant to quantum attacks. Cyber forensics experts will need to familiarize themselves with these new encryption methods and their potential impact on data collection, preservation, and analysis. Transitioning to quantum-resistant encryption standards will be vital for securing digital evidence in a quantum-enabled future.

## 3. The Implications for Forensic Investigations and Evidence Collection

Quantum computing's influence on digital forensics extends beyond cryptography. It also raises questions about the methods used to collect, preserve, and analyze evidence. As quantum computing evolves, it could affect the underlying algorithms used for data analysis and pattern recognition in forensic investigations.

**Data Decryption and Retrieval**: Investigators often rely on computationally intensive techniques to decrypt and retrieve data during an investigation. As quantum computers become more powerful, they could quickly bypass these existing encryption methods, rendering some forensic tools ineffective. For example, evidence that was previously considered protected could be decrypted far more quickly than with current decryption tools. This may lead to the need for new forensic tools designed to handle the quantum environment and maintain data integrity.

**Quantum-Enabled Forensic Tools**: The development of quantum-enabled forensic tools could enhance the ability to process large datasets. For instance, quantum computing's parallel processing capabilities could accelerate pattern recognition, anomaly detection, and statistical analysis in digital forensics. These tools could improve investigators' abilities to search vast amounts of digital evidence, especially in cases involving large-scale data breaches or cybercrimes that generate immense volumes of data.

**Quantum Key Distribution (QKD) for Secure Evidence Handling**: Quantum mechanics also offers a promising solution to data security through Quantum Key Distribution (QKD). QKD allows the secure exchange of cryptographic keys, making it nearly impossible for third parties to intercept or tamper with the transmission. This technology could be used to enhance the security of digital evidence in transit, ensuring that forensic evidence remains unaltered and maintaining its integrity for legal proceedings.

## 4. Quantum Computing's Role in Digital Forensic Data Analysis

Quantum computing also presents the potential for transforming how forensic experts analyze digital evidence. Traditional forensic data analysis often relies on pattern recognition algorithms that can process large datasets in search of anomalies, such as fraudulent transactions, malware footprints, or unauthorized access logs. Quantum computers can offer significant speed advantages in these areas.

**Faster Data Processing**: In investigations involving vast amounts of digital evidence, quantum computers could expedite the analysis process. Quantum-enhanced machine learning algorithms might be able to sift through large datasets, such as network logs, financial records, or social media posts, in a fraction of the time it would take classical computers. This would allow forensic investigators to identify key evidence more efficiently, improving the speed and accuracy of their investigations.

**Complex Algorithmic Analysis**: Quantum computing could also enable the development of more sophisticated forensic algorithms that can solve problems that are computationally intractable for classical computers. For example, quantum algorithms might be able to model complex networks, simulate the behavior of advanced malware, or predict attack vectors with a higher degree of accuracy. This could greatly enhance the ability of forensic experts to detect subtle traces of cybercrime, even in highly obfuscated or encrypted data.

### 5. The Challenges of Quantum Computing in Cyber Forensics

Despite its potential, quantum computing introduces several challenges for cyber forensics, especially as the technology matures.

**Lack of Standardization**: As quantum computing is still in its early stages, there is a lack of widely adopted standards for its use in forensic investigations. This uncertainty creates challenges for forensics professionals who need to understand how quantum tools and algorithms will fit into existing forensic frameworks and legal processes.

**Transition to Post-Quantum Forensics**: As quantum computing advances, the digital forensics field will need to transition to new tools, encryption methods, and investigative techniques. This transition could be complex, as it will require updating existing forensic protocols, retraining forensic experts, and ensuring that evidence collected from both classical and quantum systems remains admissible in court.

**Quantum Security Risks**: While quantum computing can provide faster processing and data analysis, it can also introduce new security risks. For instance, quantum computers could be used by cybercriminals to break into secure systems or compromise sensitive evidence during investigations. Forensic professionals will need to stay informed about both the positive and negative applications of quantum computing, ensuring that they are prepared for new security threats.

Quantum computing has the potential to revolutionize the field of cyber forensics by introducing both new opportunities and significant challenges. While it may enhance data analysis and pattern recognition, it also poses a major risk to current cryptographic systems and forensic tools. The forensic community must stay ahead of quantum advancements by embracing post-quantum cryptography, developing new forensic tools, and ensuring that evidence handling remains secure and legally sound in a quantum-enabled future. As quantum computing continues to evolve, cyber forensics experts will play a crucial role in adapting to this paradigm shift and protecting the integrity of digital evidence in an increasingly complex and technologically advanced world.

# 13.2 Addressing Threats in the Metaverse and Virtual Environments.

The rise of the metaverse and virtual environments is transforming the digital landscape, creating new opportunities for social interaction, business, entertainment, and even law enforcement. However, as these environments grow, so too do the risks associated with them. The metaverse, often seen as an interconnected space of virtual reality (VR), augmented reality (AR), and digital worlds, presents a complex array of security challenges that require innovative approaches in cyber forensics and cybersecurity.

In this chapter, we explore the emerging threats in the metaverse and virtual environments, examining how these spaces differ from traditional digital environments. We also discuss the tools, techniques, and strategies needed to investigate crimes and ensure security in these new digital realms, focusing on how to adapt forensic practices to meet the challenges of the metaverse.

## 1. The Metaverse and Virtual Environments: An Overview

The metaverse refers to a collective, persistent virtual environment that integrates augmented reality (AR), virtual reality (VR), and other immersive technologies. This space allows users to interact with each other and digital elements in a shared virtual world, using avatars to represent themselves and engaging in various activities, such as gaming, shopping, working, and even attending social events. With billions of dollars being invested in the development of the metaverse, it is fast becoming a part of mainstream digital culture.

Virtual environments, which may exist as standalone games, platforms, or as parts of the metaverse, provide highly interactive, often complex, and immersive experiences. These environments are typically decentralized, dynamic, and highly user-driven, which introduces new security considerations for both users and businesses operating within these spaces.

## 2. Unique Threats in the Metaverse and Virtual Environments

As the metaverse and virtual environments become more sophisticated, they are becoming targets for a variety of cyber threats. These threats extend beyond traditional digital security issues, such as hacking and data breaches, and can affect users' safety, privacy, and financial assets. The following are key threats specific to the metaverse:

**Identity Theft and Impersonation**: In the metaverse, users create avatars that represent their online presence. These avatars are often used for communication, transactions, and other activities. Cybercriminals can exploit this system to steal identities, impersonate others, or engage in fraudulent activities. Unlike in traditional digital spaces, impersonation in the metaverse may involve interactions that feel more personal, adding complexity to identifying and verifying malicious actors.

**Virtual Property Theft**: Many virtual environments involve digital assets, such as virtual real estate, items, and currencies. Just like physical goods, these assets can be stolen through various means, including hacking, phishing, or exploiting vulnerabilities in the platform. For example, a user might lose access to virtual property or items if an attacker successfully compromises their avatar or wallet.

**Harassment and Abuse**: The metaverse's immersive and interactive nature opens the door to new forms of harassment and cyberbullying, such as verbal abuse, unwanted interactions, or offensive content being directed at other users. These behaviors can affect users' experiences and even their mental health, raising concerns about how virtual environments should be policed and how to protect individuals from harmful behaviors.

**Fraud and Scams**: Cybercriminals may exploit the financial components of virtual environments. Scams, such as fake virtual products, Ponzi schemes, or phishing attacks disguised as legitimate transactions, are prevalent in the metaverse. These scams often target individuals who are less familiar with the virtual ecosystem and may suffer financial losses as a result.

**Malware and Ransomware in Virtual Spaces**: Like traditional cyberspace, virtual environments can be infected with malicious software, including viruses, malware, and ransomware. These can compromise user data, disrupt services, or lock digital assets until a ransom is paid. In a world where many financial transactions are carried out with virtual currencies or non-fungible tokens (NFTs), ransomware attacks can be particularly dangerous.

### 3. Challenges for Forensic Investigations in the Metaverse

Forensic experts face significant challenges when it comes to investigating crimes or incidents that occur within the metaverse and virtual environments. The unique features of these spaces, such as decentralization, anonymity, and immersive interaction, complicate the process of evidence collection and analysis.

**Decentralized and Pseudonymous Nature of the Metaverse**: Many virtual environments operate in decentralized ways, where there is no central authority overseeing transactions and activities. This makes it harder to trace the origin of illegal activities, such as fraud or harassment, as there is often no clear digital trail that leads to a perpetrator. The use of pseudonyms or avatars further complicates the identification of individuals involved in illicit behavior.

**Inconsistent Legal Jurisdictions**: The global, cross-border nature of virtual environments makes it difficult to apply traditional laws and regulations. In many cases, users from different countries may be involved in cybercrimes, which can create jurisdictional challenges when investigating and prosecuting offenses. This adds complexity to obtaining evidence, as different legal systems may have varying rules on privacy, data access, and admissibility of digital evidence.

**Volume and Variety of Digital Evidence**: The sheer volume and variety of data generated in virtual environments create another challenge for digital forensic investigations. Evidence may be dispersed across multiple platforms, devices, and types of digital media, ranging from chat logs and transaction records to virtual objects and interactions. Analyzing and preserving this evidence requires specialized tools and expertise.

**Dynamic and Fluid Nature of Virtual Environments**: Virtual worlds are highly dynamic, with environments that are constantly evolving. As users interact with the platform, the digital landscape changes in real-time, making it difficult to preserve evidence before it is altered or deleted. The persistence and volatility of virtual data require forensic experts to act quickly and efficiently to collect and preserve evidence before it is lost.

## 4. Tools and Techniques for Investigating the Metaverse

To effectively address the unique threats of the metaverse and virtual environments, forensic experts must adapt their tools and techniques to the virtual world. This involves developing new methods for evidence collection, analysis, and preservation while ensuring that the integrity of digital assets is maintained.

**Digital Forensics for Virtual Environments**: Specialized digital forensic tools are required to collect data from virtual environments, which include logs, chat transcripts, digital wallets, and transactional histories. These tools should be capable of handling the unique aspects of virtual environments, such as encrypted communications and decentralized systems, ensuring that evidence is admissible in legal proceedings.

**Blockchain Forensics**: Many metaverse platforms use blockchain technology to manage virtual assets, transactions, and currencies. Blockchain forensics tools are crucial for tracking transactions, identifying fraudulent activities, and ensuring that virtual property can be traced back to its rightful owner. Blockchain's transparency and immutability make it a valuable tool for investigators to establish the provenance of virtual assets.

**Behavioral Analysis and AI Integration**: Behavioral analysis and artificial intelligence (AI) can play an important role in identifying malicious actors or criminal activity within virtual environments. AI can be used to detect anomalous behavior patterns, such as unusual transactions, suspicious communications, or instances of harassment, providing investigators with actionable insights. Integrating AI into forensic tools can help speed up the analysis and reduce human error.

**Digital Evidence Preservation**: Preservation of virtual evidence is one of the most critical aspects of forensic investigations. Forensic experts must ensure that data collected from virtual environments is stored securely and without alteration, especially in environments where content changes rapidly. The use of cryptographic techniques, such as hashing, ensures that the integrity of the evidence is maintained, even in dynamic virtual spaces.

### 5. Legal and Ethical Considerations in Virtual Forensics

Investigating crimes in virtual environments presents unique legal and ethical challenges, particularly with respect to privacy and user rights. Ensuring that forensic investigations comply with international laws and respect user privacy is crucial.

**Privacy Concerns and Data Protection**: In virtual environments, where users may share sensitive personal information and engage in financial transactions, maintaining privacy is critical. Forensic experts must be mindful of data protection regulations, such as the General Data Protection Regulation (GDPR), when collecting and handling evidence.

**Jurisdictional Issues**: As mentioned earlier, the cross-border nature of virtual environments complicates the application of laws. Investigators must navigate various international legal frameworks to determine which laws apply and how evidence can be collected and used in different jurisdictions.

The metaverse and virtual environments represent a new frontier in digital interaction, but they also introduce a range of cybersecurity and forensic challenges. As these spaces evolve, so too must the tools, techniques, and practices used to investigate and protect them. By understanding the unique threats posed by these immersive virtual worlds and adopting new approaches to digital forensics, investigators can help ensure the security, safety, and integrity of the metaverse while upholding legal and ethical standards.

# 13.3 Evolution of Forensic Tools for Emerging Technologies.

As technological innovations continue to shape the digital world, forensic tools and techniques must evolve to keep pace with new challenges posed by emerging technologies. The rapid advancement of fields like artificial intelligence (AI), blockchain, cloud computing, the Internet of Things (IoT), and quantum computing has created a need for specialized forensic solutions capable of investigating complex, decentralized, and rapidly changing systems. This chapter explores the evolution of forensic tools in response to these emerging technologies, highlighting the challenges forensic investigators face, the tools developed to address these challenges, and how the field of digital forensics continues to adapt to the ever-changing landscape of technology.

## 1. The Role of Forensic Tools in Emerging Technologies

Forensic tools are essential for gathering, preserving, and analyzing digital evidence from a variety of sources. As technology evolves, so too must the forensic methodologies and tools that investigators use to maintain the integrity and admissibility of evidence. Forensic experts rely on these tools to uncover and interpret data from devices, networks, and systems that may not have been present or even conceived of a decade ago. As new technologies arise, forensic tools must be adaptable to handle new data types, architectures, and attack vectors.

Emerging technologies not only increase the volume of data available for forensic investigation but also change the structure and types of evidence investigators need to analyze. Traditional forensic tools were designed to handle static data and simple, centralized systems, whereas modern tools must handle more dynamic, decentralized, and multifaceted environments. The evolution of forensic tools involves the development of more sophisticated, scalable, and flexible solutions that can address the unique complexities of these new technologies.

## 2. Blockchain Forensics: Tracking Transactions in Decentralized Networks

Blockchain technology, the backbone of cryptocurrencies like Bitcoin and Ethereum, has revolutionized the way financial transactions are conducted by creating a decentralized ledger that is immutable, transparent, and distributed across a network of computers. While these properties offer significant benefits for privacy and security, they also pose unique challenges for digital forensics. The distributed nature of blockchain makes it difficult to identify the actors behind transactions, and the pseudonymous nature of blockchain addresses obscures the identity of users, complicating investigations into criminal activities like money laundering, fraud, and cybercrime.

To address these challenges, forensic tools for blockchain analysis have evolved. Early blockchain forensic tools were basic, focusing on transaction tracking and wallet address analysis. Today, these tools have become more sophisticated, enabling investigators to trace the flow of funds across multiple transactions and identify clusters of addresses associated with illicit activities. Tools like Chainalysis, CipherTrace, and Elliptic have emerged as leaders in blockchain forensics, offering deep packet inspection, wallet clustering, and behavioral analysis to help investigators uncover criminal activities within blockchain environments. These tools can map out entire transaction networks, even when the transactions are obfuscated through techniques like mixing services or privacy coins, thus allowing forensic experts to follow the trail of digital assets and trace back illicit transactions to their origins.

## 3. Cloud Forensics: Investigating Data in the Cloud

The widespread adoption of cloud computing has introduced new challenges in digital forensics. Data is no longer stored on local hard drives or centralized servers but is distributed across remote servers managed by third-party cloud providers. This raises questions about jurisdiction, data ownership, and the complexity of accessing cloud-based evidence. Cloud forensics requires tools capable of acquiring data from these distributed and often encrypted environments while maintaining the integrity and chain of custody.

The evolution of cloud forensics tools has focused on addressing these challenges by providing investigators with the ability to remotely acquire and analyze data stored in the cloud. Early cloud forensics tools were limited to basic file retrieval and analysis. However, with the growth of cloud technologies, modern forensic tools are now designed to interact with various cloud platforms, including Amazon Web Services (AWS), Microsoft Azure, and Google Cloud, among others. These tools allow investigators to retrieve logs, snapshots, and other evidence while circumventing issues related to data fragmentation, encryption, and access control.

Cloud forensic tools, such as X1 Social Discovery, CloudForensics, and FTK Imager, now support a range of cloud services and integrate with APIs to provide seamless access to cloud-based evidence. These tools offer cloud-specific data acquisition techniques, such as the ability to extract data from cloud storage, virtual machines, and containerized applications. Furthermore, they are designed to address the challenges of multi-tenant environments, ensuring that evidence is preserved while respecting the privacy of other tenants within the same cloud infrastructure.

## 4. The Internet of Things (IoT) and Forensic Challenges

The Internet of Things (IoT) represents a vast network of interconnected devices that communicate with each other and the internet. From smart home devices like thermostats and security cameras to industrial control systems, the IoT ecosystem is rapidly expanding. With the growing use of IoT devices, forensic experts face challenges in acquiring and analyzing the data generated by these devices. IoT devices often collect and store data in diverse formats, in various locations, and across different networks, making the task of collecting and preserving evidence complex.

The evolution of forensic tools for IoT investigations has focused on the ability to access and extract data from these devices, which often lack traditional storage systems. IoT forensics tools must be able to handle device-specific protocols, communication channels, and proprietary data formats. Additionally, they must account for the fact that many IoT devices store data in real-time or send it to cloud servers, making it essential for forensic experts to work quickly to capture volatile data before it is lost.

Tools like IoT Inspector and Paraben's IoT Forensics Suite have been developed to address these needs. These tools provide capabilities for acquiring and analyzing data from IoT devices, including sensors, cameras, wearables, and smart appliances. They can extract data from various sources, such as flash memory, SD cards, and cloud-based servers, and provide investigators with a comprehensive view of the digital trail left by IoT devices. By incorporating data from IoT networks, these tools help forensic experts reconstruct events, detect anomalies, and identify potential threats or malicious activities.

## 5. Artificial Intelligence and Forensics: Automation and Pattern Recognition

Artificial intelligence (AI) has the potential to significantly enhance forensic investigations by automating data analysis, identifying patterns, and detecting anomalies in vast datasets. Traditional forensic investigations often involve manually sifting through large volumes of data to identify evidence, which is time-consuming and prone to human error. AI-powered forensic tools are being developed to speed up this process by applying machine learning algorithms to recognize suspicious behavior, detect fraud, or even predict future attacks.

Machine learning-based tools for forensic investigations are evolving to support advanced data analysis in various domains, including network traffic, malware detection, and fraud prevention. These tools can automate the process of sorting through large datasets, identifying relationships between different data points, and making real-time decisions about potential threats. For example, AI-powered tools can analyze network logs, identify patterns indicative of a cyberattack, and alert investigators to critical evidence that warrants further investigation.

AI-based forensics tools, such as Darktrace, Palo Alto Networks' Cortex XSOAR, and Endgame, are helping cybersecurity professionals and forensic investigators detect and mitigate emerging threats faster than ever before. By using machine learning to continuously learn from new data and adapt to evolving threats, AI tools can enhance the effectiveness and efficiency of forensic investigations in real-time.

### 6. The Future of Forensic Tools: Integrating Emerging Technologies

As new technologies like quantum computing and 5G networks continue to emerge, forensic tools will need to evolve further to accommodate the unique challenges they bring. Quantum computing, for example, could enable faster and more efficient decryption of encrypted data, making it both a potential asset and a challenge for digital forensics. Likewise, 5G networks, with their higher speeds and increased connectivity, will generate vast amounts of data that may need to be analyzed in real-time, requiring forensic tools capable of managing and processing these large datasets.

Forensic tools will continue to evolve in response to these emerging technologies, leveraging advancements in AI, machine learning, blockchain analysis, and cloud forensics. To meet the demands of future investigations, forensic experts will need tools that are flexible, scalable, and capable of integrating with a wide range of systems, platforms, and technologies.

The evolution of forensic tools for emerging technologies is critical to keeping pace with the ever-changing landscape of digital threats. As new technologies like blockchain, cloud computing, IoT, AI, and quantum computing redefine the digital environment, forensic experts must develop and adopt innovative tools that can handle the complexities of these systems. By continuously evolving forensic tools and techniques, the field of digital forensics can stay ahead of cybercriminals and ensure that investigators are equipped to tackle the challenges posed by these emerging technologies.

# 13.4 Preparing the Next Generation of Forensic Professionals.

The field of forensic cybersecurity is rapidly evolving, and as technology advances, the demand for skilled professionals who can investigate complex cybercrimes and safeguard digital evidence grows exponentially. Preparing the next generation of forensic professionals requires a combination of technical expertise, practical experience, and an understanding of the legal and ethical frameworks that govern digital investigations. In this chapter, we explore the skills, knowledge, and training necessary to develop future forensic experts who can successfully navigate the challenges of an increasingly digital and interconnected world.

## 1. Bridging the Skills Gap: The Need for Multidisciplinary Training

One of the main challenges in preparing future forensic professionals is the need for a multidisciplinary skill set. Cyber forensic investigators must possess a deep understanding of both technology and law. This includes knowledge of operating systems, networking protocols, databases, digital storage devices, and emerging technologies like AI, blockchain, and cloud computing, as well as an understanding of the legal implications of evidence handling, privacy concerns, and jurisdictional issues.

Educational programs that combine elements of computer science, information technology, law, and criminal justice are essential for creating well-rounded forensic experts. Universities and institutions offering degrees or certifications in cybersecurity, digital forensics, and information assurance have begun to tailor their curricula to reflect this need. These programs are increasingly offering practical courses that incorporate the latest tools and techniques in digital forensics, such as hands-on labs, live data analysis, and mock investigations.

To fill the growing skills gap in the industry, training programs must emphasize both technical proficiency and the soft skills required to work within a legal context, including communication, problem-solving, and teamwork. This multidisciplinary approach will allow the next generation of forensic professionals to address a wide range of challenges and think critically about how to adapt to an ever-changing technological landscape.

## 2. Hands-on Experience: Learning by Doing

In addition to theoretical knowledge, hands-on experience is essential for developing proficiency in forensic cybersecurity. While classroom training provides a solid foundation, real-world exposure to live cases, simulated environments, and mock investigations is critical for honing investigative skills. Many institutions now offer specialized labs and virtual environments where students can engage in practical exercises involving data acquisition, malware analysis, network forensics, and cloud-based investigations.

Internships and industry partnerships are also invaluable for gaining real-world experience. These opportunities allow students to work alongside seasoned professionals on actual forensic investigations, providing them with insights into how forensic methods are applied in the field. Internships also help students build networks within the industry and establish mentorship relationships with experienced forensic investigators, which can be instrumental in securing future employment opportunities.

Moreover, specialized certification programs, such as the Certified Computer Forensics Examiner (CCFE), Certified Cyber Forensics Professional (CCFP), and GIAC Forensic Analyst (GCFA), offer targeted training in digital forensics, reinforcing practical skills and providing a professional credential that is recognized within the industry. These certifications ensure that forensic professionals remain up-to-date with the latest forensic methodologies, legal regulations, and emerging technologies.

## 3. Adapting to Technological Advancements

As technology continues to evolve, so must the tools and techniques used in forensic investigations. The next generation of forensic professionals must be adaptable and prepared to work with the latest technologies, including AI, machine learning, blockchain, cloud computing, and the Internet of Things (IoT). These technologies introduce new challenges and opportunities for forensic investigators, as they generate vast amounts of data that must be analyzed, preserved, and interpreted accurately.

Educators and industry leaders must emphasize the importance of continuous learning and adaptation. Digital forensics is a dynamic field, and the tools, tactics, and techniques used in investigations are constantly changing. Future forensic professionals must be able to stay ahead of the curve by developing a mindset of lifelong learning and remaining engaged with the latest developments in the cybersecurity landscape. This includes actively participating in industry conferences, reading the latest research, and experimenting with new forensic tools and techniques.

Collaborations between academia, industry, and government agencies can help ensure that training programs and certification tracks remain relevant and up-to-date. By fostering partnerships between educational institutions and tech companies, the next generation of forensic experts can gain access to cutting-edge tools and training, preparing them for the complexities of investigating cybercrimes in an ever-evolving technological environment.

## 4. The Importance of Legal and Ethical Knowledge

In addition to technical skills, forensic professionals must understand the legal and ethical frameworks that govern their work. The collection, analysis, and presentation of digital evidence must adhere to strict legal standards to ensure that the evidence is admissible in court and that the rights of individuals are respected. Forensic professionals need to be familiar with privacy laws, data protection regulations, and international conventions regarding cybercrime to avoid compromising the integrity of investigations.

Training programs should include courses on cyber law, data protection, and evidence handling to prepare future professionals for the ethical challenges they may encounter in the field. For instance, knowledge of the General Data Protection Regulation (GDPR) in the European Union or the Computer Fraud and Abuse Act (CFAA) in the United States can help forensic experts navigate complex legal landscapes and avoid legal pitfalls. In addition, ethical decision-making training will help professionals balance the technical demands of forensic investigations with their legal and moral obligations.

An understanding of the legal context will also allow forensic professionals to effectively communicate their findings in court, working with legal teams to present digital evidence in a way that is both accurate and understandable to non-technical audiences, including judges and juries. This skill is crucial for ensuring that digital forensics investigations hold up under scrutiny and lead to successful prosecutions.

## 5. Building a Collaborative Cybersecurity and Forensics Ecosystem

Cybercrime is a global issue, and tackling it requires collaboration across borders, sectors, and disciplines. The next generation of forensic professionals must be prepared to work as part of a broader cybersecurity ecosystem, collaborating with law enforcement, private companies, government agencies, and international organizations. Building relationships with colleagues from various domains will be essential for staying informed about emerging threats, sharing best practices, and addressing the increasingly sophisticated nature of cybercrimes.

Educational programs should foster teamwork and interdisciplinary collaboration, offering opportunities for students to work with professionals from other fields, such as network security, criminal justice, and law enforcement. Cyber forensics experts must understand how their role fits within a broader investigative framework, working alongside specialists in various cybersecurity domains to identify threats and mitigate risks.

In addition, the increasing complexity of cybercrimes demands that forensic professionals work closely with law enforcement agencies and government organizations to share intelligence, respond to incidents, and develop national and international strategies to combat cybercrime. As a result, collaboration skills, as well as cultural and jurisdictional sensitivity, will be critical for the next generation of forensic professionals as they navigate global cyber threats.

## 6. Encouraging Diversity in the Forensic Cybersecurity Field

The field of cybersecurity and digital forensics has traditionally been dominated by a relatively homogeneous group of professionals. However, there is an increasing recognition that a diverse workforce is essential for solving complex cybercrimes. Bringing together people with different backgrounds, perspectives, and expertise can lead to more innovative problem-solving and better decision-making in forensic investigations.

To prepare the next generation of forensic professionals, it is essential to encourage greater diversity and inclusivity in the field. This can be achieved by actively recruiting individuals from underrepresented groups, offering scholarships and mentorship opportunities, and providing support to ensure that all students have equal access to training and career advancement opportunities. A diverse workforce can help ensure that the field of forensic cybersecurity reflects the needs and challenges of the global community and is equipped to address a broad spectrum of cybercrime cases.

Preparing the next generation of forensic professionals is essential to the continued success of the field. By offering multidisciplinary training, providing hands-on experience, fostering adaptability, and emphasizing the importance of legal and ethical considerations, we can equip future investigators with the tools and knowledge needed to tackle the complex challenges of digital forensics. Collaboration across industries, countries, and disciplines, combined with a commitment to diversity and continuous learning, will ensure that the next generation of forensic experts is prepared to face the evolving threats in the digital landscape and protect against the increasing risks posed by cybercrime.

In a world where data breaches, ransomware attacks, and cyber espionage are escalating threats, the ability to protect and investigate digital data has never been more crucial. **"Forensic Cybersecurity: Protecting and Investigating Digital Data"** provides an in-depth exploration of the vital discipline that bridges the gap between digital forensics and cybersecurity.

Authored by seasoned expert **Mylan Rochefort**, this book takes you on a journey through the intricate world of cyber investigations and defense strategies. From understanding the anatomy of a cyberattack to mastering cutting-edge tools and techniques, each chapter equips readers with the knowledge and skills needed to navigate the digital battlefield.

Whether delving into network forensics, analyzing malware, or overcoming the challenges of cloud environments, this comprehensive guide combines practical insights with real-world case studies. It also looks ahead, examining how artificial intelligence, quantum computing, and other emerging technologies will shape the future of forensic cybersecurity.

Ideal for professionals, students, and anyone fascinated by the inner workings of the digital world, "Forensic Cybersecurity" is both an essential resource and an inspiring call to action. It empowers readers to not only investigate the aftermath of cyber incidents but also to proactively safeguard systems and data in an increasingly connected world.

Prepare to uncover the tools, strategies, and mindset needed to protect the digital frontier. The future of cybersecurity starts here.

www.ingramcontent.com/pod-product-compliance
Lightning Source LLC
LaVergne TN
LVHW060121070326
832902LV00019B/3069